The Waste Land
in Different Voices

The Waste Land
in Different Voices

•

The revised versions of lectures
given at the University of York in
the fiftieth year of *The Waste Land*

by

**A. C. Charity, J. S. Cunningham, Donald Davie
Dennis Donoghue, Richard Drain, D. W. Harding
Bernard Harris, John Dixon Hunt, A. D. Moody
Kathleen Nott, B. Rajan and Nicole Ward**

•

edited by

A. D. MOODY

Edward Arnold

© University of York, 1974

First published 1974
by Edward Arnold (Publishers) Ltd,
25 Hill Street, London W1X 8LL

ISBN: 0 7131 5753 4

Printed in Great Britain by
Billing & Sons Ltd., Guildford and London

Contents

Acknowledgements

The publishers' thanks are due to the following for permission to reproduce copyright material:

Faber and Faber Ltd, London, and Harcourt, Brace Jovanovich Inc., New York, for extracts from T. S. Eliot's *Four Quartets, Collected Poems 1909–1962, Selected Essays* and *The Waste Land*; Mrs Valerie Eliot, Faber and Faber Ltd and Harcourt, Brace Jovanovich Inc. for extracts from *The Waste Land: A Facsimile and Transcript of the Original Draft*, edited by Valerie Eliot; Jonathan Cape Ltd, London, and New Directions Publishing Corporation, New York, for an extract from Robert Duncan's translation of Gérard de Nerval's 'El Desdichado', from Robert Duncan's *Bending the Bow* (copyright 1968 by Robert Duncan); Faber and Faber Ltd and St Martin's Press Inc., New York, for an extract from Robert Donington's *Wagner's 'Ring' and its Symbols*; Editions Gallimard, Paris, for extracts from Charles Baudelaire, *Œuvres complètes* (Bibliothèque de la Pléiade).

The Contributors

A. C. Charity is Senior Lecturer in the Department of English and Related Literature, University of York

J. S. Cunningham is Reader in the Department of English and Related Literature, University of York

Donald Davie is a poet, and Professor of English at Stanford University, California

Denis Donoghue is Professor of Modern English and American Literature, University College Dublin

Richard Drain is Senior Lecturer in the Department of English and Related Literature, University of York

D. W. Harding is a literary critic and Emeritus Professor of Psychology, University of London

Bernard Harris is Professor in the Department of English and Related Literature, University of York

John Dixon Hunt is Lecturer in the Department of English and Related Literature, University of York

A. D. Moody is Senior Lecturer in the Department of English and Related Literature, University of York

Kathleen Nott is a poet, novelist, critic and philosopher

B. Rajan is Professor of English at the University of Western Ontario

Nicole Ward is Lecturer in the Department of English and Related Literature, University of York

List of Plates

These illustrate the essay by John Dixon Hunt, ' "Broken Images": T. S. Eliot and Modern Painting', and appear between pages 164 and 165.

1 Marcel Duchamp, *Nude Descending a Staircase, No. 2*, 1912 (The Louise and Walter Arensberg Collection, Philadelphia Museum of Art)

2 René Magritte, *Les rêveries du promeneur solitaire*, 1926 or 1927 (Collection E. L. T. Mesens, Brussels)

3a René Magritte, *Les objets familiers*, 1927 or 1928 (Collection E. L. T. Mesens, Brussels)

3b René Magritte, *Le chef d'œuvre ou Les mystères de l'horizon*, 1955 (Collection L. Arnold Weissberger, New York)

4a René Magritte, *Le fils d'homme*, 1964 (Collection Harry Torczyner, Green Castle, New York)

4b René Magritte, *Le bouquet tout fait*, 1957 (Collection Mr and Mrs Barnet Hodes, Chicago, Illinois)

5a Giorgio di Chirico, *The Dream Transformed*, 1913 (The City Art Museum, St Louis, Missouri)

5b Giorgio di Chirico, *The Uncertainty of the Poet*, 1913 (Private collection, London)

6 Giorgio di Chirico, *The Soothsayer's Recompense*, 1913 (The Louise and Walter Arensberg Collection, Philadelphia Museum of Art)

7 Juan Gris, *Still Life Before an Open Window: Place Ravignan*, 1915 (The Louise and Walter Arensberg Collection, Philadelphia Museum of Art)

8 Georges Braque, *Violin and Palette*, 1910 (The Solomon R. Guggenheim Museum)

Preface

Our occasion was the fiftieth year of *The Waste Land*. It was time for a new look at that poem: time to see it as no longer 'modern', but established; to see it as no isolated monument but an integral part of a life's work; and to see it as the product of a past era, one which ended with the death in 1972 of Ezra Pound, 'il miglior fabbro'. It was a time to ask, what does Eliot's work mean to us, now, in the next age? For we read him with different minds from the readers of fifty or even ten years ago; and we discover a different poetry. Consequently we seek new voices to speak it, and to speak of it. And we do this not for novelty's sake, but because poetry stays alive only in living and changing minds, so that what endures in it must be perpetually made new.

Precisely how Eliot's readers in the 1970s differ from those of the 1920s is more than I could say. Would it serve to cast the times into a phrase or two, or to say that where once it was Frazer, now we may read Lévi-Strauss? However, this much is certain: we are all of us altered by the working of the poetry in the minds of its readers throughout the half-century. That tells in the way we can take it as an immediate experience. Instead of asking, what does it mean? and seeking to decipher and to explain as if it were a strange object turned up in alien ground, we ask familiarly, does it work and is it a valid and useful experience? We read not from the text alone, 'out there', but from the inner life of the text, and its life within us. This, I think, must be the ground of our present collaboration: it is what brings together a diversity of authors and gives coherence to our book; and it should bring us into a close relation with other readers of Eliot now.

Whether, upon our common ground, some of us discover a common sense of Eliot's poetry, I leave our readers to make out. I want only to affirm a radical agreement, implying a real experience of the poetry, and a real concern for the use of poetry. What I would affirm after that, and as the necessary complement, are our diversity and differences. Where there can be no finally

A*

right reading, variousness is our best resource. The wide range of our special interests, and our possibly sharp differences of judgement, so long as they are rooted in the poetry, are an opening out towards further discoveries, and promise a more complete experience than we yet apprehend.

'He do the Police in different voices.' That was Sloppy in *Our Mutual Friend,* dramatising the news of crime and the courts. As the title for Parts I and II of the ur–*Waste Land*, it indicated the many alien voices caught in the poem. Yet the closing 'fragments', in such different languages, are made to compose not Babel but 'the Peace which passeth understanding'.

As to the arrangement of the dozen contributions, others were possible and quite as good as the one I have settled for. There is no straight line of argument; and no linear order can do justice to the network of inter-relations. One would need three-dimensional space for that, or the space-time of music. But the reader's own mind may serve: there may be found the scope and free play to compose our whole argument. I have given what help I can, by offering an arrangement patently arbitrary, and, below the surface, somewhat antiphonal. So the inevitable line might at least curve, cross itself, or spiral.

There is, however, a natural starting point and a proper end. Professor Rajan, twenty-five years before, had edited the first symposium on Eliot. Professor Harding was one of the pioneers in the appreciation of Eliot's work, in *Scrutiny* during the 1930s and 1940s. I place them first to honour a continuity of critical endeavour. Donald Davie's autobiographical essay I place at the end to honour the continuity of poetic endeavour. It seemed natural and fitting that his first *Collected Poems* should come out in that year, 1972, establishing a just claim to speak for the next age after that of Eliot and Pound, his acknowledged masters. Our thinking about poetry should always end, ideally, in renewed creativity.

An editor has this privilege of speaking before his betters. I would use it, finally, to thank them for giving me their best work, and for the pains very generously taken over it. I am particularly grateful to those who came as visitors to the York Department of English and Related Literature, some from far places. The lectures made up a University Open Course Series, and as such were delivered in the spring and summer of 1972. But it was intended from the first that they should be published, and all of them, whether before or after delivery, have been written and revised for printing. I wanted a book good enough to discover what Eliot means now, and I thank my contributors for having given it to me and to the reader.

May Day, 1974   *A. D. M.*

The Dialect of the Tribe

B. Rajan

Twenty years after the writing of *The Waste Land* a man treads the streets of an unreal city where the dead leaves rattle like tin over the asphalt. Death has undone many who flowed over London Bridge and much more than the bridge is tumbling down. The rain for which the limp leaves of the jungle had waited is now the fiery rain that falls on a burning metropolis. The thunder that spoke will be the dove descending. Midwinter Spring has superseded April as the season of cruelty and creativeness. At the heart of light, the hyacinth has become the lotus and the rose.

These detailed relationships make it evident that we have reached a turning of the stair and are invited to look down on what has been passed through. But in looking down we do not merely see a province of the mind more clearly because we see it in a light that is closer to finality. We are also made to recognize that the winding stair has been travelled by others, who contemplate what we understand through our own eyes and help us to draw the shape of an understanding which is both within us and beyond ourselves. The familiar compound ghost is a reminder of how the historical sense calls on us to respond to the presence of the past as well as to its pastness. Unidentifiable because it is intimate, it is so much a part of the writer's being that to discourse with it is virtually to assume a double part in the dialogue with one's self.

It is possible to apply some useless scholarship to the delineating of those 'brown, baked features' but there are certain basic resemblances which it is instructive as well as intriguing to discern. To talk about the bitterness of age and the wreckage of the body is to summon to the stair the poetry of Yeats, but more is involved than this unavoidable acknowledgement. The style of the encounter itself evokes the elder poet's views upon the mask, while differentiating Eliot's treatment from that of Yeats. The reference to 'the rending pain of re-enactment' recalls with exactness the anguish of *Purgatory*. The mention of 'honour' reminds us of the *Dialogue of Self and Soul*, with honour finding the self in the wintry blast. The exasperated spirit proceeding from wrong to wrong directs us once again to *Purgatory* and to the climax which extends the chain of error in seeking to cut it. The dancer is one of Yeats's more celebrated images, and the dancer in the fires of purification is the summit of the upward effort in *Byzantium*. Others besides Yeats have blown their horns in poetry but, given the accumulations of detail, it may not be without significance that the 'fabulous horn' in Yeats is linked to the 'sudden shower'.[1]

There is however another remembrance in the compound ghost that haunts Eliot more tellingly and creatively than Yeats. Though Laforgue taught Eliot 'how to speak' and Baudelaire showed him 'the possibility of fusion between the sordidly realistic and the phantasmagoric'[2] which he put to such decisive use in *The Waste Land*, it was Dante who, after forty years, remained 'the most persistent and deepest influence' on his work. It was moreover a cumulative influence: 'the older you grow, the stronger the domination becomes.'[3] The encounter scene in 'Little Gidding'—the closest approximation that has been achieved in English to the effect of *terza rima* in Italian—pays appropriate tribute to this influence. Twenty years ago it was Dante's words which were chosen to characterize the unreal city and to suggest in the last lines of the poem the means of escape from that city into reality. 'Little Gidding' confirms the conjecture that it is Dante, rather than Stetson, who has been with the poet in the ships at Mylae. But the dead master's presence is not easy to accommodate, and Eliot admits that this section of 'Little Gidding' 'cost me far more time and trouble and vexation than any passage of the same length that I had ever written'.[4] We can either pine for the discarded drafts or respond to the tautness and the fluency which is the result of all this stitching and unstitching. Whatever our preferences, we would be less than just if we did not discern that the thing said is as Dantesque as the way of saying it, particularly in the final recurrence of those

---

[1] W. B. Yeats, *Collected Poems* (New York, 1950), 232, 244, 196.
[2] *To Criticize the Critic* (London, 1965), 125–6. Cp. 22.
[3] *Ibid.*, 130.
[4] *Ibid.*, 129.

lines from the twenty-sixth canto of the *Purgatorio* which have so dominated Eliot's creative memory.

This crucial passage provides the title for the third volume of poems that Eliot published in England. A line from it appears in one of the discarded poems in the *Waste Land* manuscript. A phrase furnishes yet another title, this time for a section of *Ash-Wednesday* as it was first published. A further phrase is embodied in the text of another section. Finally, the crucial line in which the ghost tells us that deliverance from error is only possible when we make ourselves new in the refining fire is one of those carefully chosen fragments which the protagonist in *The Waste Land* shores against his ruins.[5] The advance into meaning so scrupulously achieved by the intervening poetry invites us again to look down the stairway and to understand more fully what the thunder said.

The third ingredient in the ghost is not altogether expected. Laforgue may have taught Eliot how to speak but it is Mallarmé not Laforgue who tells us what it means to be concerned with speech. We know that Eliot came to prefer Mallarmé to Laforgue as he came to prefer Herbert to Donne.[6] But the ghost is not compounded as it is merely to state Mr Eliot's preferences. It stands in the poem to declare the poem's nature and the nature of those previous acts of exploration that have helped to make possible whatever truth is found here. A varied company is joined and justly joined in the unearthly community where two worlds overlap. We find the arch-symbolist and the poet who moved beyond symbolism in order to find that he had no speech but symbol. There is the poet of the rose and the poet who cultivated the rose, in learning how the holy tree grows like the lotus in man's heart. There are two men who cast their lives into their rhymes and whose rhymes tell of more than medieval Florence and the indomitable Irishry. There are the swordsman, the saint and the esthete, the poet of the swan and of the swan in shadow. In responding to a collective presence which the poem rightly describes as 'both one and many', we learn something of the

---

[5] *The Waste Land. A Facsimile and Transcript of the Original Draft*, ed. Valerie Eliot (London, 1971), 100–1; *Ara Vus* [sic] *Prec* (The Ovid Press, London, 1920); 'Al Som de L'Escalina', *Commerce* (Autumn 1929); *Ash-Wednesday* IV, *Collected Poems* (New York, 1962), 90; *The Waste Land*, line 428.

[6] *To Criticize the Critic*, 22–3.

width of a poet's apprenticeship and of the responsibility laid on us in our concern with speech.

Concern with speech is also made evident by the manner in which three of the four Quartets turn to language during their final sections, moving first through its betrayals and then to its fulfilment in the complete consort dancing together, the commerce of high and low as well as of old and new. The formal decorum points as it must to the deeper coherence to which it is connected. Since its symbol is the dance, we are called on to remember that the dance in the same three Quartets has been used to signify matrimony, the meeting of stillness and motion, and the joining of two worlds in measured movement through the purgatorial fire. Thus, even the tactics of speech enact the recognitions which speech seeks to convey. Our concern is with words because for those born to use them, words are the best way of finding what stands for ever in the wheeling and turning of words.

The ghost's next line raises a variety of interesting issues entangled in a manner which we must hopefully call creative. Since Eliot associated himself with a revolution in poetry characterized by a return to the language of common speech,[7] we might argue that his main aim in poetry was to restore rather than to purify dialect. But poetic language in its remoter reaches—and it is also the language of a tribe in this sense—has itself been castigated as a Babylonish dialect harsh and barbarous.[8] Are we then concerned with a golden mean or 'an easy commerce', anticipated by previous efforts to raise the vernacular into literary dignity? This is the accomplishment frequently credited to Dante in Italian and Ben Jonson in English. We can observe with scholarly prudence that this is undoubtedly part of what the ghost meant, particularly if we supplement our caution with the platitude that the boundaries of the vernacular are indefinite. Though large slabs of dialect were eliminated in the final version of *The Waste Land*,[9] enough remains to instruct us on the function of low life in high poetry. Yet *The Waste Land* is not simply a twentieth-century achievement in the plain style, and though Eliot can affirm that 'history is now and in England' we refrain from

---

[7] *On Poetry and Poets* (London, 1957), 31.

[8] Samuel Johnson, 'John Milton', *Lives of the English Poets* (London, 1925), I, 112.

[9] See in particular *Facsimile*, 4-5, 54-9.

underlining too heavily the Englishness of Eliot. Perhaps we restrain ourselves because the ghost has convinced us.

The word 'tribe' is generously inclusive in the first place. Dante, Mallarmé and Yeats have different ways of purifying dialect. But if we extend the term even further to cover the efforts of all those who think and live by thought, the followers of the lotus and the rose, of Buddha, of Krishna and of Augustine, if we think of the many dialects of comprehension behind which stands the unchanging language of truth, we see more and see better in looking down the stairway. The fragment from Heraclitus which forms the second of the epigraphs to *Four Quartets* supports such a reading. So too does the ghost's suggestion that the purpose of purifying the tribe's dialect is 'to urge the mind to aftersight and foresight'.

Eliot's poetry is an advance, an inch-by-inch movement up the stairway in which the end is significant because it both remembers and fulfils the beginning. 'The end is where we start from' and therefore to some degree the final cause which defines the full accomplishment. Though *The Waste Land* largely stands by itself, it is not fully itself until it is placed in a continuum and until we look back on it along what the later work discloses as the path of its potentiality, the direction it must take to achieve its own becoming.

Enough has been said to allow the simplification that the poet advances from dialect into speech and eloquence, and more particularly into that deeper eloquence which is the discovery and celebration of the meaningful. One way of considering *The Waste Land* is to see it as assiduously assembling the potential components of that eloquence. We encounter in it the polyglot poem ranging laterally across cultures, ranging backwards into the literary past and ranging up and down the social ladder through the disguises and declarations of emptiness. The effort at inclusiveness is strenuous. Significance *should* come out of the talk and the gestures, out of the relics of meaning which the mind has sifted through and the memory hoarded. The directing voice is civilized enough and has travelled sufficiently far to be dissatisfied with Burbank and his Baedeker. All it lacks are the resources of speech, the shared understanding between man and man, or even the pattern given to the mind within which the mind's contents can be located and understood. The units of awareness may be present but what cannot quite be achieved are the connective forces, the grammar of comprehension.

This is modern man and the sound of the key turning is the proof of a prison which might otherwise not be recognized. This is man not only east of Eden, but probably too far east of it for creative or even nostalgic remembrance. Paradise is not lost but destroyed, as it is at a decisive moment in Milton's poem. The mind can voyage through the strange seas of itself. It will find not Ithaca, but a whirlpool.

Ithaca in our time has been a popular destination. The shaping presence of the *Odyssey* is of course prominent in Joyce and Pound, and Eliot's claim that we must use the mythical instead of the narrative method is frequently intoned, though some doubt can be expressed about the degree of method in his myths. What is also important is the strong recollection, in the discarded drafts of *The Waste Land*, of Ulysses's final voyage as recounted by Dante. The Dry Salvages are a milestone in that voyage,[10] so it is no accident that the third Quartet sets before us a journey to the limits of the known and a death by drowning which, unlike the death of Phlebas the Phoenician, is what Marvell would call a shipwreck into life. There are other recollections which are also evolutions. Belladonna, the lady of the rocks, becomes the lady whose shrine stands on the promontory. The *Gita* supersedes the Fire Sermon. The three imperatives which end *The Waste Land*— give, sympathize, control—are replaced by 'Ardour and self-lessness and self-surrender'. Finally, Madame Sosostris (or rather her paraphernalia) make what can only be called an appropriate reappearance at a time when Hitler was busy with his astrologers. But the inventory of clairvoyant tactics—Eliot's parody of the epic catalogue—takes place *after* that death by water which Madame Sosostris had warned us to avoid. We are therefore no longer prisoners of the parody but are able to see beyond it and to reach around it to the truth which it deforms but also hints at. We learn the limitations of that dimension which man's curiosity searches but to which it also clings. There is more than one way in which the coming of Christ can silence the oracles.

We have moved forward from *The Waste Land* in taking up some of its images, and how we have moved forward is suggested by a crucial passage in 'The Dry Salvages':

We had the experience but missed the meaning,
And approach to the experience restores the meaning

[10] *Facsimile,* 54–69, 128 n.

In a different form, beyond any meaning
We can assign to happiness. I have said before
That the past experience revived in the meaning
Is not the experience of one life only
But of many generations . . .

We may note in passing how 'many generations' reminds us of the
multiple ingredients of the familiar compound ghost, of the
citations of the past that in *The Waste Land* flow into and frame
the sterile present, and of that simultaneous presence of the
totality of literature which constitutes tradition for the individual
talent. But our immediate concern must be those insistent inter-
twinings which bind experience and meaning together in spread-
ing yet gathered relationships, so that we are made aware of meaning as something both attained by experience and itself
experienced. We recall that thought, to Donne, was an experience
which modified his sensibility. Thus the pattern by which language
is able to touch the central stillness cannot be imposed. We also
stand at a point in the mind's history where the pattern can no
longer be assumed or even discovered. The main intermediate
possibility is the one taken up by Eliot's poetic development.
If meaning cannot be found it must be heard. The search for
significance must be driven forward to a boundary at which the
thunder can legitimately speak.

It is in the end not simply Madame Sosostris, but the poetic act
in its stubborn integrity, which clings to the dimension of past
and future. That clinging is not necessarily a failing. It must be
seen against a complementary truth which Eliot's writing also
puts to us, which is that time is only conquered through time.
If the birth of meaning is to take place at the edge of experience,
then experience itself must find its way to the edge. The poem of the
whole mind, which *The Waste Land* certainly is in a crucial sense,
must end in the partial defeat of the mind. But the defeat would
be frustrating rather than meaningful if the poem did not proceed
to it and to some degree achieve it through a full and honest
exposure of the mind's contents.

It is necessary to put everything on the table and in this sense
the polyglot poem is today's version of the encyclopedic epic.
It too, like *Paradise Lost*, attempts to be the infinite receptacle,
but its principles of organization are not evident from its creden-
tials. The traditional poem either declares itself or puts forward
and progressively puts together the ingredients of an under-

standing that is able to complete and to shape it. *The Waste Land* is purposefully limited to ascertaining the conditions under which understanding might be reached. To proceed even this far and to know itself even to this degree, it must call upon everything in the mind that seems capable of significance and, having convened itself, subject itself to scrutiny. It is east of Babel as well as east of Eden. If the possibility of speech exists, it can only exist at the heart of the medley of voices.

It is not only the landscape of *The Waste Land* to which we should attend. The earth thirsting for rain is the mind thirsting for meaning. To find a structure not alien to itself it must put down the nuclei of significance, the broken images in their felt juxtapositions, shuffling them like cards and rearranging them like tea-leaves. It must widen its resources, the hinterland by which it is civilized. Many languages and the literature of many periods can uncover between themselves more surely the principles by which the mind is made. Wisdom should be the accumulation of many dialects, the gist of the best that has been known and thought. Or is it, ironically, lodged in the mind's trivia? The search for significance would be less than conclusive if it did not take in all pertinent possibilities.

It is apparent by now that the search has to fail. To say this is not to imply that it was designed to fail, or even that what the failure meant was seen with clarity at the time of the failure. A boundary is reached, and it is only by looking backwards from what is subsequently achieved beyond the boundary that we understand the poem which the boundary encloses. When we have been led to aftersight we are able to recognize that the failure must be comprehensive in order to be meaningful. Until the possibilities of the dimension are exhausted, the mind's curiosity will cling to past and future. More than one journey is needed before it can reach the conclusion that it cannot know its nature through its geography.

Despite appearances, the poetry of failure is by no means easy to write. The finding of meaning is so bound up with the achievement of form that it can seem to be part of a poem's natural density. Doubt may threaten the poem but the climactic chords resound. Moreover, at the time that Eliot wrote *The Waste Land*, an accomplished failure-artist, W. B. Yeats, was turning failure into his greatest success. At the other extreme the failure of incompetence is easy enough to avoid; but the failure of meaning-

8

lessness, of an abyss so deep that the thunder cannot speak to it, must also be turned aside though the poem may be called on by its integrity to confront it. The ironies of a poem such as *The Waste Land* can be made to circumvent this threat by implying more than the participating voices are capable of saying. But these ironies must carefully stop short of defining shaping principles, limiting themselves to the recognitions which will enable those principles to be announced and to be placed in relation to the poem's necessities.

Even the 'placing' may be something which other poems in the continuum have to accomplish. What the thunder says is a succession of imperatives, not necessarily felt as more authentic than the poem's other voices. The response is the familiar disjointedness, the shoring of fragments in a gesture like those many other gestures to which the poem has fruitlessly submitted. If more is meant, it is the turn in the stairway which shows us what else has entered our condition.

To this extent criticisms of *The Waste Land* that draw attention to its residual unrelatedness, to the failure of its various elements to cohere, testify obliquely to the poem's integrity. It can indeed be argued without perversity that *The Waste Land* not only has to fail but fail in the particular way in which it does fail if it is to prepare the way for the movement forward in subsequent poems and so take its proper and productive place within the achievement of the poetry as a whole. What is important is that the elements in *The Waste Land* should be brought together not so as to achieve a meaning, but to particularize an experience and a dialect which will make possible an advance into meaning and speech. The poem is not self-sufficient. It is part of a progress which began before it and will continue beyond it. Gerontion's phrase 'We have not reached conclusion'—a phrase which his own withering away from the source of life has emptied—is one which it is the concern of the whole movement to restore.

It is for this reason that, despite Eliot's brave words in his *Dial* review of *Ulysses*, the mythical method can be no more successful than the narrative method. It does not control, order and give significance to the immense panorama of futility and anarchy which is contemporary history.[11] It is, in fact, an arrangement rather than a structure. Similarly deceptive is the observa-

[11] 'Ulysses, Order and Myth', *The Dial* LXXV (5 November 1923), 483.

tion in the footnotes on the locus of *The Waste Land*. What Tiresias sees may very well be the whole poem, but what he sees is not meaningful unless it is found in the poem. That it is not found suggests that the integrative force of vision is alien to the poem on its chosen plane of existence; it is an alienation embodied in the emptiness of the poem's ritual gestures of renewal. These gestures were once life-giving acts. But in the climate of the waste land, divination has been debased into fortune-telling and love has been mechanized as lust. The connections with the past fail to provide a basis for transformation. They define the diminuendo of the present but the music they invoke is louder rather than different: the bang is not superior to the whimper. Fear in a handful of dust may seem to promise something in its menaces, but it is actually closer to Gerontion's sterile terror than it is to the creative fear of the holy. The cage in which the Sibyl wished to die serves not to intensify the longing for escape but to provide instead, according to the manuscript, the setting for the calculations of a chess-game.[12] Even that celebrated collocation of 'two representatives of eastern and western asceticism', which Eliot heavily advises us is not accidental, does not provide us with the terms of renewal. It is the sense of destruction which is dominant in the immediacies of the verse, with the word 'burning' standing finally in isolation as if all qualifications to it had been burned away. The restorative implications which the thought can carry (as in Donne's fourteenth Sonnet or in 'Good Friday Riding Westward') remain indecisive in the verbal energies. If we remind ourselves of the relationship between burning and refining, we must also recognize that the poem's progress so far has not achieved possession of that relationship. Thus when death comes in the next section, its implications are limited to a studious reminder of the skull beneath the skin. There are no dolphins to carry Phlebas to Byzantium and no voice to assure us that Lycidas is not dead. The great vision of the guarded mount may stand at the horizon of the poem in what the thunder says, but only when the poem has exhausted its own insufficiency.

It remains to us to consider the words heard in the voice of the Thunder and the sequence in which they are heard. Eliot's

[12] *Facsimile*, 10–11. Pound's objections to the original epigraph from Conrad (*Facsimile*, 125 n.) led to the epigraph we know, Conrad being remembered in the epigraph to 'The Hollow Men'.

reference to the *Brihadaranyaka Upanishad* is inaccurate,[13] so it can be argued that in altering the order of the three imperatives he was merely providing us with a second case of faulty recollection. The Editorial Board which produced *The Waste Land* was not infallible, and one of the words in the fragment from the *Pervigilium Veneris* is persistently misquoted in the manuscripts.[14] The Board has no comment on what the Thunder said unless Pound's 'O.K. from here on *I think*'[15] is taken as applying to the whole final section. But perhaps the altered order can be made to submit to a better explanation than individual forgetfulness and collective negligence.

The Thunder's single seed-word, DA, is apprehended in three ways by three orders of existence. The Gods hear it as *Damyata*, man as *Datta* and the Asuras as *Dayadhvam*. This is the sequence in the Sanskrit, and it has the obvious advantage of providing us with an orderly descent through the scale of existence as well as with an indication of the main shortcoming of each of the three orders. Eliot begins with man, and it can be argued that he does so not because of reckless egocentricity but because all three imperatives are heard in the poem as addressed to the human condition.

A further and more important justification of the sequence is that it enables Eliot to put 'control' (*Damyata*) at the end, and it is precisely control which the poem has failed to achieve in contemplating and ransacking its contents and in administering to them the vestigial rites of renewal. Moreover, two movements of commitment now precede the attainment of control, and it can be suggested that the former bring about the latter. The elaboration of *Datta* is heavily revised in the manuscript and it is apparent that changes such as 'blood shaking the heart' for 'blood beating in the heart' and 'can never retract' for 'cannot retract' are made to increase the intensity of commitment. In the comment on *Dayadhvam*, the deletion of 'friend, my friend' stresses the isolation of the prison of the self; the same effect is underlined by the replacement of 'murmurs' by 'rumours'; and the substitution of 'confirms a prison' for 'has built a prison' indicates that the first stage in the liberation of ourselves must come from the recogni-

[13] The correct reference is V, 2.
[14] *Facsimile*, 80–81, 88–9. The error persists in the Boni and Liveright text (*Facsimile*, 146).
[15] *Facsimile*, 70–71.

tion of our own imprisonment.[16] All the restorative efforts in the waste land have in truth been acts of self-immurement, fearing the flow of life, coveting the dead gestures, degrading love into lust, contemplating only as annihilation what could be the passage to a fuller and higher existence, till we reach a point where the voice of the thunder is needed to remind us that we once heard the sound of the key turning. Only by blood shaking the heart, by an act of reaching out deep enough to imperil the structures of our lives, can we re-establish the conditions of our being.

As the re-establishment takes place, the commitment beyond the self and the abandonment of the self result not in the losing but in the finding of control. The sea is calm enough for gaiety to transfigure what on the other side of the venture seemed like dread.[17] The 'you' of the third declension (contrasted with the 'we' of the first and the 'I' of the second) enables us to imagine that the Thunder is addressing the speaker of the last lines. The speaker would then be one who had been unable to make the transforming commitment. This is not the effect of the earlier stages of the manuscript, but the revisions may well have been directed to securing such an effect.[18]

The final words are a promise of control, preceded by acts which seem to establish its opposite and succeeded by images in which the old disintegration appears to return and even to be intensified. As the end loops back to the beginning, we are invited to ask ourselves whether we only see a deeper chaos or whether we are able to know the place for the first time. The appearances are those of fragmentation, a delirious babble effective only in suggesting that Hieronimo has attained the peace of madness. If the Thunder had not spoken it would be no more than ingenious to point out that the arid plain is now behind the speaker, or that the erstwhile heap of broken images is now *shored* against his ruins in what may be read as an initial act of retrieval. Since the Thunder has spoken we are able to see how, at the poem's limit, the promise of control announces itself notwithstanding and even paradoxically, because of the images of fragmentation with which it is juxtaposed. We realize that 'Shall I at least put my lands in order' is more than an inquiry

[16] *Facsimile*, 76–9.
[17] Yeats, 'Lapis Lazuli', *Collected Poems* (London, 1950), 292.
[18] *Facsimile*, 79.

as to what can be saved from the holocaust. Behind the ingrained habits of the waste land, the clutching at personal identity and private relics, there remains the possibility of inner restoration. A later poem will say 'This is the land. We have our inheritance',[19] and the modulation will define how experience misses the meaning.

If we consider the shored fragments as the lands which are set in order—a construction which intensifies the movement of disintegration with which the poem ends on one of its levels—we can see how the fire which Arnaut Daniel enters extends the teachings of 'The Fire Sermon' and will, in its turn, extend into the many meanings of fire which dance in 'Little Gidding' round the revival of the same words. To be young like the swallow, the aged eagle must refuse to stretch its wings. He who was advised to guard against death by water must learn in *Ash-Wednesday* to accept death by devouring and must learn in 'The Dry Salvages' how to submit and what is achieved by submission to the on- slaught of that sea which is all about us. The ruined tower, already the symbolic home of another poet, will be found in *Ash-Wednesday* to conceal a winding stair. Though it leads into a garden, a further cycle of poems will make it clear that the peace of the garden can only be momentary, and that we must embark upon a perilous flood, more threatening and therefore more life-giving than the waste land's sterility. If traditions have been found wanting, it is so that a dead master can instruct a living pupil in what is truly creative in the presence of the past. To study the shored fragments is to appreciate that to make an end (in both senses) is truly to make a beginning; but the realiza- tion is brought about by the pointing forward of the poem even more than by its self-evaluative ironies.

The dimension must be searched and its failings felt. Its rites of renewal must be tested and found insufficient. At the edge to which the poem brings itself another dimension can then be manifested, declaring at the point of intersection what is latent in the experience that seems to have been explored. It is typical of the integrity of the poem we are considering that even at this point the meaning is not triumphantly proclaimed. It is not even indisputably recognized. When the declensions of the Thunder are repeated in the last lines, it is almost as if they were another series of fragments, part of the lands which are to be set in order

[19] *Ash-Wednesday, Collected Poems 1909–62*, 98.

instead of the shaping principles which are to order those lands. The final benediction—'Shantih, Shantih, Shantih'—can be read as reflecting the peace of enlightenment, or as indicating no more than exhausted subsidence into a consolatory formula, a termination rather than an ending. We are left with the debris of dialect. If the terms of renewal have been heard on the poem's horizon, it is the subsequent poems that Eliot writes which, by embodying the advance into meaning and speech, will enable us to look back on an earlier journey and to see its significance 'in a different form'.

In recent years there has been a growing understanding that Eliot's work composes a continuity and that his individual poems can only be fully themselves when they are placed and explored in that continuity. 'The constituent things', Dr Leavis writes, 'are in their concentration so completely what they are, the development is so unforeseeable, and yet so compelling in its logic, that the whole body of the poetry affects us as one astonishing major work.'[20] Frank Kermode comments that 'when the Quartets speak of a pattern of timeless moments, of the point of intersection, they speak *about* that pattern and that point; the true image of them is *The Waste Land*. There the dreams cross, the dreams in which begin responsibilities.'[21] My own attempt to characterize the concerns that underlie and integrate Eliot's poetry was published in 1966.[22] This essay has sought to elaborate an important chapter in the response of a mind, distinctive both in its tenacity and in its literary percipience, to the overwhelming questions by which its growth was shaped.

[20] F. R. Leavis and Q. D. Leavis, *Lectures in America* (London, 1969), 55. See also *Education in our Time and the University* (London, 1969).

[21] 'A Babylonish Dialect', *T. S. Eliot: The Man and his Work,* ed. Allen Tate (London, 1967), 243. The movement from *The Waste Land* to *Four Quartets* is perhaps not best described as the movement from image to idea. It could be better—though not altogether adequately—described as the movement from an enabling experience to a subsequent experience that bestows meanings on the previous experience. We should also note that if, as D. W. Harding points out (*Experience into Words*, London, 1963, 106), 'Burnt Norton' is characterized by its creation of concepts, the movement of the Quartets then is from concepts, through experience, to an order built upon and looking back on both.

[22] 'The Overwhelming Question', *The Sewanee Review* LXXIV (Winter, 1966). This issue, with additions, was reprinted as *T. S. Eliot: The Man and his Work.*

What the Thunder Said

D. W. Harding

For people of student age at the present time it takes an effort of historical imagination to realize what *The Waste Land* seemed like when it was a new poem. I met it first in 1925 when I went to Cambridge and found that *Poems 1909–1925* was admired and enjoyed by the stimulating people in the English school, M. D. Forbes, I. A. Richards, F. R. Leavis, who were making a dent in the academic rigidities that had dominated English studies, people who were not just fashionable iconoclasts but disciplined and exacting teachers. They took *The Waste Land* in a very different spirit from the *Times Literary Supplement*, which complained of 'a disinclination to awake in us a direct emotional response', objected to 'blatancies like "the young man carbuncular"', and decided that 'we do not derive from this poem as a whole the satisfaction we ask from poetry'.[1] With its challenging newness of technique, the range of its social reference, the intensity but at the same time the astringency and control of its emotional response to contemporary existence, the poem was a formidable piece of anti-establishment writing. To find it studied now in sixth forms, with prepared notes and predigested opinions to be memorized, is a shock, rather as if you'd watched a magnificent animal in its natural habitat and then years later come on it stuffed in a museum case.

Eliot brushed off the highfalutin literary clichés about its expressing the disillusionment of a generation or being a criticism of contemporary society. Leavis has referred to the poem as too personal compared with the greater achievement of *Four Quartets*, and Eliot had spoken of it in the same terms, saying 'To me it was only the relief of a personal and wholly insignificant grouse against life; it is just a piece of rhythmical grumbling.' We may want to put that beside Tolstoy's dismissal of *Anna Karenina*

[1] *TLS* (20 September 1923).

in his later years as just the story of a loose woman. At the same time there can be no doubt, from the scraps of biographical evidence that are now available, that the poem did emerge from a background of great personal stress. Eliot was struggling in the poem with his own problem, but it was one that highlights similar problems facing innumerable other people of his and later generations.

Central to the strains in his situation was his very difficult first marriage. The details have not been made available, but he was devoted to his intelligent and extremely neurotic wife who suffered from endless ill-health, presumably psychosomatic; to what extent Eliot's own psychological difficulties contributed to hers can only be guessed at. Her illnesses brought heavy expenses for doctors and nursing, this at a time when, because of his marriage and his refusal to return to an academic career in America, his father no longer paid him the allowance on which he had lived during his long years of university study. His family were inclined to believe, he told John Quinn, that he had made a mess of his life. He was anxious to bring out a book as a step towards reconciling them to the path he had chosen, and his father's death in 1919 'does not weaken the need for a book at all—it really reinforces it—my mother is still alive. . . '. Although the conflict with his family was civilized and muted, it must have been an appreciable strain, especially to someone as closely attached to his mother as Eliot evidently was; in 1920 he wrote to his brother: 'I am thinking all the time of my desire to see her. I cannot get away from it. Unless I can really *see* her again I shall never be happy.'[2] Bertrand Russell, who let Eliot and his wife share his flat, aided them financially and gave Vivien Eliot personal help of some kind, but before the publication of *The Waste Land* their relationship with him too had become for Eliot a source of discomfort, evident in the uneasiness and doubt that make painful reading in one of his letters to Russell.[3] Moreover, the work at which he was earning his living at the bank—handling the accounts of former enemy aliens within the terms of the various peace treaties—was demanding and, combined with his private difficulties, left him little energy for the 'long poem' which he said at the end of 1919 'I have had on my mind for a long time'.

Under these strains he became exhausted and a specialist

[2] *Facsimile*, xviii.
[3] *Autobiography of Bertrand Russell* (London, 1968), vol. ii.

ordered him to rest completely for three months, 'quite alone, and away from anyone'. He went first to Margate, but with his wife ('I could not bear the idea of starting this treatment quite alone in a strange place'); after a few weeks there he went alone to a sanatorium in Switzerland for five or six weeks and there had enough rest and uninterrupted time to complete *The Waste Land* in its first, long form. His treatment seems to have been only palliative, neither exploring his personal difficulties nor giving him further insight into them. At that period it was far from easy to get effective psychotherapy. Although some doctors were practising it they were ridiculed, denigrated and obstructed by establishment medicine. Eliot had in the first place gone to a nerve specialist, but as he wrote to Julian Huxley, 'I want rather a specialist in psychological troubles', and he complained that English doctors 'seem to specialise either in nerves or insanity!'

The poem, then, was written during recovery from a nervous breakdown; in the background, during some years of its incuba-tion, was a depressed and anxious and increasingly exhausted man, tied to demanding work in the City instead of being able to do the writing he wanted, and above all involved in the difficulties produced by marriage with a highly neurotic woman. In the poem itself the relation of men and women is central. It has been suggested (e.g. by Hugh Kenner) that the notes to the poem are not to be taken seriously since Eliot supplied them partly to fill up space in the first edition. Though some of them were erudite padding written with his tongue in his cheek others are certainly significant as explicit, straightforward statements of what Eliot saw in the poem, the way he understood it. One of the most important, perhaps the most important, is the note on Tiresias in the scene between the typist and her young man. Eliot is careful to say in the text that Tiresias, 'though blind . . . can see', and his note says 'What Tiresias *sees*, in fact, is the substance of the poem.' What he sees is one version of youthful sexuality, young love we can say ironically, in the debased form given it by city life in London. He has foresuffered both sides of such a sexual encounter and records the nullity of it: for the young man carbuncular only a boost for his ego ('bestows one final patroniz-ing kiss') and for the typist bored indifference ('Well now that's done: and I'm glad it's over').

But, says the same note, the personages of the poem merge, the men melt one into the other and 'all the women are one woman'. So the failure of true relation in sex, of any real communication between persons, in the squalid scene in the typist's bedsitter, is at least one potentiality of the more conventional romantic and lyrical young love of the earlier passage:

'You gave me hyacinths first a year ago;
'They called me the hyacinth girl.'
—Yet when we came back, late, from the hyacinth garden,
Your arms full, and your hair wet, I could not
Speak, and my eyes failed, I was neither
Living nor dead, and I knew nothing,
Looking into the heart of light, the silence.
Oed' und leer das Meer.

The characters, say Eliot, merge; and therefore both young couples are earlier versions of the older pair in 'A Game of Chess'. Here by contrast with the bedsitter the scene is one of opulent luxury, and by contrast with the hyacinth garden oppressively enclosed. The allusions are to Antony and Cleopatra, Dido's feast for Aeneas, the Garden of Eden—all examples of love that comes to grief. Then comes the more brutal sexuality of Tereus towards Philomela, and the dismissal of the whole romantic delusion with the phrase 'And other withered stumps of time'. The hyacinth girl, romantic and overwhelmingly lovely, merges into a querulous neurotic; and the fabulously luxurious interior with its opulent art becomes an unhappy modern flat or hotel—the opulence is Edwardian, as if the Queen of Sheba had furnished at Harrods—with the wind moaning under the door. And the lovers are two people who remain drearily together in spite of neurotic and weary exasperation with each other.

A total failure of communication is a salient part of the misery:

'My nerves are bad tonight. Yes, bad. Stay with me.
'Speak to me. Why do you never speak. Speak.
'What are you thinking of? What thinking? What?
'I never know what you are thinking. Think.'

I think we are in rats' alley
Where the dead men lost their bones.

The lack of communication echoes not only the episode with the typist where nothing but physical contact is attempted, but also the words about the return from the hyacinth garden, 'I could not/Speak'. At first glance that speech might mean that he was just overwhelmed by love, but I think the less happy implication of a failure to communicate lurks even here. Otherwise it would be hard to account for the word 'Yet', which modifies what had seemed romantically happy; and this accords with the final reference to the Tristan story with its frustration of the lovers' reunion.

There are more positive, constructive elements in the poem, and they form an essential part of it, but for the moment we may take these three episodes as a nucleus of the negative aspects. Other passages are organized around them: the typist episode is extended at a slightly more prosperous level in the three Thames daughters and the loitering heirs of City directors; Queen Elizabeth in her obscure and unsatisfactory relation with the Earl of Leicester (whom for political reasons she dare not marry) becomes another Thames daughter at a vastly higher social level, and merges with the neurotic woman of the Game of Chess, since Eliot places Elizabeth in a barge on the Thames, calling up the idea of Cleopatra's barge which in the Game of Chess becomes 'The Chair she sat in, like a burnished throne . . .'; the failed romance links Elizabeth and Leicester with the hyacinth girl; and finally, at a very much lower social level, Eliot epitomizes some of these miseries in the marriage of Lil and her demobbed husband.

It is easy enough to connect these themes of the poem with the personal background of Eliot's life at the time. But if in that sense the poem is personal, it still reflects what have always been problems for a vast number of people. In face of the misery of failing to resolve problems arising out of sexual desire and its involvement with the relations between persons, one resort, all through history, has been to asceticism—sometimes desperate, sometimes dignified. Sex and the pleasures of the senses generally are treated as traps to be avoided. And so the end of Part III of *The Waste Land* culminates, as Eliot's note says, in allusions to St Augustine and the Buddha, 'these two representatives of eastern and western asceticism'. The note is rather prim and pedagogical in manner, in the way Eliot has of exaggerating and slightly mocking his own actual characteristics ('How unpleasant to meet Mr Eliot!/With his features of clerical cut,/And his brow so grim/And his mouth so prim . . .'). But in substance it is of crucial importance, a brief reminder of great religious teachers who found sexuality a false path leading to triviality and dissatisfaction, and who saw no way out except to renounce everything associated with it, including of course the romantic love glimpsed as a possibility in the visit to the hyacinth garden.

And then, appropriately, after the resort to asceticism which concludes Part III, there comes a statement of death, Part IV, 'Death by Water'. The life of the merchant voyager picks up some of the romantic threads of the early parts and weaves them together with its mercantile, commercial features. Phlebas is Mr Eugenides but also, as Eliot notes, is not wholly distinct from Ferdinand Prince of Naples. The references to *The Tempest*— 'This music crept by me upon the waters', 'Musing upon the king my father's death', 'Those are pearls that were his eyes'—bring a romantic story and a rather romanticized handling of death into relation with the realities of the sea-change that Phlebas undergoes—'A current under sea/Picked his bones in whispers.' The cry of gulls and the deep-sea swell again bring up something of the early reference to the romantic Tristan and Isolde story, and this reinforces the allusions to the romantically perfect love of Ferdinand and Miranda.

In spite of the fact that Part IV is a version of an earlier poem and that Eliot had some doubts about including it, there are ample links tying it to what went before. So 'Death by Water' follows immediately on the statement of asceticism that ends Part III, picks up the possibilities of romantic love but submerges them in references to commercialism, with the debased sexuality of the big cities, whether London or Carthage, and sees the end of it all in the dead body disintegrating in the ocean currents. 'He passed the stages of his age and youth'—the phrase covers everyone in the poem from Marie to Tiresias and at the same time suggests the regression from living body to decaying corpse.

The view sometimes put forward that the drowned sailor is meant, among other things, to suggest the god of the fertility cults whose image was thrown into the water each year, to return with the spring and the sprouting corn, seems difficult to reconcile with the dominant feeling of this section of the poem— the sense of ending, the inevitable conclusion of life: 'Consider Phlebas, who was once handsome and tall as you.' It is true that he is prominent among the cards of Madame Sosostris, some of which at all events refer, by way of the Grail legend, to the fertility religions; and if we are meant to have this allusion in mind its hint at renewal does cohere with the effort in the final

Part V to find some positive possibilities, some conceivable recovery from the futility and sterility of the waste land.

Running all through the first four parts of the poem is the failure of vitality, associated with the failure in personal relations, which Eliot represents as the waste land. Soon after he had broken off work with his nervous breakdown, Eliot told Aldington that the trouble was 'due not to overwork but to an aboulie and emotional derangement which has been a lifelong affliction'. It seems to be a lack of zest and drive, a failure of the hope and eagerness that accompany action emerging from deep need and promising its fulfilment, which Eliot essentially represents in the sterile land waiting for rain. The land is waiting also for its king to be cured of his impotence; in the Grail legend the Fisher King is restored from his wound by Parzival. But notice that the theme of the poem is really a failure of vitality in the emotional sense, not literally a failure of fertility. Lil has been more than fertile enough, but her dreary life is all part of the emotionally sterile waste land. At first sight, surprisingly in view of the main theme, the poem actually starts with the coming of rain—April stirs 'Dull roots with spring rain'—but this only emphasizes by contrast the gloomy failure to enjoy, the apparently stony rubbish of the situation he describes:

> What are the roots that clutch, what branches grow
> Out of this stony rubbish? Son of man,
> You cannot say, or guess, for you know only
> A heap of broken images, where the sun beats,
> And the dead tree gives no shelter, the cricket no relief,
> And the dry stone no sound of water . . .

The son of man knows only the infertility. Yet even here the implication is that something is surviving, something is growing out of this stony rubbish. Discontent, disillusionment, misery are not the whole content of *The Waste Land*. There are hints of better possibilities and implicit alternatives all through, especially in the allusions to the fertility rites and the notion of fertility restored. Part V more explicitly concerns itself with the positive possibilities which have been lost or not actualized in what Eliot sees as the desert of postwar life in London.

Although Part V opens with a reference to the Crucifixion, this is not Eliot in his Christian phase and we should not suppose that he was at this time feeling his way towards conversion.

His distance from what he later found in Christianity is suggested by his note on 'Shantih' in the first edition of the poem. There after saying that the repetition of 'Shantih' is a formal ending to an Upanishad, he adds: ' "The Peace which passeth understanding" is a feeble translation of the content of this word'. It is only in later editions that his changed attitude is conveyed in the revised note which reads: ' "The Peace which passeth understanding" is our equivalent to this word.' The Christian story is here one example of the widespread myth of the god who has to be slain (the Adonis, Attis, Osiris whose cults Frazer studied in *The Golden Bough*). The Crucifixion is thus part of the fertility cycle, with resurrection promised but yet to come. Eliot therefore uses the point in the Christian story where the disciples are in a waste land between the Crucifixion and the appearance of the resurrected god—on the journey to Emmaus. This is made into the desperation of a journey through waterless desert, the verse conveying the impression of phantasmagoria and delirium:

> If there were only water amongst the rock
> Dead mountain mouth of carious teeth that cannot spit
> Here one can neither stand nor lie nor sit
> These is not even silence in the mountains
> But dry sterile thunder without rain
> There is not even solitude in the mountains
> But red sullen faces sneer and snarl
> From doors of mudcracked houses
> > If there were water
> And no rock
> If there were rock
> And also water
> And water
> A spring
> A pool among the rock
> If there were the sound of water only
> Not the cicada
> And dry grass singing . . .

At the end of this section comes a hint of the reappearance of Christ, but this (according to Eliot's note) is also the delusion reported by explorers 'at the extremity of their strength' that there was one more member of their party than could actually be counted.

The impression of phantasmagoria and the delirium of people

at the limit of their endurance are widened into an historical vision of cities falling into ruin, with a suggestion of barbarian hordes on the move, and a reference in the notes to the postwar chaos of eastern Europe. The suggestion of lost civilizations and abandoned dwelling places is combined with the ruined chapel of the Grail legend, Chapel Perilous, where the Knight's courage is tested with nightmare visions, including (according to medieval versions of the legend) bats with baby faces.

Tracing out these sources matters much less than feeling what a magnificent climax of exhaustion and near despair Eliot creates. At this extreme, 'In this decayed hole among the mountains', we arrive at the culminating point where sufferings reach their limit and relief comes:

> Only a cock stood on the rooftree
> Co co rico co co rico
> In a flash of lightning. Then a damp gust
> Bringing rain . . .

The extent of the relief that comes, perhaps even the reality of the relief, are left uncertain in the poem. Although the damp gust is said to bring rain, the injunctions spoken by the Thunder are followed by a passage (the final paragraph of the poem) in which we are back with the Fisher King, with the arid plain behind him, still wondering what the future holds—

> Shall I at least set my lands in order?

It is however in the positive values and possibilities expressed through the Hindu legend of the Thunder that Eliot comes nearest to stating psychological alternatives to the sterility of the waste land, or of his own state of 'aboulie and emotional derangement'. What gives added importance to his positive formulations is that he has made highly significant changes from what the Thunder said in the original legend. There we are told that Prajāpati, the Lord of Creation, gives an injunction to each of three groups of students of sacred knowledge, gods, men and devils (asura), who were his threefold offspring. He puts a question to each group, they make their reply, and he confirms that they are right. To the gods his injunction is, Restrain yourselves (Damyata); to the men, Give (Datta); to the devils, Be compassionate (Dayadhvam). This is the translation by R. E.

Hume.[4] In a brief guide meant for schools and colleges, B. C. Southam[5] uses a translation that simplifies the message still further: 'Control yourselves; give alms; be compassionate.'

Eliot alters the order and gives each injunction either a wider or—in one case at least—a quite different meaning from the simple moral precept offered by the more literal translations of the legend. 'Give' comes first. It goes far beyond any simple idea of material benefaction. As Eliot's enlargement of the injunction shows, he is making it refer to self-surrender and commitment. There can be no doubt of the high value he places on it:

> By this, and this only, we have existed . . .

The second injunction, 'Sympathize', implies something much wider than the 'Be compassionate' of the original. It affirms the possibility and the duty of sharing the feelings and outlook of someone else. This seems to be a desperate affirmation, made in defiance of the philosophical position of F. H. Bradley on whose work Eliot had written his doctoral thesis. Eliot in his note quotes from Bradley, 'My external sensations are no less private to myself than are my thoughts or my feelings . . . in brief, regarded as an existence which appears in the soul, the whole world for each is peculiar and private to that soul.' This, in the text of the poem, Eliot converts into the idea of an imprisoned self:

> I have heard the key
> Turn in the door once and turn once only
> We think of the key, each in his prison
> Thinking of the key, each confirms a prison. . . .

Apart from the philosophical position that Bradley was adopting, this standpoint has obvious reference to the failures of communication between people which forms one of the psychological themes of the earlier parts of the poem.

The third injunction, 'Control', is given a totally different meaning in Eliot's formulation from what it has in the Hindu legend. Instead of 'Restrain yourselves' it refers to an action directed to the other person in a relation:

---

[4] *The Thirteen Principal Upanishads* (Oxford, 1931).
[5] *Student's Guide to the Selected Poems of T. S. Eliot* (London, 1969).

> your heart would have responded
> Gaily, when invited, beating obedient
> To controlling hands. . . .

In the abstract, the notion of 'controlling' the other person may seem at odds with contemporary ideas of allowing the other complete autonomy, *not* trying to control him or her. But what Eliot understood by this imperative is indicated much more clearly in the full expository passage: as the boat responded, so her heart would have responded if he had been able to offer an effective invitation. And she would have responded 'gaily', a word that strikes a sharp contrast with the prevailing mood of the poem. The tense, 'would have responded', is crucial: he reproaches himself with failing to elicit something that his partner would have been able to give, with failing to achieve what might have been if he had been able to obey this third imperative.

The importance of Eliot's choice of the conditional tense is emphasized by the fact that it represents a change from an early draft; he first wrote 'your heart responded' and inserted 'would have' as a revision. In fact for each of the three injunctions of the Thunder his explanatory lines fall into a significantly different grammatical form. For the first—'Give'—there is an affirmation implying that the injunction has been obeyed:

> what have we given?
> My friend, blood shaking my heart,
> The awful daring of a moment's surrender
> Which an age of prudence can never retract
> By this, and this only, we have existed . . .

The self-commitment has been achieved and is fully in the past.

For the second word of the Thunder the only statement of what has been done refers to a failure to follow the injunction:

> I have heard the key
> Turn in the door and turn once only . . .

This is a failure to get outside ourselves and obey the injunction of sympathizing; the past records failure, and in the concluding lines the present offers only a doubtful possibility:

> Only at nightfall, aetherial rumours
> Revive for a moment a broken Coriolanus. . . .

The reference to Coriolanus is cryptic, probably condensing a great deal for Eliot personally. Shakespeare's Coriolanus was lacking in sympathy, locked in the prison of his own personality, and he was broken when he gave way to his mother's pleading—broken when he approached sympathy, if indeed that can be seen as an approach to sympathy. Possibly Eliot's lines convey the bare possibility of reviving for a moment a Coriolanus who has learnt to sympathize; they can scarcely imply a recovery of the earlier unbroken man. This passage and the unfinished Coriolan sequence suggest that the figure of Coriolanus focused a conflict not fully explored by Eliot. It is at any rate clear from the form of the passage and its contrast with the lines on 'Give' that while self-commitment is viewed as something that has been achieved, the possibility of any intimate sharing of feelings with another person seems remote, barely conceivable.

With the third injunction, 'Control', we get the past conditional tense and the implication of an irrevocably lost opportunity. The reference by means of the verbal tense to what might have been is crucial. 'What might have been' becomes later one of the important concepts in *Four Quartets*, stated directly as the opening of 'Burnt Norton':

> Time present and time past
> Are both perhaps present in time future,
> And time future contained in time past.
> If all time is eternally present
> All time is unredeemable.
> What might have been is an abstraction
> Remaining a perpetual possibility
> Only in a world of speculation.
> What might have been and what has been
> Point to one end, which is always present.

In *The Waste Land* what might have been is still a matter for self-reproach.

The poem stands by itself, and its achievements and limitations can be assessed without any biographical reference. Since the publication of the facsimile, however, with its admirable introduction by Valerie Eliot, we know enough of Eliot's personal situation at the time to use this as a convenient, though not necessary, approach. Recovering from the worst exhaustion of his nervous breakdown and groping towards faint possibilities of renewal and reconstruction, Eliot was at the same time sufficiently self-aware not to delude himself with hopes or resolutions that could not be fulfilled. He drew three great injunctions from a remote religion, ethical injunctions consistent with any religion or none; but the borrowing was nominal and he gave the three imperatives an interpretation of his own. In his interpretation their bearing on the making of a personal relation is kept to the fore, a relation which can be sexual but is less sterile than the sexual relations glimpsed in the earlier parts of the poem, and so offers an alternative to the flight into asceticism. The words of the Thunder seem to stand quite outside the framework provided for the poem by the fertility cults; they come within it only because, by implication, the emotional sterility conveyed in the first three Parts is essentially the result of a failure in personal relations.

The way in which Eliot formulated his commentary on the three injunctions expressed the degrees of uncertainty he felt about the possibility of putting them into action. Self commitment he saw as achievable; it evidently was so for himself, to judge by his two marriages (which for a man like Eliot could not have been conventional social undertakings) and his conversion to the Anglican Church. These decisions, his rejection of the academic career awaiting him in America, his British naturalization, all point to a man who found it possible to make choices 'Which an age of prudence can never retract'.

The other two injunctions evidently presented greater problems and difficulties. Even in the plays, in fact, he was still preoccupied with the question whether two people can make full and trustful contact with each other and whether fully confiding invitation and response are possible. It was not until *The Elder Statesman* that he could affirm that these are possibilities—and it was a remarkable affirmation in view of the intense psychological difficulties that they involve.

The whole of Part V, 'What the Thunder Said', is highly complex and to some extent ambiguous, corresponding to the precarious situation of a man who has partially recovered from a psychological collapse but remains aware of the formidable obstacles still ahead of him. That situation is reflected not only in the handling of the three injunctions but in the uncertainty which hedges the outcome of the poem. The fertility cults themselves were optimistic; the rain came, the impotent king was cured, the sacrificed god returned with spring and the new vegetation. The ending of Eliot's poem is much less confident. After the Fisher King's hesitant hope

> Shall I at least set my lands in order?

there come brief allusions recalling the theme of ruined cities, rape, and the purgation of lust. The quotation 'Hieronymo's mad againe' suggests the danger of relapse. But the final lines repeat the three injunctions as if they were still valid and still pointed to possibilities; and 'Shantih' expresses the acceptance of things as they are in all their uncertainty.

'The Waste Land':
The Prison and the Key

Richard Drain

> We think of the key, each in his prison
> Thinking of the key, each confirms a prison

The Waste Land is a poem of the isolated sensibility. In it the human dialogue has failed—is shown to fail:

> 'Speak to me. Why do you never speak? Speak.
> 'What are you thinking of? What thinking? What?'

Between the couples that inhabit the poem there is no way of speaking, and no response or responsiveness that might lead to one. The poem's recourse is to conduct a different dialogue: to escape the squirrel cage of the isolated personal condition, to evade the romantic cult of the individual agony, it enters into a dialogue with other literature. This, while no doubt a salutary challenge to the blinkered provincialism into which English poetry had sunk, remains the poem's most notorious technique. It offers to the isolated intellectual the comfort that he still holds the key to a common cultural heritage. But common to whom? Only to intellectuals—if to them. The poem presents its broken or disfigured quotations like the salvaged fragments of some archaeological dig; the heritage, it seems, has been engulfed by the present as by a mass of grey lava. The key confirms the prison.

What it fails to confirm is the nature of the prison. The prison is the self; or else it is the world we live in. To know which it is, or at least which is the real cause of the condition suffered, is vital; or else how can we know what action to take to free ourselves? But within the poem the two cannot be distinguished; this is part of the predicament it expresses. If the poem struggles against this, it is a struggle in a quicksand where each movement submerges it deeper. Thus, its technique of cross-cutting from the immediate scene to a range of different cultures acts like a ceaseless attempt to transcend its own subjectivity: by taking bearings at all points of the compass, it seems to promise an objective and impersonal assessment of where we are. But the effect created is equally that of a head full of echoes, in which experience is filtered through memories of other men's writings, and the boundary between the inner and outer world dissolves in a Bradleyan blur. Appropriately the poem's linking theme is drawn from the Grail legends. For in them the sickness of the King and the sickness of the land are inextricably linked. And so, if *The Waste Land* touches us, it disables us. We might do something about our inner sterility if we were not half persuaded that it is an inevitable consequence of living in our time. We might do something about our time if we were not half persuaded that it appears as it does only through the distorting lens of our inner condition. As it is, we can do nothing, and hopelessness begins to seem like a form of wisdom.

For some time, however, most readings of *The Waste Land* have been content to accept more readily than Eliot that the poem testifies to a sick land rather than a sick mind; that the malaise it expresses is the effect of a decaying culture, and not that the effect of decay is an expression of a malaise. It has been generally agreed that the modern world is the waste land, and the human sensibility its victim. Conservative taste, once so shocked by Eliot's work, has recognized here a theme of its own, and, mollified by its author's later conduct, granted the poem classic status. It is an irony half deserved. Addressed to an élite and leaning upon the fine things of the past, it seems to present itself as the ultimate poem, plucked from the mouth of cultural disaster, a last mutilated survivor from forgotten times, surveying a scene in which poetry must be unnatural and is likely to be impossible— 'Voices singing out of empty cisterns and exhausted wells'. In such circumstances, criticism has tended to give way to a kind of higher fatalism: if the poem's procedures are rarefied, how can they be anything else? Can civilization today hope to do more than shore fragments against its own ruin? Elitism and defeatism have joined to justify each other, discerning in Eliot's poem a spiritual ally.

It may not support them quite as well as they thought. *The*

Waste Land makes it clear that 'culture' in the narrow sense— (a knowledge of the best books)—cannot be relied upon to save us: which is not defeatism, but a simple truth, that in no way encourages the admiring self-regard of a passive elite. However, this is probably not enough to prevent among those impatient of such attitudes a reaction away from Eliot's poem. It is too leading an instance, after all, of the way in which poets, isolated within their culture, have responded by turning poetry into a form of cultural isolationism. And this is likely to lead now to a distrust of Eliot's procedures and a denial of his vision.

This could happen in two ways. On the one hand it is likely that attention will shift from the sickness of the land to the sickness of the King—or in other words, that the criticism of life the poem attempts may find itself explained away in terms of the personal psychological crisis Eliot was suffering at the time he wrote it (as he himself later attempted to do). On the other hand, the poem may come to be viewed more and more as an expression of the moods and attitudes of a class. That class would seem to be an intelligentsia that had reached the point of no return. Mistaking redundancy for independence, aspiring to mandarin status only to find itself on the street, it found itself now obliged to palate the world made by its real family, the bourgeoisie, or else go hungry. It dreamt still of evading a pact with these relations and with 'reality' as they conceived it, and of winning some higher salvation through determined faith in the now invisible world of spiritual values. But stultified by its own ironies, it lacked that faith. Self-accusing in consequence, dispossessed in both the outward and the inner life, it found itself forced at last to face the iron law: that you could not hope for ever to lick the cream of culture and flout those who paid for it.

It is good to recognize that *The Waste Land* was not handed down from God and that its moods are not necessarily incumbent on all men of superior sensibility when they survey their time. It is therefore useful to understand the personal and social pressures that forced it to the shape and bias it has. Yet neither of the responses sketched above is fully adequate to the poem Eliot has written. To find in it the plight only of a particular man, or a particular narrow class of intellectuals, is to amputate what it has to tell us. Whether or not the poem records 'the disillusion of a generation', it certainly expresses moods that were not confined to Eliot, nor to his fellow readers of the classics. It is now a platitude that the nature of modern social life in Western countries is liable to induce feelings of alienation such as the poem treats—not only in that functionless figure, the artist, but equally in the typist, who is a pure functionary. The issues raised by the poem are too wide rather than too narrow, and it will not do to think we have placed and surpassed them. On the other hand, it is no real testimony to the poem to accept it as a final and unequivocal reading of those issues—or to think it offers that. To do so is to ignore the tension out of which it was created. It is to miss the conflicting awareness it strives to express, and the alternatives between which it is so painfully suspended.

It is this conflict and these alternatives that I wish to explore. To this end I want to consider two of the quotations that Eliot brings together at the very end of his poem:

> Le Prince d'Aquitaine à la tour abolie
> These fragments I have shored against my ruins
> Why then Ile fit you. Hieronymo's mad againe.

To explore these lines may seem an academic diversion, unlikely at this late stage of the annotation game to be of much profit. One knows by now that to follow up Eliot's allusions in the poem is to become persuaded of their unfailing suggestive relevance. The question is whether the poem can support the weight of consciousness it thereby takes upon itself—whether it can make it over into full poetic experience. I am not, though, trying to add yet another resonance to the echo-chamber that the poem already is. In choosing these two quotations, Eliot represents the two poetic traditions that by his own testimony most influenced the development of his poetry: symbolism and Elizabethan drama. It is often suggested that these influences are readily compatible. I think they are not, but that they attract Eliot in contrary directions, and represent finally a choice he cannot resolve: a choice not simply of literary modes, but of ways of speaking that would relate him to different hearers; that suggest different conceptions of the dialogue a writer might have with his society; or in short, different keys to his prison. By closing the poem with these lines, he suggests the importance of this to the body of the whole work and the dilemma it treats.

'Le Prince d'Aquitaine' figures in Nerval's sonnet, 'El Desdichado'.

> Je suis le ténébreux,— le veuf,— l'inconsolé,

Le prince d'Aquitaine à la tour abolie:
Ma seule *étoile* est morte,— et mon luth constellé
Porte le *soleil* noir de la *Mélancolie*.

Dans la nuit du tombeau, toi qui m'a consolé,
Rends-moi le Pausilippe et la mer d'Italie,
La *fleur* qui plaisait tant à mon cœur désolé,
Et la treille où le pampre à la rose s'allie.

Suis-je Amour ou Phébus?... Lusignan ou Biron?
Mon front est rouge encore du baiser de la reine;
J'ai rêvé dans la grotte où nage la sirène....

Et j'ai deux fois vainqueur traversé l'Achéron:
Modulant tour à tour sur la lyre d'Orphée
Les soupirs de la sainte et les cris de la fée.[1]

Prufrock, too, had lingered with mermaids—

I have heard the mermaid singing, each to each.
I do not think that they will sing to me.

—and there is the difference: they sing to Nerval as they do not
to Prufrock. Nerval's poem also is a poem of isolation. He
mourns something lost—a lost star, a lost flower, a lost love.
And yet as it moves into its dream grotto, the poem succeeds in
affirming them as mysteriously real and transcendent. In the
process the imprisoning boundaries of the isolated self dissolve;
the poet loses his individual identity; he is equally the Prince of
Aquitaine, Amor or Phoebus, Lusignan or Biron; in him a range
of figures from different cultures can come together, their opposed

---

[1] In Robert Duncan's translation:

I am the dark one,—the widower,—the unconsoled,
The prince of Aquitaine at his stricken tower:
My sole *star* is dead,—and my constellated lute
Bears the black *sun* of the *Melencolia*.

In the night of the tomb, you who consoled me,
Give me back Mount Posilipo and the Italian sea,
The *flower* which pleased so my desolate heart,
And the trellis where the grape vine unites with the rose.

Am I Amor or Phoebus?... Lusignan or Biron?
My forehead is still red from the kiss of the queen;
I have dreamd in the grotto where the mermaid swims....

And two times victorious I have crosst the Acheron:
Modulating turn by turn on the lyre of Orpheus
The sighs of the saint and the cries of the fay.

Bending the Bow (London, 1971)

aspirations reconciled. 'We think of the key, each in his prison'—
the lone poet has found the key; he is released through dream,
and enters a community that knows no frontiers: the self-created
community of the imagination. He discovers the secret identity of
alien civilizations. On the lyre of Orpheus he modulates 'the
sighs of the saint and the cries of the fay'. He becomes a god.

This in the early nineteenth century is to break down the
categories of the reasoning mind. Nerval can achieve this free-
floating elevation only by resorting to the occult—or, finally,
to insanity. When asked why he had taken to leading a lobster
down the road on a ribbon, Nerval replied that it didn't bark
and knew the secrets of the sea—reasons that are cogent enough
from his own point of view, though by the norms of his society
they meant he was demented. To claim before others that one was
holding the Queen of Sheba's garter was tantamount to hanging
oneself in it—which is what Nerval finally did. But in the early
twentieth century no poet needed to resort to such extremes. To
modulate the sighs of the saint and the cries of the fay is a modest
achievement compared to reconciling the knights of the Holy
Grail with pagan fertility rites—and this had been done in a
thoroughly reasonable manner, quite without benefit of madness,
in Jessie Weston's book, *From Ritual to Romance*, from which
Eliot took his guiding ideas for *The Waste Land*. It is as if modern
inquiry simultaneously vindicates Nerval's procedures and outdates them—outdates, that is, their need for occult and irrational
modes. Without incurring any charge of mysticism, Eliot can
make Nerval's connections and more, shaking his cultural
kaleidoscope so that its fragments combine in ever-varying
patterns.

And yet—

> I can connect
> Nothing with nothing

—the variety of patterns the mind can make may defeat its search
for inner coherence. The process may lead nowhere, as Eliot's
verse suggests by its recurrent disconnections, mental blanks
and evocations of meaninglessness. Our sophisticated intellectual
procedures may be just another version of Middleton's game of
chess—a skilled diversionary game, behind which the cynical
initiate can discern the human animal moving automatically to its
banal vices. And behind that again—'In spite of the works of

Watman and Puncher . . . man wastes and pines.' The intellectual
is condemned to futility. Like a latter-day Casaubon, he is still
hankering despite himself for a key to all mythologies, in quest
of a Grail that he has proved to be a Freudian deception.

But Eliot, for all his critical awareness, is not here writing
satire as he did in *Prufrock*; he is not, that is, out to secure that
kind of insulating critical distance between his poem and the
predicament it describes. His poem is immersed in that predicament. It is itself committed to the quest—the quest it can barely
believe in. This is its inconsistency—to continue to strive against
a failure it has all but accepted. Backed by the spirit of modern
knowledge, the poet's mind dallies with beguiling concepts out
of the past: redeeming fires and magic waters, transformations,
mystical unions, surpassings of the self—but all this proves one
thing only: that the mind is haunted by delusions; that 'Hieronymo's mad againe'.

Like Nerval, Kyd allows himself substantial dealings with the
irrational. His play *The Spanish Tragedy*, in which Hieronimo
figures, established mental aberration as a theatrical winner;
and it remained so until the theatres closed down. Whether or
not England became famous for insanity, as the gravedigger in
Hamlet suggests, English drama might well have done. Lunacy
remains arguably our most striking contribution to world theatre.
All the dramatists in whom Eliot is most interested pay it considerable attention.

In *The Spanish Tragedy*, Hieronimo, finding his son brutally
murdered, cannot accept the fact. Bereaved like the speaker in
Nerval's sonnet, he spasmodically persuades himself that his
son still lives, that he sees and talks to him: that he communes
with him as Nerval communes with Amor and Phoebus.

> That corpse you planted last year in your garden,
> Has it begun to sprout?

For Hieronimo, who planted the tree on which his son was hung,
it does sprout, for his son appears to him within the aged form
of Don Bazulto—or so he believes.

Of course, the clear daylight conditions of the Elizabethan
playhouse are different from the private mental world in which
we read symbolist poetry. There is no chance that Kyd's audience
will confuse the living and the dead; no chance that Hieronimo

will persuade them that his subjective visions are in any way true. And Kyd correspondingly confines his delusions to brief spasms, and in between returns him to his senses. Nonetheless, though delusion and reality are plainly separated, Hieronimo returns from the one to the other with a changed perception—with new eyes:

> Oh eyes! no eyes, but fountains fraught with tears;
> O life! no life, but lively form of death.

Eliot's poem similarly deals with transformed vision ('Those are pearls that were his eyes. Look!'). And Kyd's rhetorical conjuring trick, 'O life! no life', can be said to express in summary form the paradox of 'April is the cruellest month', and the poem's essential verdict on the visible world. Hence at the end of the first sequence of 'A Game of Chess', the image that comes to Eliot's mind as the most disturbing is that of lidless eyes ('Pressing lidless eyes and waiting for a knock upon the door'). If one's eyes were lidless, one would have to stare at reality for ever, vulnerable to every speck of the grit and dust into which, under such scrutiny, it decomposes. The effect is to make the reader thankful he can close his eyes; and wishful that he might subsist from time to time, like Nerval, on his inner visions.

But this last image is not one that would have occurred to Kyd. He, naturally, wants his audience to keep its eyes open. He is like the dramatists who follow him—those dramatists who influenced Eliot so much: for his play to survive, he is out to induce not dream, but wakeful attention. So the effect of Eliot's Elizabethan allusion 'Hieronymo's mad againe'—whose obsolete spelling makes it an allusion to a period and not simply a play—is that of an open-eyed demolition of any hopes or consolations that his gathered fragments may have hinted at. And this effect is not properly countered by the wise Sanskrit injunctions and final blessing that he then offers—'Datta. Dayadhvam. Damyata. Shantih shantih shantih'; for they may be nothing but Hieronimo's play—'Ile fit you'—which was a piece written in foreign tongues to enable various deserved killings to be conveniently effected. They may be, that is, one final game of chess, a last learned babbling before the poet, like Hieronimo, bites his tongue out and so finishes; and so too perhaps becomes another Philomel—but one who has finally seen through that beguiling old tale of being changed in recompense for his suffering to a swallow ('O swallow

swallow') or nightingale of 'inviolable voice'; or of transforming
reality with the lyre of Orpheus.

Such an effect makes one reconsider the relation of Eliot's
poem to the symbolist movement, for that relation begins to
seem distinctly equivocal. Consider one of the first passages we
come to in the poem—the Madame Sosostris sequence. It is often
suggested that here we have a characteristic instance of the
breakdown of ancient religious wisdoms in our time. But the
clairvoyant is surely a very marginal figure to pick if one were
wanting to evoke the nature of our times. And the tarot pack
does not embody any wisdom that Eliot was particularly interested in; indeed, his note would suggest that he knew little more
about the tarot than he had picked up from Jessie Weston's book.
Nerval on the other hand was deeply involved in tarot symbolism,
as 'El Desdichado' shows. And an interest in the occult consorted very naturally with the concerns of symbolist poetry
throughout the century. 'Chaque lame du Tarot, suggérant une
multitude de sense harmoniques, résume les rapports subtils qui
unissent les différents octaves de la gamme universelle des
correspondances.'[2] The pack of cards that constitutes *The Waste
Land*, however, suggests a multitude of disharmonies. The
passage that immediately precedes Madame Sosostris is that of
the hyacinth girl. The experience it expresses could be read as
transcendent, though it might equally be seen as disabling:

> . . . I could not
> Speak, and my eyes failed. . . .

Another perhaps is strangling in the Queen of Sheba's garter,
choked by the intensity of his own illusions. And so Eliot
shuffles his cards, and the symbolist poet, who aspires towards
comparable experiences beyond eyesight and rational explanation,
is replaced by Madame Sosostris of the bad cold and the carefully
guarded horoscope. The effect is to satirize these leanings in
the symbolist movement—and equally in the poet of *The Waste
Land* who is still drawn to them.

But these leanings are part of a faith Eliot cannot so easily
relinquish; the faith so frequently expressed by nineteenth-
century poetry in the existence of a reality other than and superior
to the daily material reality, which is supposedly the only one
recognized by the poet's society—bourgeois society, totally

[2] J. Richer, *Gérard de Nerval et les doctrines ésotériques* (Paris, 1947), 106.

preoccupied with getting and spending. This faith was never more radiantly expressed than in the book which introduced Eliot to the symbolists: Arthur Symons's *The Symbolist Movement in Literature*. 'After the world has starved its soul long enough in the contemplation and the re-arrangement of material things, comes the turn of the soul; and with it comes the literature of which I write in this volume, a literature in which the visible world is no longer a reality, and the unseen world no longer a dream.' In fact, like Eliot, the poets of whom Symons writes do not reach that unseen world so painlessly. For example, Mallarmé, in his Baudelairean poem 'Les Fenêtres', sees himself as trapped in a sickening material world, imprisoned among the stupid. This intensifies his yearning for release into the blue purity of the skies beyond the window, even at the risk of failing in his flight and 'falling throughout eternity'. But the absolute dichotomy of his two worlds is not to be broached, and so he remains arrested: unable to break the glass, finding nothing precious save that imagined ineffable draught of life, or death, or both together: 'the heart of light, the silence':

> Mais hélas! Ici-bas est maître: sa hantise
> Vient m'écœurer parfois jusqu'en cet abri sûr,
> Et le vomissement impur de la Bêtise
> Me force à me boucher le nez devant l'azur.
>
> Est-il moyen, ô Moi qui connais l'amertume,
> D'enfoncer le cristal par le monstre insulté
> Et de m'enfuir, avec mes deux ailes sans plume
> — Au risque de tomber pendant l'éternité?[3]

Poetry of this kind, one may say, posits a Holy Grail. And in this way the Grail myth that Eliot treats in *The Waste Land* may be related to the immediate literary tradition, and by implication the whole phase of culture, that he is heir to. But is the poem a critique of that phase pointing a way ahead? Or is it rather a

---

[3] In C. F. MacIntyre's translation:

> But, alas, Here-below is master, his intimacy
> sickens me sometimes in this certain shelter,
> and the dirty vomit of Stupidity
> makes me hold my nose before the azure.
>
> Are there ways, O Self who know asperity
> to break the crystal outraged by this monster
> and to escape, on these wings without feathers
> —at the risk of falling throughout eternity?

self-critical elegy for a collapsed faith—a faith upon which it
nonetheless depends? The 'azur' of Mallarmé's poem—a heaven
strained pure of all theological suggestion—is close to being pure
void. To the generation who suffered the first world war, it was
really not possible to go on proposing this as something to live by.
Eliot does not. The chapel is empty. But without that, what?
Nothing remains but to hope for some miracle or act of grace—
and the poem, with its echoes from Shakespeare's late plays,
stretches to achieve its subtlest music in order to keep that hope
alive. 'Who is that third who walks always beside you?' It is
Godot, and the poem waits for him. It is as if Eliot has seen
through those values by which poets in an alien world had sustained themselves and out of which they had shaped their work;
and yet in the last resort he is unable to break with them.

I am suggesting that the inertia the poem treats is the outcome
not of a doctrinaire pessimism but of an acute ambivalence.
Consider, for instance, the effect of the various allusions to
water in the poem. Water is the element that Eliot substitutes
for Mallarmé's blue air as the element hungered for: the arid
waste land waits for rain. The change is significant in that water
sustains earthly life and satisfies physical thirsts in a more tangible
way than does air. The bodily life and the spiritual life are thus
not set in opposition. And yet neither is there any way of distinguishing the life-giving redemptive water from the water in
which one drowns—the water that picks the flesh from the
bones of Phlebas the Phoenician. The different parts of the poem
work to confuse the sense, like the lady's perfumes in 'A Game
of Chess'. We cannot tell where life lies. What might seem to be
the life forces are suspect or treacherous: April is the cruellest
month. The sexual forces are invoked, yet turned from with
disgust. This creates a form of paralysis in the poem, and puts at
its centre an image of the human being as inert raped female—
'Supine on the floor of a narrow canoe'—without response to
that which divides its knees, or by the same act its psyche. There
are some lines by Yannis Ritsos:

> . . . and simultaneously the age-old clatter
> of those keys about which he could never with certainty
> discover whether they were unlocking or locking up.[4]

---

[4] Yannis Ritsos, 'Dusk', from *Twelve Poems for Cavafy*, translated by
Paul Merchant (London, 1971).

Eliot is similarly uncertain.

Whatever the limits this ambivalence finally sets upon the poem's grasp of life, it allows it to draw on a more native heritage than that of French symbolism or English drama. For all its European influences, *The Waste Land* seems a distinctly American work, looking back to that American literary heritage in which, in response to the sharp ethnic oppositions within American culture, the meaning of black and white, can be totally transferred. It is the heritage of Poe's *Gordon Pym*—in which we cannot tell whether the strange whiteness of the waters is that of ashes or milk, their warmth that of life or of some ultimate fire. It is the heritage of Melville, Twain, Hawthorne and James—writers in whom the possibility of some phantasmogoric reversal (of values, roles, or even the physical environment) is always present. Ishmael's moral doubts find visionary expression when he wakes to find his ship seemingly flying backwards. In *The Waste Land*, the world turns upside down—

> And bats with baby faces in the violet light
> Whistled, and beat their wings
> And crawled head downward down a blackened wall
> And upside down in air were towers
> Tolling reminiscent bells, that kept the hours

In accordance with such inversions, Tiresias is male or female—but Eliot's American roots are such that the notional figure at the poem's centre often seems closer to James's Lambert Strether (whose sexuality is also neutralized) than to Tiresias: Strether who, in an alien country, seeks vainly to distinguish life from corruption: 'Then there was something in the great world covertly tigerish, which came to him across the lawn and in the charming air, as a waft from the jungle. . . . These absurdities of the stirred sense, fruits of suggestion ripening on the instant—' such fruits of suggestion ripen again in *The Waste Land*. 'The chair she sat in, like a gilded throne'—the rich European bric-à-brac receives once more the alien American scrutiny, in which hypnotized fascination gives way to intimations of decadence and sterility.

These critical misgivings, reflected as they are in an imagery of drought distinctly foreign to our climate, have today an unexpected effect: it is as if *The Waste Land* is the first poem to imagine how Europe might appear within the perspectives of the Third World. But the vision of ourselves we are given is touched with a sense of hallucination and nightmare that disturbs the critical focus of the poem. Despite the consciousness of varied cultures that is sustained in us, we are given no firm vantage point from which to judge whether life beneath its deceptive styles and appearances has ever been of a truly higher order than it is now—or than it is now in the vision of the poem. True, the verse often juxtaposes a banal present against an apparently richer past. But as the richness itself is made morally suspect, where we expect a contrast we are often left with an implied analogy, as if behind the period façades the same emptiness might be found in any age. 'Jerusalem Athens Alexandria Vienna London'—the cities dissolve into a featureless horizon, in which we are hard put not to discern the universal human condition. *'Oed' und leer das Meer.'* True that lovely lady of the eighteenth century had her moral anguish where the modern typist has only her gramophone. But this distinction dwindles if history itself is a gramophone. The poem often suggests as much, and more. Life is a gramophone, and the poem too: voices from the past issue distortedly from it, caught within an eternally replayable present that has no hope of change, nor of vital meaning.

This mocks the historical reach of the poem, and nullifies the sense of perspective that it seems to promise. It also twists a knife in the poetry it is made of. If the difference between cultures and cultural styles ultimately makes no difference, why bother to cultivate those differences with such unprecedented care in the texture of one's verse? The poem is alienated from its own subtly-studied surface. It practises an art that it does not trust. It cuts off its own fine ear.

But in the insecurity of its aims and its art and the diminishing of its outward perspectives the poem reaches its true centre. It lives as an expression of acute deprivation. It speaks of a life deprived of relationship with others, and of sexual or spiritual fulfilment; a life deprived of meaning. The deep need for a code or faith or myth by which this condition can itself be given meaning is the motive of the poem. But by allowing it to fail (still, at the close of the poem, 'The limp leaves/Waited for rain'), Eliot realizes the essence of the condition, and wins the power to communicate it with a disturbing intensity. As we read we view not simply a landscape of the mind, but a territory of

human experience. It unfolds before our eyes with an unreal
immediacy, like the hallucinations of a starving man:

> Above the antique mantel was displayed
> As though a window gave upon the sylvan scene
> The change of Philomel, by the barbarous king
> So rudely forced; yet there the nightingale
> Filled all the desert with inviolable voice
> And still she cried, and still the world pursues,
> 'Jug Jug' to dirty ears.
> And other withered stumps of time
> Were told upon the walls; staring forms
> Leaned out, leaning, hushing the room enclosed.
> Footsteps shuffled on the stair.
> Under the firelight, under the brush, her hair
> Spread out in fiery points
> Glowed into words, then would be savagely still.
>
> 'My nerves are bad tonight. Yes, bad. Stay with me.
> 'Speak to me. Why do you never speak? Speak.
> 'What are you thinking of? What thinking? What?
> 'I never know what you are thinking. Think.'

The language here, at first even, cool and simple, safe in its
museum, swells in romantic beauty ('Filled all the desert with
inviolable voice'), and then betrays us. A word sways out of
sequence, repeating itself ('Leaned out, leaning') throwing our
sense of progression minutely off balance; across the borders of
logic, things and emotions infect each other, with a sensory
immediacy: her hair 'Glowed into words, then would be savagely
still'. And the words that come, ('My nerves—') come with the
staccato starts and stuck-needle repeats of the neurotic mind;
the spoken language of those who cannot converse.

It is the range and flexibility of Eliot's language that is striking;
a range and flexibility we can only compare with the developed
achievements of Elizabethan or Jacobean dramatic verse; and
that testifies to his study of that verse quite as surely as his
closing reference to *The Spanish Tragedy*. But the playwrights of
that earlier tradition did not achieve those qualities by such
study, or at least by such study alone. Their verbal effects were
not bred in a linguistic test-tube. Their range developed because
they were addressing a range of people, their audience; their
flexibility because they needed to keep them all interested at
once. We do not need to idealize their situation: it encouraged

the pointless sensationalism and capitulation to majority prejudice that all too often mark the plays of the time. But the dramatist of that period, whoever he is, is not locked in his prison dreaming of the key. He is exposed to a public; his actors must hold their own, usually in daylight on an open stage, with his words. Those words in consequence must match the range of his audience's knowledge, experience, awareness and wit, meet them not only in the special rhetoric of the theatre but also in their own idiom. His language is therefore not simply *his* language, nor simply a language he has found in books. His words spring from the dialogue of a living society, and it is this brought to dramatic focus that we hear in the major plays.

It makes no sense finally to cultivate a flexible language unless you are choosing to be involved in a comparable situation: unless you have listened and wish to speak to a range of people. In Elizabethan drama, Eliot found a key different from that offered by Nerval—a language that could do so. But in *The Waste Land* he tries both to accept it and reject it. He unlocks an inner vision, but the prison gates stay shut. He frames the key and hangs it on the wall.

For all the genius of the poem, it cannot escape being affected by this. For comparison, consider Marlowe's *Faustus* and the way in which its hero's visions can be succeeded by the following exchange:

Wagner: The villain is out of service, and so hungry that I know he would give his soul to the devil for a shoulder of mutton, though 'twere blood raw.

Clown: Not so, good friend. By'r Lady, I had need have it well roasted and good sauce to it, if I pay so dear.

Faustus is the clown, but the clown is not Faustus. Humanity is common, but its voices are different enough. These might have broken in from the audience if the play had not forestalled them. It does, exposing its theme to the repartee of the non-privileged, and thereby to a full range of human impulse and reaction. Compare the equivalent effect in *The Waste Land*:

Well, that Sunday Albert was home, they had a hot gammon,
And they asked me in to dinner, to get the beauty of it hot—
HURRY UP PLEASE ITS TIME

The clown is ordered off the stage before he can begin. The

dissenting voice which speaks up for its ordinary appetites and the beauty of hot gammon cannot be accommodated—whereas in the Elizabethan playhouse it cannot be kept out.

If the mood of Eliot's poem is deepened by this, its range is circumscribed. The rapid changes of tone the poem practises distract us from the narrowness of its emotional content rather than fill it out. The series of null sexual relationships the poem sketches, consummated or not consummated under the shadow of a library bookshelf, do not provide a spectrum of life so much as reiterate a theme. They have been chosen as selectively as the quotations that set them off. And that the poem should strive for impersonality when the bias of its attention is so personal seems self-defeating. It is as if Eliot sought to turn alienation to account as a way of objectively distancing his subject. Yet the distancing effects the poem's practises—the cooling changes of tone, the dissonant juxtapositions, the stylistic framing of scenes—are expressive above all of alienation.

It is an alienation not only from the life of the times, and the life of the sexes, but also from the self. Impersonality may be the ideal of a person attempting to turn away from himself—or away from that person he fears he might be: he perhaps who, faced with the injunctions of the Thunder, has no sins to confess, but only incapacity and lack of courage. The poem cultivates an art of poetic ventriloquism in which the personal voice is muffled, a forest of references to life and literature elsewhere in which the self is evaded. The poem's brilliance diverts its energies in a game of intellectual cat's-cradle, and this allows it inwardly to remain sunk in pervasive emotional states that will not come to a head. Its visions are compelling but the poem will not rise to certain intensities—the intensity it almost mutely points to in the line

Burning burning burning burning

There is much in 'The Fire Sermon' but nothing to burn us—as perhaps there needs to be for it to move us forwards through the ritual-dramatic arc of the poem into Death ('Death by Water') and beyond. 'Poetry is the language of a state of crisis': Mallarmé's saying is true of *The Waste Land*; but the crisis will not break, and that is the nature of the crisis.

The injunctions of the Thunder in the final section do not go very far towards changing this. The application they are given in the lines following them seems, like the 'hyacinth girl' passage, to be a surfacing of personal preoccupations that we have not been allowed fully to understand. They cannot resolve a poem which has extended its cultural concerns so widely. They hint at a salvation to be found through simple relationship with another; and the efficacy of this, in the given world of *The Waste Land*, we cannot trust.

The problem lies in the relation a man has with people at large—with society—and not simply with this friend or that woman. Eliot's preoccupation with Elizabethan drama and the suppleness of its language implicitly acknowledges this. It offers him a key quite opposed to the poetry of the previous century which had most shaped his own. It beckons him towards a different confrontation with his world. He moves to follow, but opens the wrong door; and walks into the prison of Culture—where his poem lives after him, illustrious and trapped.

'To fill all the desert with inviolable voice'

A. D. Moody

'Gesang ist Dasein'
(Rilke, *Sonette an Orpheus*, I. 3)

A poem may evolve in the minds of its readers. It will not change essentially; yet it grows as our ways of experiencing and conceiving it develop. For each generation and all readers must make their own the works which they inherit, by rediscovering their original force, and so conserving and continuing it. *The Waste Land* after fifty years is a live poem, but ours only if we can 'make it new'.

Proof of its vitality is its outliving the established ways of reading it. While the poem compels, the received criticism ceases to convince. That it is a poem about a crisis or breakdown of European culture, and that it seriously invokes primitive fertility myths—such accounts, for so long found persuasive, now seem out of touch with the actual experience.

The accounts which will replace them will be as partial, but they should have the advantage of expressing our own best sense. I think it likely that in the next phase of the poem's life much more attention will be paid to the element of deep personal emotion. Its presence is not a new discovery. But earlier critics hardly knew what to make of it; or they took Eliot's idea of Impersonality—that poetry 'is not a turning loose of emotion, but an escape from emotion; . . . not the expression of personality, but an escape from personality'[1]—to mean that it would be illicit to take notice of the personal element. But there is a great difference between directing attention upon the poet's private life,

---

[1] 'Tradition and the Individual Talent' (1919), *Selected Essays* (London, 1951), 21.

outside the poem, and directing it upon the poetic persona, or personality enacted within the poem.

It is the poet within the poem that concerns me, not the man he was nor the experience behind it. I suppose that as we come to know more and speculate more about Eliot's private life, we will be drawn towards reading the poetry by its light. The publication of the original drafts of *The Waste Land* has had that effect, both helpfully and distractingly. There have been memoirs, and no doubt there will be more, which seem to add mainly to the distraction. But we may prevent the error of reading the poem as a document of the early years of Eliot's first marriage—an error as extreme as to read it as a document of European culture—by seeing that it *is* the expression of intense personal feeling, but only in an impersonal form. We are wrong to think that the personal ceases to be personal when it achieves impersonal expression. It is rather intensified and verified.

When Eliot said he wrote *The Waste Land* 'simply to relieve his own feelings'[2] he was perhaps speaking for effect, in reaction against the prevalent opposite view. Yet a true and profound meaning can be given to the remark. It is a meaning which turns the established views inside out. Within the notion that the poem is about the breakdown of Europe, is the fact that it does express the process of breakdown and reintegration which may occur in the individual psyche. And the inner aspect of the fertility ritual (as one might gather indeed from Miss Weston's *From Ritual to Romance*) also enacts the process of spiritual and psychic regeneration, as a *rite de passage* from a fallen or failed state to a perfected one.

If Eliot's criticism in the early 1920s spoke with another voice, it was perhaps to divert attention from what most nearly concerned him. He could confess later that 'a poet may believe that he is expressing only his private experience; his lines may be for him only a means of talking about himself without giving himself away; yet for his readers what he has written may come to be the expression both of their own secret feelings and of the exultation or despair of a generation'.[3] At the time though he tended to put it just the other way, as in his approval of the method of *Ulysses*:

[2] *On Poetry*, an address at Concord Academy (Concord, Mass., 1947), 10.
[3] 'Virgil and the Christian World' (1951), *On Poetry and Poets*, 122–3.

In using the myth, in manipulating a continuous parallel between contemporaneity and antiquity, Mr Joyce is pursuing a method which others must pursue after him. . . . It is simply a way of controlling, of ordering, of giving a shape and a significance to the immense panorama of futility and anarchy which is contemporary history. . . . It is a method for which the horoscope is auspicious. Psychology (such as it is, and whether our reaction to it be comic or serious), ethnology, and *The Golden Bough* have concurred to make possible what was impossible even a few years ago. Instead of narrative method, we may now use the mythical method. It is, I seriously believe, a step towards making the modern world possible for art. . . .[4]

Obviously that asks to be applied to *The Waste Land*. But in that poem (as we can now see quite clearly from the drafts[5]) the method served to make possible for art, not the modern world but his own disordered inner world. He was oppressed by the problem which in 1919 he attributed to Hamlet and to Shakespeare:

The subject might conceivably have expanded into a tragedy . . . intelligible, self-complete, in the sunlight. [But] *Hamlet*, like the sonnets, is full of some stuff that the writer could not drag to light, contemplate, or manipulate into art.[6]

The problem is that of giving expression to feelings which otherwise remain 'to poison life and obstruct action'. His way of putting this in 1927 is much more illuminating for *The Waste Land* than those remarks about the mythical method—or the impersonal theory of poetry:

What every poet starts from is his own emotions. . . . Shakespeare, too, was occupied with the struggle—which alone constitutes life for a poet—to transmute his personal and private agonies into something rich and strange, something universal and impersonal. The rage of Dante against Florence, or Pistoia, or what not, the deep surge of Shakespeare's general

[4] '*Ulysses*, Order and Myth', reprinted from *The Dial* (November 1923) in *Forms of Modern Fiction*, ed. W. Van O'Connor (Bloomington, Indiana, 1948), 123–4.
[5] I have made a case for this view of the drafts in a review in *The Cambridge Quarterly* (Summer 1972).
[6] 'Hamlet' (1919), *Selected Essays*, 144.

cynicism and disillusionment, are merely gigantic efforts to metamorphose private failures and disappointments.[7]

He added: 'The great poet, in writing himself, writes his time.' But in the case of *The Waste Land*, in writing himself he wrote a work which expressed, not history, but a permanent truth about the inner life of the individual.

I am not proposing to unwrite the poem by trying to get back to the 'personal and private agonies'. But I am concerned to observe the poet, within the poem, engaged in the struggle which alone constitutes his life, to enter into lucid possession of his experience of frustration and failure, and to transmute it into a creative form. The process is one of self-knowledge and of a progressive integration of the self; and its climax comes when wholeness of being is achieved in song.

Read in this way the poem may become charged with a drama of direct interest to our own inner life. We may come to see that the waste land is not the modern world, so much as the landscape of an inward desolation. It is the poetic mind or psyche that is as if dead. Yet at the same time it is struggling against its death. The death might be described as an inability to feel or to express feeling—what Harry in *The Family Reunion* calls 'the partial anaesthesia of suffering without feeling'. The struggle is to recover feeling through lyrical expression. In the poem's own terms, it is a struggle to get beyond the state of Tiresias, who because he has foresuffered all is now 'the mere spectator', and to become like Philomela and Arnaut Daniel who can sing their suffering. If the mind in the poem is successful, the poem will be not simply the expression of its desolate disorder, but the very process of its regeneration. For in transforming its inner waste into lyrical utterance it will have come alive.

This may be offering a new reading, and yet it is only to place *The Waste Land* within the tradition of Orphic poetry.[8] Orpheus' song was held to animate nature, to bring alive the souls of things. (A more contemporary way of thinking about the matter could be found in Jung, but the story is to me more suggestive than the psychology.) From this point of view the English poet whose

---

[7] 'Shakespeare and the Stoicism of Seneca' (1927), *Selected Essays*, 137.
[8] A very good book in this connection is Walter A. Straus's *Descent and Return: the Orphic Theme in Modern Literature* (Cambridge, Mass., 1971).

work is most nearly related to Eliot's is Coleridge—with whom he felt a particular affinity, as it happens. *The Ancient Mariner* closely parallels *The Waste Land* in its inner process and meaning. And 'Dejection' diagnoses a disorder which Eliot too had to 'make move and live'—

> A grief without a pang, void, dark, and drear,
> A stifled, drowsy, unimpassioned grief,
> Which finds no natural outlet, no relief. . . .

Colderidge's images and ethos are quite distinct from Eliot's; and yet there is an essential correspondence between his invocation of 'The passion and the life, whose fountains are within', and the inviolable voice which at the climax fills the waste land:

> And would we ought behold, of higher worth,
> Than that inanimate cold world allowed
> To the poor loveless ever-anxious crowd,
> Ah! from the soul itself must issue forth . . .
> A sweet and potent voice, of its own birth. . . .

Coleridge had perhaps experienced as profoundly as anyone the ecstasy of being wholly and fully expressed in lyric form, if only in rare and privileged visitations:

> Could I revive within me
> Her symphony and song,
> To such a deep delight 'twould win me,
> That with music loud and long,
> I would build that dome in air,
> That sunny dome! those caves of ice!

*

The phases of the process now to be traced through *The Waste Land* are these: first, the primary experience of passion and its burnt-out aftermath; second, the deepening sense of emptiness in personal existence and of alienation from all life; third, the state of alienated vision in which a 'dead' world objectifies the 'dead' mind; but then in the presentation of the deadened state as others suffer it there appears a strain of sympathetic response along with the revulsion; and from this sympathy comes a direct suffering of the poet's own deprivation and loss. In this last state the primary experience is immediately felt and expressed; and the poet's at last finding his own voice in song is the token of the reintegration of the self that had been alienated.

The personal predicament at the heart of the poem is first revealed in lines 31–42: an intimate instance of the classic tale of romantic passion—or Wagner's *Tristan* distilled. The quotations, from the opening and from the final act of the opera, establish far-reaching perspectives. Within them, what the woman says, and what the poet reflects, are charged within intense and ambivalent feelings. Her words evoke the hyacinthine experience, but retrospectively and through the sad echo of others' words: so that the present experience is of loss. His wondering retrospect recovers the moment more directly only to bring out more clearly its defeating doubleness: this ecstasy annihilates ordinary sense, and afterwards it is the desolation which persists. Thus in this instance romantic passion seems to mean an empty ending.

Eliot's way of developing and shaping this primary material is to surround that passage with analogies and contrasts which will expand and objectify it, as 'hyacinth' and 'heart of light' are expanded by the *Tristan* allusions. The opening paragraph declares a generalized, choric weariness at the endless recurrence of seasons which bring no inner renewal; then modulates into a particular voicing of the bleak prospect (it might be the hyacinth girl's) beyond the death of passion. Here, and even more in the prophetic voice which follows, one can see why Eliot should have thought of putting 'Gerontion' as a preface. This voice expresses a reflex of consciousness contending with the loss of passion, attempting to maintain integrity and a sense of control by insisting that things are as they are. Instead of Marie's nostalgia and pathos, it finds through denunciation the strength to renounce the life that is lost. Yet that is only another way of fixing the state, and can show no more than 'fear in a handful of dust'. Its effect is to make inevitable and universal what we are about to see in the particular instance.

There is an interesting parallel to this prophetic voice in Tennyson's 'Tiresias'—one passage of which suggests a near connection between prophecy and passion:

> the winds were dead for heat;
> The noonday crag made the hand burn; and sick
> For shadow—not one bush was near—I rose
> Following a torrent till its myriad falls
> Found silence in the hollows underneath.
>   There in a secret olive-glade I saw
> Pallas Athene climbing from the bath

In anger; yet one glittering foot disturbed
The lucid well; one snowy knee was prest
Against the margin flowers; a dreadful light
Came from her golden hair; her golden helm
And all her golden armour on the grass,
And from her virgin breast, and virgin eyes
Remaining fixt on mine, till mine grew dark
For ever, and I heard a voice that said
'Henceforth be blind, for thou hast seen too much. . . . '

Madame Sosostris, the contemporary soothsayer, I am inclined
to take as the parody of the prophetic voice. Perhaps she speaks
more sense than she can know. Yet she speaks only to our fears,
and her dealings in the occult simply confirm mortality in passion.

The final paragraph of Part I answers to the first (as the outer
panels of a pentaptych), presenting in the Unreal City the general
state of men who have lost their passion, and whose time-bound
existence generates no significant life or feeling. The corpse
that figures so fantastically at the end is, like Hamlet's levity,
'a form of emotional relief': only by something so violent and
unreal can the need for a burial of these walking dead be asserted.
The generalization, however, as the line from Baudelaire's
'Au Lecteur' insists, would include us all in this universe of death.
If the heart of 'The Burial of the Dead' is a specific personal
experience, the whole would confirm its negative conclusion as
the ultimate truth of experience.

Thus the tone of Part I enforces the Sybil's dusty 'I would die',
as it would have done this epigraph in the drafts from *The Heart
of Darkness*:

Did he live his life again in every detail of desire, temptation,
and surrender during that supreme moment of complete
knowledge? He cried in a whisper at some image, at some
vision,—he cried out twice, a cry that was no more than a
breath—
'The horror! the horror!'

Eliot allows very little to relieve the horror of death in life, and no
promise at all of release from it. To invest hope in the fertility-cult
associations of certain images would be to mistake their tones,
which range from despair through disbelief to buffoonery without
ever becoming serious or positive. In particular, 'That corpse
you planted last year in your garden' must be 'the buffoonery

of an emotion which can find no outlet in action'. And that places the protagonist in the predicament of Tennyson's Tiresias:

> Virtue must shape itself in deed, and those
> Whom weakness or necessity have cramped
> Within themselves, immerging each, his urn
> In his own well, draw solace as he may.

Much later there will be 'voices singing out of empty cisterns and exhausted wells'.

At the centre of 'A Game of Chess' is the passage of dialogue which expands the aftermath of the hyacinth garden experience into a stark drama. His dead response can only confirm her hysterical terror of a void at the heart of life. His state is the more terrible in that he seems not to feel what he sees. His violence, savagery and burlesque are perhaps desperate efforts to stir feelings. But they are the reverse of sympathy—rather a matter of 'Thinking of the key, each confirms a prison'.

The objectifying material surrounding that passage is more directly related to it than was the case in Part I. The long opening passage fills in a far-reaching background to this sad end to romantic love, associating the former hyacinth girl with the long line of *femmes fatales* stretching back to Eve. That is to make her the exemplary present moment of that history, However, that this Cleopatra is not Shakespeare's, nor the Dido Virgil's, nor the Belinda Pope's, shows that all here is being seen by that same sad-eyed, blank-souled man who will confirm that the woman has real cause for her neurosis. The pub monologue is just as much 'what he sees', for all the apparent objectivity conferred by the demotic idiom. If this is what romantic passion comes down to in the London of the day, it may be because that is all he is able to perceive. For while there is a show, here as in Part I, of doing the Police in different voices, the felt fact is that everything is shaped and coloured by just the one powerful point of view.

The only relieving feeling is the woman's hysteria, with which must be associated the strikingly distinct 'inviolable voice' of Philomel—how her picture speaks from the midst of that verbal desert!—and also Ophelia's farewell to Hamlet's mother. That is, the poet does register, as well as death-in-life, the anguish of those who feel it, and go mad or transmute it into song. These voices, which exceed the poet's own responses, are the significant

development from Part I. There the voices were all subdued to
the poet's own disillusion. These, though brief and broken, are
urgently passionate; and in feeling their tragedy they stand
against mere dulled despair.

In this paradox begins the poem's major development. For the
initially dominant voice, which resembles those of Gerontion or
The Hollow Men, is first countered by these suffering ones, then
will become like them. The difference between the two states is
subtle yet radical, a difference in the way of experiencing the
same facts which will amount to exchanging the fixity of death
for return to life. In the imagery of *The Hollow Men*, a poem which
was more a continuation of *The Waste Land* than a new departure,
there is on the one side the 'sightless' vision of 'our dried voices'

> quiet and meaningless
> As wind in dry grass
> Or rats' feet over broken glass

and on the other

> There, the eyes are
> Sunlight on a broken column . . .
> And voices are
> In the wind's singing
> More distant and more solemn
> Than a fading star.

In 'The Fire Sermon' the dramatic tension between these two
elements is fully developed. And what Tiresias sees is succeeded
by what the Thames-daughters sing. Eliot's notes, misleadingly
helpful as ever, direct attention only to Tiresias, in whom the
several male voices merge. But I do not find that the women
meet in him as the note would have it. Indeed, it is just their
retaining a distinct expression that saves the work from his
blank nihilism.

There is no difficulty in following the modulation of the poet's
voice from Part II into that of Ferdinand-Tiresias. The preoccupation with rats and bones, the dead resonances out of *The
Tempest* and *Hamlet*, the twisted levity of lines 185–201, and the
sightless vision of typist and young man carbuncular, are all
expression of the one predominant state. But now, instead of
realizing itself in a dramatic relationship, this state is projected
upon the 'objective' world of the 'Unreal city'. The poet is ventur-

ing an ambitious generalization from his personal experience: as he is, so is all the world. If his passion's end is emptiness, then all passion is vain and without meaning.

However, while this part of the poem does very effectively find no meaning in the life it observes, the reader needs to see that what *he* has to reckon with is the projection of a state of mind. In the hyacinth garden or the nerves dialogue, or in the Thames-daughters song, the voices have an objective identity to which we may respond directly with our own eyes and ears. But when Tiresias speaks we see only what he sees, and hear only his voice. The typist, of all the women in the poem, is the only one to feel nothing; but the tired boredom may be more his than hers. At any rate we should take what he says critically, not as authoritative. What Eliot wrote of Tourneur seems pertinent:

> 'Tourneur's great defect as a dramatic poet', says Collins, 'is undoubtedly the narrowness of his range of vision': and this narrowness of range might be that of a young man. The cynicism, the loathing and disgust of humanity, expressed consummately in *The Revenger's Tragedy*, are immature in the respect that they exceed the object. Their objective equivalents are characters practising the grossest vices; characters which seem to be spectres projected from the poet's inner world of nightmare, some horror beyond words. So the play is a document on humanity chiefly because it is a document on one human being, Tourneur; its motive is truly the death motive, for it is the loathing and horror of life itself. To have realized this motive so well is a triumph; for the hatred of life is an important phase—even, if you like, a mystical experience—in life itself.[9]

This gives a new gloss to the blindness of Tiresias; and connects it with Bradley's 'the whole world for each is peculiar and private to that soul'. To object that the presentation of the typist and clerk does less than justice to life's potentialities is to see only half of the matter. For the further and greater point is that this is how life appears to one in whom it has failed.

While that is the dominant voice and vision, others offer themselves to our attention. Spenser's nymphs, and Goldsmith's, are evoked in this waste of passion neither nostalgically nor sardonically: the tone is nearer to elegy, in that the dismissal preserves a direct feeling for what is lost. This makes the opening

[9] 'Cyril Tourneur' (1930), *Selected Essays*, 189–90.

paragraph antiphonal, from its first statement: 'The river's tent/ is broken'. Though the weighting is strongly towards 'But at my back in a cold blast I hear', that urging to despair is checked in the refrain 'Sweet Thames run softly till I end my song'— which we hear with its own harmony, as well as discordantly in this new context—and in the more piercing music of the Biblical exile's lament. Compared with the surrounding flat or harsh musings, these feel and utter a kind of love. Surprisingly, in the final two quatrains of the typist episode there is a related softening of detached observation towards anguished sympathy. The visual account would dissolve 'lovely woman' to 'automatic hand', and the rhyme would mock 'alone' with the mechanical 'gramophone'. Yet the movement is closer to Goldsmith in feeling than to that brittle satire. The music sympathizes with what the seer would repudiate.

This counterpoint of what the ear may hear against what the eye sees becomes more telling from here to the end of Part III. 'This music crept by me upon the waters', with the eight lines following, might appear to set up sardonic contrasts between the evoked past and actuality. But there is a music actual and immediate in the verse itself, which is not the primitive gramophone's bray, but nearer to Ariel's song than anything heard in the poem as yet. The mandoline and the fishmen's chatter are accepted with the 'inexplicable splendour': what lies beyond them does not sour them (as was the case in 'Lune de Miel'). Possibly this is contrary to the conscious intention; but then the music of poetry does surpass what the conscious mind can conceive. Moreover, it is vital in *The Waste Land* that our sympathetic life should be stirred, not fixed in Tiresias' basilisk stare.

The very form of the Thames-daughters song follows the pressure in the poem towards lyricism. Of course if one does not (in Hopkins' phrase) 'read it with the ears and not the eyes only', it is possible to register only broken phrases and lines and find no difference, unless intensification, between 'I can connect/Nothing with nothing' and 'Nothing again nothing' at line 120. But the latter led naturally to the self-lacerating recollection of 'that Shakespeherian rag'; while this is a song that does strangely allay the fury and the passion. (Or the difference can be measured by reference to the original drafts, where at first the voice was that of Tiresias' seeing, but then a genuinely objective voice was refined out to speak itself simply and directly.)

With the movement from observation to immediate utterance, the distance between poet and object is dissolved, and so too is the gap between perception and feeling. That the nymphs' predicament of numbed negation should be felt, as it is, appears a paradox. Yet is not such a state precisely what is to be felt, in the poem as a whole? Their state is a continuation of that of all the other characters who have lost their passion—only with the creative difference that now the dulled or desperate reactions are being replaced by the first direct expressions of that state of loss. Their song is not the projection of a state of mind into alienated images, but the simple acknowledgement of it: an acknowledgement in which the poet participates by a sensitive responsiveness to *their* voices and rhythms. Thus the poet begins to recover himself through sympathy with others, whom previously he had rejected as he sought to escape himself. And the springs of feeling, so painfully sealed up, at last begin to flow in the poem: for as these nymphs are transformed towards the nightingale's state, the transmutation of the poem's burden of anguish into song is begun.

The correspondence with *The Ancient Mariner* is revealing. The mariner too sees all about him a universe of death, as the expression or consequence of his deadened imagination, until (as the gloss puts it) 'By the light of the moon he beholdeth God's creatures of the great calm, their beauty and their happiness' and blesses them unawares. The response in 'The Fire Sermon' is very different in its object, and yet essentially the same action. The mariner had seen as loathsome what he now can bless: it is in and through his perceptions and rhythmical expression of them that the great change occurs from death to life. In *The Waste Land*, to sympathize with instead of coldly judging the Thames-daughters—to accept them implicitly as fellow-beings, not spectres and grotesques—is to begin to break out of the prison of the alienated self, and to reintegrate the 'dead' conscious mind with the suppressed realm of feeling. In this process the vital agent is the power of music to express the feelings the conscious mind cannot admit.

'Death by Water', by its coolly-detached tone and resolved music, confirms the conquest of the earlier negative states of fear, terror and revulsion. This death is not grotesquely horrifying, nor the expression of a hatred of life itself—as 'Dirge' in the original drafts was—but simply the final end of nature. Yet to be able to see and feel death in this way involves the purgation of frustrated desire, and of the terror of nothingness. In this *memento mori* we are shown, not 'fear in a handful of dust', but something closer to 'dry bones can harm no one'. In fact this lyric effects the transition from the one state to the other.

The culmination of the poem's struggle for releasing expression comes in the 'water-dripping song' (lines 331–58). The most remarkable feature is its direct lyric voice—the voice of immediate experience. This is something quite new in the poem, and indeed in Eliot's work up to this time. It is no longer 'Tiresias' nor any persona who speaks; nor is it an 'observation' as in *Prufrock and Other Observations*—that is, a point of view defined in what it perceives. It is of course the voice of the poem, of the poet in the poem. But then its novelty shows how he is transformed. The poet is no longer to be identified as Ferdinand-Tiresias, though his predicament is the same. But now he suffers in the manner of Philomel, Ophelia and the Thames-daughters. It is here then that 'the two sexes meet' and the poet's self becomes whole: not in the seer, but in the voice which sings what it suffers.

The transformation can be measured by the way this desert differs from the prophet's vision in lines 19–30:

> What are the roots that clutch, what branches grow
> Out of this stony rubbish? Son of man,
> You cannot say, or guess, for you know only
> A heap of broken images, where the sun beats,
> And the dead tree gives no shelter, the cricket no relief,
> And the dry stone no sound of water.

>

>   If there were water
> And no rock
> If there were rock
> And also water
> And water
> A spring
> A pool among the rock
> If there were the sound of water only
> Not the cicada
> And dry grass singing
> But sound of water over a rock
> Where the hermit-thrush sings in the pine trees
> Drip drop drip drop drop drop drop
> But there is no water   (346–58)

And yet there is—in the way its lack is felt, whereas the earlier passage is simply arid, and only confirms the 'handful of dust'. The difference is that between a hell where there is no hope, and purgatory's refining fire in which an Arnaut Daniel *plor e vau cantan . . . e vei jausen lo jorn, qu'esper, denan*, weeps and goes singing, and sees with joy the dawn he hopes for.

Of course, to have come through to this mode of suffering frustration and loss is not to have risen above them nor escaped them. Precisely not that. It is to have become able to suffer what before had been too intolerable to be acknowledged or felt. Moreover, this expression of unfulfilment intensifies the desire which before had been deadened; and so it recovers, not the lost object of love, but the suppressed passion for it. And to recover that passion even in the aspect of loss—but refined out from its usual fulfilments and frustrations—is to recover a motive for life. Although it is a motive, a desire, at this point detached from any specific object, it has at least been freed from a dead form to seek some further form that may prove more viable. It is a waterless *road* that replaces the hyacinth garden, as in *Ash-Wednesday* the desert where the bones sing will replace the rose garden. This is not yet an and, but a way of suffering one kind of death so that it may be not the end.

Eliot's account of the writing of this song is deeply interesting.[10] He had been trying for months to complete the poem, and been unable to make any progress. The trouble, as he told his brother, was an emotional block, some deep derangement of the power of feeling and expressing feeling. He became ill and suffered a form of breakdown; then towards the end of 1921 went to a Lausanne clinic to recover. There the final part 'took shape and word' in an 'incantation, an outburst of words' so effortless as to seem not his own. Of this release of what had so long been 'incubating within the poet' he said:

> To me it seems that at these moments, which are characterised by the sudden lifting of the burden of anxiety and fear which presses upon our daily life so steadily that we are unaware of it, what happens is something *negative*: that is to say, not

[10] See Valerie Eliot's introduction and notes to her facsimile edition of the original drafts of *The Waste Land*; also 'The *Pensées* of Pascal' (1931), *Selected Essays*, 405; 'Conclusion', *The Use of Poetry and The Use of Criticism* (London, 1933); 'The Three Voices of Poetry' (1953), *On Poetry and Poets*, 98.

'inspiration' as we commonly think of it, but the breaking down of strong habitual barriers—which tend to reform very quickly. Some obstruction is momentarily whisked away. The accompanying feeling is less like what we know as positive pleasure, than a sudden relief from an intolerable burden.[11]

The danger in connecting that with the poem is that here the borderline between the man and the poet in the poem nearly disappears. Yet we can keep within the realm of the poem and still find that account illuminating as an analogous experience. Something of that sort has taken place, but in images and rhythms which are at once more precise and more open. In its own terms the water-dripping song is to be connected with the allusions to Philomela and Arnaut Daniel, and to the swallow of whom the the poet in the *Pervigilium Veneris* asks 'quando fiam uti chelidon ut tacere desinam', when I become as the swallow shall I sing as the nightingale? That the poet at the end of *The Waste Land* must still put that question confirms that the barriers and the burden fall again very quickly. For the space of the song he has found his own voice and inward self. But he must then return into the confused and divisive world of change and history; in which—or, in Eliot's case, against which—the poet struggles to attain that completeness of being of which song is an expression: *Gesang ist Dasein*.

The rest of Part V after the water-dripping song may be seen as a return, a flowing back from the deep source of self towards wholeness and reintegration: a return which involves repassing the stages of experience which previously had meant negation and alienation. Now, as it were in the sunlight of sane consciousness, the uncertainty of the other's presence, the falling of the unreal cities, the nightmare visions and intimations of death, are all contemplated with virtual serenity. There is sympathy and involvement, yet the fullest effect is of cool detachment. The images which would appal have a music which accepts their associations undisturbed, accommodates them to the harmonies of patience and resolution. The nightmare becomes unreal, a mere grotesquerie of the disordered mind without power over the newly-integrated self; while that self gives an affirmative stress to the 'voices singing'. What testifies most to the spirit's recovery of its powers is the absence of fear of death:

> In this decayed hole among the mountains

[11] *The Use of Poetry and the Use of Criticism*, 144–5.

> In the faint moonlight, the grass is singing
> Over the tumbled graves, about the chapel
> There is the empty chapel, only the wind's home.
> It has no windows, and the door swings,
> Dry bones can harm no one.

Here is no taint of 'rattled by the rat's foot only, year to year'—the mind is freed from that condition.

The final proving of the poet's recovered powers, beyond the realm of a nightmare at once private and in history, is his responding to the Thunder's challenge with a just account of his experience. Instead of guilt and terror, or evasive denunciation of the world, he plainly acknowledges and compassionately revalues his relationships with others. These matter-of-fact assessments of limitation and failure are a form of arriving (as 'Little Gidding' will put it, having gone much further) where he started, to know the place for the first time. They are the final stage of integrating into the psyche the intolerable experience which had been alienating him from himself and from life. The water-dripping song effected a resurgence of his vital powers; these reponses show that he is whole and sane enough to be able to live with himself.

*

However, the complete being towards which this achievement points is not attained in *The Waste Land*. This poem, hardly final nor complete in itself, is rather the basis of the major work which evolves continuously from 'What the Thunder Said' to 'Little Gidding'. It has its deepest significance as part of that larger *œuvre*. To put the emphasis upon its quest for the integrity of the lyric voice is to recognize the essential creative achievement. Whereas to neglect or minimize that lyric voice, in favour of some supposed critique of the modern world or myth of culture, is to emphasize only the negative and alienated elements and to identify the work with just those states which it strives to overcome. The poet has not yet attained 'a condition of complete simplicity'; but he has passed beyond Tiresias, transformed that stifling anguish into lyric being whose 'suffering is action'.[12]

Perhaps my emphasis does not depart from the received readings so much as attempt to penetrate more deeply. Our

[12] Cf. Thomas's first speech in *Murder in the Cathedral*.

ordinary understanding of primitive ritual and myth, or of religious mysteries in general, as of civilization and poetry, tends to stop short at appearance and explanation. A remark of Eliot's in the introduction to his mother's dramatic poem *Savonarola* (1926) is to the point:

> Some years ago, in a paper on *The Interpretation of Primitive Ritual*, I made an humble attempt to show that in many cases *no* interpretation of a rite could explain its origin. For the meaning of a series of acts is to the performers themselves an interpretation; the same ritual remaining practically unchanged may assume different meanings for different generations of performers; and the rite may even have originated before 'meaning' meant anything at all. The persons concerned may believe that the ritual is performed in order to induce a fall of rain; but this innocent belief throws no light on the genesis of their behaviour. . . .

Fully and inwardly understood, all our significantly human acts have a common and mysterious source: arising from and returning into that secret realm where our being generates itself.

This would in any case be the proper way of regarding the fertility rites and the Grail legend. Frazer did just acknowledge, what Jessie Weston stressed, that within the overt concern with natural fertility was veiled a more profound mystery. At Eleusis, for instance, the symbol of the golden ear of wheat had a double significance. To the non-initiate it meant a ripened harvest; but to the initiate it meant a spiritual transformation, a new life beyond a death. The initiates had undergone a ritual experience of the horrors of life and terrors of death, hoping to attain through catharsis to the ecstasy of illumination.[13] This, however, is the essential action of all religious rites; as it is a basic and permanent process of the psyche. In a secular time we may perceive it more readily as the form of tragedy; or as the experience of breakdown and reintegration in the personality.

The experience of *The Waste Land* is of course more specific than that: it is quite precisely a love-experience. The allusions to *Tristan* connect it with the psychology of courtly love. And the allusion to Arnaut Daniel, praised in *Purgatorio* xxvi as supreme among the troubador poets though his song there is 'Ara vos

[13] Colin Still's *Shakespeare's Mystery Play: a study of 'The Tempest'* (London, 1921) has much to interest the reader of *The Waste Land* and certain of Eliot's later poems.

prec' and 'Sovegna vos', marks a connection with Dante, in whose work that tradition of love poetry was given a form which Eliot wholeheartedly approved. *The Waste Land* is only the first stage in his following after Dante—but it may mean more to more readers on that account. The beloved is not here recovered in an ideal form. There is simply the failure of romantic love, the desolation consequent upon that, and then the mobilizing of psychic resources to live through the failure—so to live the experience that being is not negated but refined.

Deeper than the generic religious form and the specific transformation of romantic love, at the very heart of the poem, is the fact that it is the mind of a poet which is undergoing the experience. Eliot remarked (paraphrasing Lévy-Bruhl) that 'the prelogical mentality persists in civilised man, but becomes available only to or through the poet'.[14] The force of the remark may be even stronger in an age when the established religious forms have ceased to express the inner processes of the psyche. The poet may be for most of us the one who most clearly and fully voices those processes which make us human. In the struggle which is his life he brings us into touch with powers, which are ours also, which can metamorphose into life-giving song what threatens to negate life.

If the water-dripping song is the climax of the poem's vital process, and if its value is not in any 'meaning' we can attach to it, but simply in the direct power of its transmutations, then we are in the presence of something mysterious which we cannot hope to explain but only to clarify. To that end I would invoke as an analogy the myth of Orpheus, type of the lyric poet. It is told that his song had power to make even the inanimate universe move and live; and his power is associated, obscurely but significantly, with the Dionysiac mysteries. When Eurydice died he followed her into the underworld, where his song relieved the shades from their labours, and so charmed Pluto and Proserpine that they allowed Eurydice to return with him. This underworld of death might correspond to both the subconscious in its 'Tiresias' state and the alien world of the 'Unreal city'. When Orpheus had looked back and lost Eurydice for ever, he ceased to sing the natural world and invoked instead she who was within or beyond —the pure lost Anima. In a similar way Eliot's poetry after *The Waste Land* mainly cultivates renunciation and purgation.

[14] *The Use of Poetry and the Use of Criticism*, 148 n.

There are limits to be registered here, which do not however question the validity of the achievement—indeed they may confirm it. If the poem turns away from the Dionysiac basis of a wholly fulfilled human life, and becomes indifferent to fulfilment in this life, that is because it has lost all hope of renewal except in the Orphic form where being enacts itself in the ideal mode of song. We may feel, if we have not lost hope and will not renounce, that the process of regeneration effected in *The Waste Land*, like the experiences which require it, may be not final but repeated over and over, so long as we have the courage and fortune to be caught up in the destructive element within and by which we mortally live. From this point of view Eliot has taken up only one phase of the experience which the myth expresses: he has made absolute the end when the beloved is irretrievably lost, and there is no recourse except in song and death. Nevertheless, to be 'absolute for death' may be the condition of his enacting so powerfully and completely that potentiality for psychic renewal.

We wish for art to celebrate and enhance our life. Yet the most positive and necessary achievements in art and life are those which triumph over what would negate us. *The Waste Land* is a creative achievement, and a creative experience, because it does come through its negative state to one of intensely-felt suffering. The recovery of the ability to feel is vital. That it is here inseparable from lyric utterance suggests that the song arises from, and penetrates to, the deep levels of the psyche where all experience must be positive. What is negative in experience is what attacks the ego and the self of consciousness. But the deepest sources of our being are not so differentiated or characterized. Lyric song, proceeding from them, must be affirmative; and must affirm the essential powers of being. Eliot put this more modestly: poetry 'may make us from time to time a little more aware of the deeper, unnamed feelings which form the substratum of our being, to which we rarely penetrate'.[15]

Yet as the poet differs from ordinary men only in being more gifted in the exercise of powers by which we all live, we may say that the great poet in realizing himself realizes powers vital to the health of his civilization. If *The Waste Land* is a significant work of self-transformation and self-creation, which has value as it mobilizes the psyche's resources, then it would establish those

[15] *Ibid.*, 155.

resources at the heart of our civilization. Behind *The Waste Land* (and *The Hollow Men* also) is a pervasive allusion to Conrad's *Heart of Darkness*, and to Kurtz who was 'hollow at the core' with the hollowness of his culture. Eliot's poem is the expression of a similar hollowness, and the answer to it. Far from being merely about emptiness and waste, it is a triumph over the waste regions of the self and its world.

Pope, Eliot, and
'The Mind of Europe'

J. S. Cunningham

> This labour past, by Bridewell all descend,
> (As morning pray'r, and flagellation end)
> To where Fleet-ditch with disemboguing streams
> Rolls the large tribute of dead dogs to Thames,
> The King of dykes! than whom no sluice of mud
> With deeper sable blots the silver flood.

So, in 1742, London's complicated river: its coal wharves the black grottos of obscenity; polluted mythologically by venereal modern hybrids, the mud-nymphs; a mingled wave of Styx and Lethe, darkness and oblivion, with a tincture of 'Vapours from the Land of dreams'. As a soporific, it lulls the flaccid and the ponderous, ensuring that 'all from Paul's to Aldgate drink and sleep'—*The Dunciad* and *The Waste Land* agree that Hell has London landmarks and London thoroughfares. As an intoxicant, it peps up the pert in farces of post-Hellenic rivalry—not chariot and javelin, but scurrilous pamphleteering and the tickling of patrons, sweaty pursuits of a ghostly immortality. Pope's crowds— 'so many'—chase spectres in an absurd provincial variant of Virgil's underworld, where the equivalent of

> Stetson!
> You who were with me in the ships at Mylae!

is Dulness's greeting to Colley Cibber at his baptism of opium:

> All hail! and hail again,
> My son! the promis'd land expects thy reign.   (I, 291–2)

Stetson was accosted as an *alter ego* in a nervously jocular Hell; Dr Busby rises dressed in an outfit happily assumed from Moloch in the Hell of *Paradise Lost*:

67

When lo! a Spectre rose, whose index-hand
Held forth the Virtue of the dreadful wand;
His beaver'd brow a birchen garland wears,
Dropping with Infant's blood, and Mother's tears.
(IV, 139–42)

His wand is the school cane, and he proclaims a pedagogue's
necromancy, whereby words alone, purged of responsibility, will
be *all* any child has to learn. His arrogance and egotism culminates
in no more—but, alas, no less—than the literal equivalent of his
spiritual sleep. Europe snores:

See Christians, Jews, one heavy sabbath keep,
And all the western world believe and sleep.
(III, 99–100)

The 'vast involuntary throng' forms and reforms, displays the
dusky solidarity of bees, or locusts, or opaque metaphysicians:

Thick and more thick the black blockade extends,
A hundred head of Aristotle's friends.   (IV, 191–2)

Their unity *and* their squabbles, their apathy *and* their euphoria,
are all owed equally to lead, 'the might of gravitation'. In a
contest that would suit Mr Eugenides, a pig of lead rewards the
pornographic diver's 'dark dexterity of groping well'. Some,
for all their good intentions, hardly sink at all, and are 'number'd
with the puppies in the mud'. Concanen, of dying memory, will
never rise again:

No noise, no stir, no motion can'st thou make,
Th'unconscious stream sleeps o'er thee like a lake.
(II, 303–4)

But William Arnall boasts both energy and mass:

with a weight of skull,
Furious he dives, precipitately dull.   (II, 315–16)

What is ineptly ponderous is ephemeral; ephemeral writers, 'true
to the bottom', rake the depths; to sink is to rise, and to do either
with zeal is to vanish for good. Lead flies from wind-guns; clocks
tick away briskly to heavy pendulums. Dipped in Lethe, the
souls of poets instantly scale heavens of absurd invention. The
opiates of Dulness start Utopian visions in the mad prophet's
empty head. A culture disinherited of its past is, for Pope, to be

seen idolizing the resourcefulness of vacancy, a doctrinaire form of 'living in the present'. Not inconsistently, it is prolific of laborious mimicries of antique rhetorics and sonorous locutions.

In both *The Waste Land* and *The Dunciad*, the sense of people as figures *in* a nightmare or dream farce answers to the sense that the figures themselves live kinds of non-existence: live by dream, by fixation, by hallucination, by being 'distracted from distraction by distraction'.[1] 'Each man fixed his eyes before his feet'; 'her brain allows one half-formed thought to pass'; 'pressing lidless eyes and waiting for a knock upon the door'; or

> Soft creeping, words on words, the sense compose,
> At ev'ry line they stretch, they yawn, they doze.
> (II, 389–90)

This last example comes from Book III of Pope's poem, where the vision of Dulness flies through Virgil's gate of false dreams, like the 'empty forms between the ivory gates' of 'Ash Wednesday'. Phlebas, Eliot, Tiresias; Silenus, Pope, the 'gloomy clerk': we are provoked to seek distinctions among them and to know the thresholds beyond which such distinctions will not hold. False dreams, a sense of life warped or starved through the agency of bigotry, or moral cowardice, or terror, or contempt: the concern with such things in *The Dunciad* and *The Waste Land* will often sharpen into satiric focus, but both poems also register, implicitly and explicitly, the stresses such material imposes on the creative sensibility. 'Hieronymo's mad againe':

> Ye Pow'rs! whose Mysteries restor'd I sing,
> To whom Time bears me on his rapid wing,
> Suspend a while your Force inertly strong,
> Then take at once the Poet and the Song.   (IV, 5–8)

Pope's hollow men, on the beach of their tumid river, are deaf to the poem they are gathered in. They do not hear the rumours of Virgil (or Milton or the New Testament or *The Iliad*) which attend them:

> Thro' Lud's fam'd gates, along the well-known Fleet
> Rolls the black troop, and overshades the street,
> 'Till show'rs of Sermons, Characters, Essays,
> In circling fleeces whiten all the ways:

---

[1] *Four Quartets*, 'Burnt Norton', III.

> So clouds replenish'd from some bog below,
> Mount in dark volumes, and descend in snow.   (II, 359–64)

Their sensibilities being so strictly lethal, an apt immortality awaits them by 'th'oblivious lake', where they will not comprehend the mocking compliment that describes them after Milton's fallen angels:

> Millions and millions on these banks he views,
> Thick as the stars of night, or morning dews,
> As thick as bees o'er vernal blossoms fly,
> As thick as eggs at Ward in Pillory.   (III, 31–4)

This Gothic Elysium offers a vision of an ultimate Endarkenment, Ignorance and Apathy Regained—a forgetful snow thawed by no future April. There is rejoicing over the burning of the Ptolemaic Library:

> Heav'ns! what a pile! whole ages perish there.   (III, 77)

Coriolanus has been broken beyond repair in the zealous demolition of pagan culture:

> Streets pav'd with Heroes, Tyber choak'd with Gods.
> (III, 108)

Were a spirit of true inquiry to revive, the universities and schools could cure it promptly:

> In ancient Sense if any needs will deal,
> Be sure I give them Fragments, not a Meal.   (IV, 229–30)

In the despair of *The Dunciad*, which is to say, in the genuinely-felt and serious outcome of its spirited game with the philistines, there is nothing *left* for such fragments to shore up. Each head becomes 'a lumberhouse of books'. Endless superficial explanations obsure what they are supposed to clarify:

> Like buoys, that never sink into the flood,
> On Learning's surface we but lie and nod.   (IV, 241–2)

The busy attentiveness of the specialist in trivialities is, Pope asserts, culpably neglectful of both the genuinely difficult and the great simple things. He identifies this with spiritual feebleness:

> The common Soul, of Heav'n's more frugal make,
> Serves but to keep fools pert, and knaves awake:
> A drowsy Watchman, that just gives a knock,
> And breaks our rest, to tell us what's a clock.   (IV, 441–4)

The sentiment here (though not the tone) may remind us of a number of passages in Eliot, among them this from his essay on Pascal:

> The majority of mankind is lazy-minded, incurious, absorbed in vanities, and tepid in emotion, and is therefore incapable of much doubt or much faith; and when the ordinary man calls himself a sceptic or an unbeliever, that is ordinarily a simple pose, cloaking a disinclination to think anything out to a conclusion.[2]

We move here from a generous inventive engagement with human inadequacy to a Johnsonian austerity that keeps a bleak distance from what it contemplates. Observing affinities between the work of Eliot and Pope frequently brings us in face of contrasts as sharp as this.

Elements in the Eliot sentence just quoted engage readily with movements of sensibility in *The Waste Land*. The poem isolates, more and less sardonically, creatures of apathy or self-centred turpitude, as does *The Dunciad*. And both poems move us to reflect on the relation between the moral ill and the loss of those finer bearings that might still be taken from the artistic achievement and religious faith of a major civilization: 'Jug jug to dirty ears'. Listening to another Eliot essay, published in 1935, we can match point after point with convictions which Pope's poem had enforced about the state of culture some two centuries earlier:

> the reader of contemporary literature is not, like the reader of the established great literature of all time, exposing himself to the influence of divers and contradictory personalities; he is exposing himself to a mass movement of writers who, each of them, think that they have something individually to offer, but are really all working together in the same direction. And there never was a time, I believe, when the reading public was so large, or so helplessly exposed to the influences of its own time. There never was a time, I believe, when those who read at all, read so many more books by living authors than books by dead authors; there never was a time so completely parochial, so shut off from the past. There may be too many publishers; there are certainly too many books published; and the journals ever incite the reader to 'keep up' with what is

[2] 'The *Pensées* of Pascal', *Selected Essays*, 411–12.

71

being published. Individualistic democracy has come to high tide: and it is more difficult today to be an individual than it ever was before.[3]

In that these emphatic judgements do convey quite precisely elements of Pope's sense of the abuse of literacy in the 1730s, they may be rather less true of the 1930s than Eliot supposed. But they are not convictions that can stand or fall according to some conceivable statistical test, for all their confident display of informed awareness of contemporary culture. They have little directly to do with *The Waste Land*, although a reader of that poem is not *wholly* surprised that Eliot came to sound so confident and so scornful in allowing the contrast to harden between the demotic present and the exalted past. In their light, *The Waste Land* will appear a poem whose essentially nostalgic and satiric art brought adroit mandarin ironies to bear upon the disorder, anarchy and futility which *a fortiori* characterize the present. Some commentaries treat it contentedly in such terms—a poem we can, as it were, 'agree with', and feel we have aligned ourselves with an impregnable cultural cause: love, not lust; faith, not its lack; past, not present. Seen unfavourably from a similar angle, this is the poem which William Carlos Williams felt had handed poetry back to the academics. But we should surely reject such outright judgements, or restrict their scope to parts or aspects of the poem. This would be to deny ourselves the gratifications that are to be gained from tracing plausible relations between Eliot's prose assertions and his poetry, and from codifying the encounters between conflicting elements and values, among them those of the present and those of the past, as they live in the poetry itself.

Criticism of *The Dunciad* is faced with broadly similar questions, and with similar temptations. Like Eliot's prose passage, it sets the parochial against the cosmopolitan (in a good sense—*not* the Grand Tour and going south in the winter). Against the factitiously original it sets the traditional (but *not* the antiquated). It, too, finds in the mere *multiplication* of authors, publishers and things published evidence of incoherence: hectic activity, but only feebly individualistic, and therefore all the more apt to erode standards by flattering the incompetent. Pope would have found much to agree with elsewhere in Eliot's essays. 'Tradition and the Individual Talent', described by Eliot as 'juvenile' but not

[3] 'Religion and Literature', *Selected Essays*, 397–8.

repudiated altogether, affirms as confidently as Pope's precocious *Essay on Criticism* the 'historical sense' which

> involves a perception, not only of the pastness of the past, but of its presence; [it] compels a man to write not merely with his own generation in his bones, but with a feeling that the whole literature of Europe from Homer and within it the whole of the literature of his own country has a simultaneous existence and composes a simultaneous order.

For the poet to perceive this is for him to be aware that

> the mind of Europe—the mind of his own country—a mind which he learns in time to be much more important than his own private mind—is a mind which changes, and that this change is a development which abandons nothing *en route*, which does not superannuate either Shakespeare, or Homer, or the rock drawing of the Magdalenian draughtsmen.[4]

Pope's *Essay* roundly defends the attainment of a matured knowledge of the creative past—the 'distant Scenes of *endless* Science' (l. 224)—and affirms that past as enshrining an exemplary Order:

> Still green with Bays each *ancient* Altar stands,
> Above the reach of *Sacrilegious* Hands. (181-2)

'The existing monuments form an ideal order among themselves', Eliot declares.[5] How such 'simultaneous existence' and 'simultaneous order' are registered in *The Dunciad* and *The Waste Land* is, of course, a crucial question for interpretative reading. We would expect their life in poetry to be more challengingly complex and various than statements of classicist convictions are able to convey. Simultaneous existence may make against simultaneous order, crowding it with fragmentary echoes which resist simple control. The past may be redeemed in innumerable ways, and held in innumerable modes of contrast with the present. The encounter between lucid and muddled or deranged conditions of 'the mind of Europe' can in imaginative literature excite ranges of awareness and start implications well beyond the scope of critical polemic or generalizations about the state of civilization, and all without being wholly at odds with these.

Pope's lines about the sleepy common soul, the 'drowsy Watchman', sharpen rather than dull our interest in the lazy and

---

[4] *Selected Essays*, 14, 16.
[5] *Selected Essays*, 15.

incurious. His couplets continually offer a quick-witted imaginative playfulness that awakens *us*:

> Yet by some object ev'ry brain is stirr'd;
> The dull may waken to a Humming-bird;
> The most recluse, discreetly open'd, find
> Congenial matter in the Cockle-kind;
> The mind, in Metaphysics at a loss,
> May wander in a wilderness of Moss. (IV, 445–50)

We, more than the dull, wake to the humming-bird, and relish that expanse of mosses. The witty play on shellfish as an image for the mind of the collector of cockles gives us a delight beyond his scope. Milton's Satan was reduced to some ungainly improvisations in crossing Chaos:

> So eagerly the Fiend
> O'er bog or steep, through strait, rough, dense, or rare,
> With head, hands, wings, or feet, pursues his way,
> And swims, or sinks, or wades, or creeps, or flies.[6]

When Pope models the antics of rival publishers on this titanic amphibian, there is a hilarious satiric aptness-in-discrepancy; but there is also the delight of things vividly seen and authentically imagined:

> As when a dab-chick waddles thro' the copse
> On feet and wings, and flies, and wades, and hops;
> So lab'ring on, with shoulders, hands, and head,
> Wide as a wind-mill all his figures spread,
> With arms expanded Bernard rows his state,
> And left-legg'd Jacob seems to emulate. (II, 63–8)

In *The Waste Land*, what the 'common soul', reading the author's notes, might learn to call '*Turdus aonalaschkae pallasii*, the hermit-thrush', is *heard* singing where it cannot *be*:

> Drip drop drip drop drop drop drop
> But there is no water.

In such cases as these, we might broadly say, the quality of the creative enterprise has a redeeming influence on its objects of attention. The diabolic little grebe provokes a delight that lives independent of the local satiric purpose, although it serves that with piquant aptness—we look *through*, as well as *into*, the poetry,

---

[6] *Paradise Lost*, II, 947–50.

as if a window gave upon a deviant sylvan scene. Registering a state of privation, Eliot's lines open (as frequently happens in his work elsewhere) to the irreducible sensuous delight that such a state essentially excludes—and the thrush's syllables fulfil the needs of a definite, if irregular, verse measure, and satisfy our ear. Both poems are rich in such events: 'a dead sound on the final stroke of nine'; 'keen, hollow winds howl through the bleak recess'. Torpor precisely felt; chaos inventively imaged: the play between such opposites lingers in the mind, with kinds of osmosis happening between them. Precision and invention prevent our attention suffering too thoroughly the contagion of the negative—scorn, loss, dejection. But the creativity of both poems is more continuously redemptive than picking out small incidents can convey.

Of both it is partly true to say that they bring special kinds of remembering to bear upon a culture that has lost its memory or suffered its memory to grow random and chaotic. In each, the remembering is frequently surprising, even bizarre, whether in how it is activated or in the nature of its bearing on the context. A kind of model is the inconsequential

> I remember
> Those are pearls that were his eyes

uttered in response to a neurotic's appeal for help rather than for English literature. But the allusive events work very variously, and their complexion changes as our sense of the poem develops: an immediately registered anomaly frequently modulates into one or more kinds of aptness, without the aptness quite displacing our first response.

> Sweet Thames, run softly, till I end my song.
> The river bears no empty bottles, sandwich papers,
> Silk handkerchiefs, cardboard boxes, cigarette ends
> Or other testimony of summer nights. The nymphs are departed.
> And their friends, the loitering heirs of city directors;
> Departed, have left no addresses.
> By the waters of Leman I sat down and wept . . .
> Sweet Thames, run softly till I end my song,
> Sweet Thames, run softly, for I speak not loud or long.

The enumeration of pollutants is fastidious in revulsion—one instance of that arm's-length primness which frequently marks Eliot's encounter with the squalid. It is a tone, we might note,

very different from Pope's exuberant indulgence in such details—
his overt delight in finding apt modes of ironic celebration of the
sordid. Pope *names* the mud-nymphs, his Thames-daughters,
with glee. He obliges pastoral and heroic idioms to accomplish
uncouth blasphemies:

> In ev'ry loom our labours shall be seen,
> And the fresh vomit run for ever green!   (II, 155–6)

or

> When lo! a burst of thunder shook the flood.
> Slow rose a form, in majesty of Mud;
> Shaking the horrors of his sable brows,
> And each ferocious feature grim with ooze.   (II, 325–8)

'Those are pearls that were his eyes' ... with a vengeance,
achieved with wicked mirth. By contrast, in Eliot's lines,
Spenser's refrain keeps formally separate from the besmirching
scene. But immediately after the line

> Sweet Thames, run softly, for I speak not loud or long

we have Marvell, not held aloof, an ethereal rumour, but modulating into words whose distinctive grotesquerie revives our sense
of that same element in Marvell's own poem:

> But at my back in a cold blast I hear
> The rattle of the bones, and chuckle spread from ear to ear.

And again, a slightly different case, Ferdinand's words from *The
Tempest* fall in with a ruminative verse rhythm that assimilates
them despite the incongruous elements:

> While I was fishing in the dull canal
> On a winter evening round behind the gashouse
> Musing upon the king my brother's wreck
> And on the king my father's death before him.

Ariel's music is not so much an allusion, as an event: it can creep
by us 'along the Strand, up Queen Victoria Street' and gain a
local habitation there, however short the lease—it lives *where*
it gains our ear. It can be heard, among other hints and guesses, in
the prison of selfhood we share with 'a broken Coriolanus', and in
the singing grass about a ruined chapel. The incongruous elements
offer repeatedly to reject each other; but they also, and often
more compellingly, require each other, and cling together,

provoking in us a distinct new awareness which is a compound of kinds of discrepancy and kinds of aptness. We pass through anomaly into recreation, but recreation which expressively enhances our awareness of resistance to it.

Repeatedly, then, the 'remembered' element suffers the contagion of its present environment, but also heightens our awareness of the present—and at a certain point, discrepancy and irony can dissolve. Goldsmith's 'When lovely woman stoops to folly', so strikingly at odds with the context of a bored, permitted rape, informs our sense of it, gives us in alteration better access to the event it also furnishes with a tonal frame. The poem may recoil from 'the gramophone', as from 'food in tins' or 'camisoles and stays', but the girl's condition is *discovered*, not just ironically placed, by the way the Goldsmith quatrain modulates into Eliot's decisive newcomer. We reflect that the interplay is not merely between the present soiled fact and the immaculate eloquence of the past, but between *any* cruel actuality and the expression that seeks to redeem it in a given sensibility. The Goldsmith lines would not redeem the typist's apathy; but the creative event of Eliot's quatrain simultaneously redeems both—they become *available* to us through their interaction. Across the distance in time and in *ethos*, the Goldsmith lyric works in its new, hostile environment, enduring defacement; and that environment receives it with a witty pointedness which recalls another Augustan mode, and which puts us in possession of this different stooping to folly. Behind the Goldsmith decorum there has to lie, after all, an event with edges and the odour of the actual.

The Spenser refrain itself, the higher dream, is redeemed in 'The Fire Sermon', for all its formal separateness in the disposition of lines on the page. Its first occurrence in the section has, in fact, a more harmonious relation with the context than the second:

> The river's tent is broken; the last fingers of leaf
> Clutch and sink into the wet bank. The wind
> Crosses the brown land, unheard. The nymphs are departed.
> Sweet Thames, run softly, till I end my song.

Here, the quality of attention merits the Spenserian eloquence, even if the broken leaf-arch images a distance from it. Then, as we read the whole long first section of 'The Fire Sermon', we encounter a sensibility which is making its way among materials drawn from widely different sectors of experience, and across major, even at times absurd, tonal alterations ('horns and motors'), but *within* a sustained measure that speaks a distinct, special climate of attention. The offered discrepancies are sharp, and in some senses witty, but they are lodged in the verse as if, after all, they had *asked* to occur. Assonance, echo, modulated repetition, rhyme, fall on the ear with discreet emphasis as they require to, at variable intervals: they 'weave the wind', to use a phrase shared by 'Geriontion' and Joyce's *Ulysses* . . . 'hear/ear to ear . . . year to year/from time to time I hear'. These are not the expedients of a formal, imposed ordering. They tell of the *behaviour* of a consciousness as it moves, within a governing *condition*, a ruminative, guarded, watchful attentiveness with a keen sense of the bizarre and the macabre. The sensibility moves, cat-like; the metrics bell the cat. Analogical or metaphoric possibilities are hinted at: the rat creeping softly, the fishing in the dull canal, help to enforce our sense of the activity of feeling— its furtiveness, its indirection, and in part its atrophy. The poetry is, we might say, self-coloured—without our wanting to endorse any search for the 'biographical' Eliot. And if the measure speaks a sustained, indrawn attention, we find that this chimes with what we might call (here and elsewhere in the poem) a preoccupation with the attenuated—the prudential, the shrinking, and the privative: 'little low dry garret', 'a little life', 'a little patience'. These phrases are among the signatures of selfhood in the poem, and felt as such.

A prudent spiritual husbandry is something 'What The Thunder Said' encounters in its own way. This whole section exhibits the authentic integrity I have been trying to speak of. A plangent opening—'torchlight red on sweaty faces.'—declines, with a characteristic binding rhyme, into the privative mode:

> He who was living is now dead
> We who were living are now dying
> With a little patience.

The privation is borne in upon us insistently with the force of a mind's encounter with itself as that occurs: the alternation of 'here is' and 'if there were' generates an intolerable pressure. Something similar occurred in the second passage of 'A Game of Chess'—but there, the panic came of neurasthenia. The feeling here, by contrast, is responsive to the whole poem—all it has been and has become; and its denser context exacerbates the

sense of impending collapse. Relatedly, this part of *The Waste
Land* is full of anxious questions—who is that? what is that
sound? what is the city over the mountans? what have we given?
History's insistences—migrations, ruins, tribulations—*require* the
poetry, have the urgency of presences long felt, now issuing as
nightmare. Spectrally immediate; clamorously unreal:

> Falling towers
> Jerusalem Athens Alexandria
> Vienna London
> Unreal.

This has none of the hurt and weary *déjà vu* of Tiresias in the
passage that explicitly involved him: the sense of mediation
through a peculiar sensibility is displaced by the compelling
force of the encounter itself. We do the poem harm if, with one
academic explainer, we persist here in speaking of a 'quester'—
as if a *persona* (and one with such a coy name) is what the
poetry directs our attention to. And the Thunder's imperatives,
breaking through pent-up expectancy, confront no mere eccentric
selfhood, no sick state we can diagnose, aloof; nor are the
answers to the thunder rightly classed as 'denials'. The 'awful
daring of a moment's surrender' is there as a human event in the
poetry, carried by that authentic discovery, 'blood shaking my
heart'. The 'would have' of the response to *Damyata* expresses
regret, but what is regretted is present in the lines with a lively
inwardness that partly redeems, if it partly exacerbates, the
declared failure to achieve that very thing:

> The sea was calm, your heart would have responded
> Gaily, when invited, beating obedient
> To controlling hands.

In the closing paragraphs of *The Waste Land*, intimations of
release, expansive and captivating, jostle for attention along with
those of collapse and *dérèglement*. The 'simultaneous existence' of
the resources of 'the mind of Europe' threatens here, we might
say, whatever order might else be derived from it. But it is not a
literary or mere esoteric crisis—a rare library fallen into the hands
of the mad catalogue assistant—though the esoteric ingredients
(especially 'Shantih') are expressive, *whatever* they mean, of
isolation and distance. Nor does it dramatize a simple antithesis
between sick and healthy, or ruined and restored. The lines offer,

as it were, an accelerated and cryptic response to the poem itself, and in particular to the rich diversity, and the frequent inconsequential working, of its remembering. That so many things press in vividly upon the exposed consciousness here is itself part of the condition; so that the redeeming alternative is not really to be sought *among* the fragments (O swallow swallow) but in some redeeming frame where their intimations might collectively create a new order of feeling, a new style. In one sense, that *is* what the poem's creativity has been seeking to accomplish, almost accomplishing, though we need to maintain a distinction between a style uniquely registering *possibilities*, and one which uniquely achieves them. We might also say that the poem's last lines visit the poem upon itself; and in this they have a counterpart in Pope's concluding Book to *The Dunciad*, where the tragic sense is conveyed that the creative intelligence may itself suffer defeat under the pressures exerted by its own materials:

> Suspend a while your Force inertly strong,
> Then take at once the Poet and the Song.   (IV, 7–8)

The impact of Pope's concluding lines is, like Eliot's, vertiginous; and they answer in this to the frenzy and disintegration he found virtually throughout the moral and intellectual and political life of his time. If the tensions of Eliot's poem are aptly closed on a note poised between (say) weariness and redemptive peace, then Pope's are equally fulfilled in the acclaim for irreversible negation:

> Lo! thy dread Empire, CHAOS! is restor'd;
> Light dies before thy uncreating word:
> Thy hand, great Anarch! lets the curtain fall;
> And Universal Darkness buries All.   (IV, 653–6)

The rhetoric echoes stirringly in the empty theatre. The creating word sonorously celebrates Uncreation.

'Those are pearls that were his eyes'. When Eliot tolled this particular reminiscent bell some twelve years after *The Waste Land*, it was in the context of his discussion of a particular kind of creative experience. In some circumstances, he observed, the poet will find himself producing 'an incantation, an outburst of words', irresistibly—poetry he may hardly recognize as his own work, so obscure are its sources, and so involuntary the moment of expression. It wells up from mysterious depths, and may only occur because some obstacle usually present has been 'momentarily whisked away'. Neither the mystery nor the spontaneity could guarantee, of course, that the poetry would be good: to Eliot, *Kubla Khan* is not completely articulate and coherent even though it embodies material which 'sank to the depths of Coleridge's feeling, was saturated, transformed there—"those are pearls that were his eyes"—and brought up to daylight again'. But poetry produced in this way—by some kind of 'capricious release'—Eliot relates, as Wordsworth did, to a protracted period of subliminal preparation:

> What one writes in this way may succeed in standing the examination of a more normal state of mind; it gives me the impression, as I have just said, of having undergone a long incubation, though we do not know until the shell breaks what kind of egg we have been sitting on.[7]

A state of 'ill-health, debility, or anaemia' was one that Eliot found conducive to the spontaneous overflow; and he was interested to find this corroborated by A. E. Housman, who punningly related his experience to that of the oyster, producing the pearl by a process of 'morbid secretion'.[8]

Discussion of *The Waste Land* would not be advanced by trying to establish a pathology of its composition based on such hints as these. But several passages in the poem have the deep inscape of creative unity, such as we might associate with some profound movement 'where all the waters meet'. And the poem persistently brings us close to the points of stress between the creative and the uncreative, between the redeemed and the irredeemable. In *The Dunciad*, too, creativity is in intimate contact with uncreation, which is also part of Pope's explicit subject-matter. The depraved creators, in Pope's poem, write by 'inspiration' in a travesty of the Holy Spirit. Their mock literary theorist anticipated Eliot and Housman in saying 'Poetry is a *natural* or morbid *Secretion from the Brain*'[9]—which meant for him 'write whenever the fit is on you, for reasons of abdominal hygiene'. The random and the fragmentary have unparalleled status in duncely creativity:

---

[7] *The Use of Poetry and the Use of Criticism*, 144.
[8] *The Name and Nature of Poetry* (London, 1933), 48–9.
[9] *The Art of Sinking in Poetry*, ed. E. L. Steeves (Columbia University Press, 1952), 12.

Round him much Embryo, much Abortion lay,
Much future Ode, and abdicated Play;
Nonsense precipitate, like running Lead,
That slip'd thro' Cracks and Zig-zags of the Head.   (I, 121-4)

The dull sensibility gestates its 'nameless somethings' with
dispatch, brings them forth half-formed, and licks them into
impressive bears. The resources of 'the mind of Europe' are to be
forgotten, or let rot, or deftly plagiarized for the delectation of
the London stage:

Small thanks to France, and none to Rome or Greece,
A past, vamp'd, future, old, reviv'd, new piece,
'Twixt Plautus, Fletcher, Shakespear, and Corneille,
Can make a Cibber, Tibbald, or Ozell.   (I, 283-6)

The Augustan equivalent of

O O O O that Shakespeherian Rag

is the actor-manager's preference for the 'wond'rous pow'r of
Noise' over the subtleties of 'Shakespeare's nature, or . . . Johnson's art':

'Tis yours to shake the soul
With Thunder rumbling from the mustard bowl,
With horns and trumpets now to madness swell,
Now sink in sorrows with a tolling bell;
Such happy arts attention can command,
When fancy flags, and sense is at a stand.   (II, 225-30)

As the arts devote themselves to the gratification of what Wordsworth was to call 'this degrading thirst after outrageous stimula-
tion',[10] there is a sense that civilization has become a tricksy
harlequinade, the stage machinery for an absurd necromancer:

All sudden, Gorgons hiss, and Dragons glare,
And ten-horn'd fiends and Giants rush to war.
Hell rises, Heav'n descends, and dance on Earth:
Gods, imps, and monsters, music, rage, and mirth,
A fire, a jigg, a battle, and a ball,
'Till one wide conflagration swallows all.
   Thence a new world to Nature's laws unknown,
Breaks out refulgent, with a heavn' its own:
Another Cynthia her new journey runs,

---

[10] Preface to *Lyrical Ballads* (1800).

And other planets circle other suns.
The forests dance, the rivers upward rise,
Whales sport in woods, and dolphins in the skies;
And last, to give the whole creation grace,
Lo! one vast Egg produces human race.   (III, 235-48)

This is the egg hatched by your Theobald and your Rich, and the poem is quick to say that 'each monster meets its likeness' in the mad mind of its theatrical creator. In Pope's truer creativity, however, something no less audacious is occurring. The lines amuse but also seduce the reader (*hypocrite lecteur*), with their vividness and their acclaim for the liberation of art from the tedious cosmic rules. The comic apocalypse of a debauched public taste is, in Pope's lines, made able to refresh that delight in true miracle that lies at the base of our hunger for the arts. That delight is not readily conveyed in terms of classical appeals to Order and Nature: the creative accomplishment of the poetry *is* the only criterion. An uncreator could be attacked for breaking decorum if he got his seasons muddled; but in truly creative hands the attack is conducted with a touch that turns muddle to miracle:

Glitt'ring with ice here hoary hills are seen,
There painted vallies of eternal green,
In cold December fragrant chaplets blow,
And heavy harvests nod beneath the snow.   (I, 75-8)

The Augustan stage could, obviously, have made an entrancing spectacle of the apocalyptic disfigurements and inversions of *The Waste Land*—what our current jargon would call The Hieronymus Bosch Show:

A woman drew her long black hair out tight
And fiddled whisper music on those strings
And bats with baby faces in the violet light
Whistled, and beat their wings
And crawled head downward down a blackened wall
And upside down in air were towers
Tolling reminiscent bells, that kept the hours
And voices singing out of empty cisterns and exhausted wells.

Eliot does not, of course, distance this nightmare by locating it in the mind of an uncreator. But it stands as another antitype of a conceived harmony and order, of a creativity in which the voices would sing from plenitude, not from vacancy. And yet (*hypocrite auteur*) how keenly that emptiness sings, and how resoundingly the bells chime; and how closely those images, of hollowness singing, answer to our sense of the special eloquence which recalled lyric fragments have in the poem's privative and needy consciousness.

Had Eliot submitted the draft material for *The Waste Land*, not to Pound in 1922, but to Pope in the 1730s, joining the queue of aspirants for the Twickenham *fiat*, his reception could hardly have been hospitable. In particular, for Pope to praise the *pastiche* heroic couplets that were to have opened 'The Fire Sermon' would have been for a dog to praise his fleas. The couplets gloat; they are willed, unskilful mimicry. They are as repellently knowing, on Eliot's own part, as Sweeney is, who 'knows the female temperament',[11] or the house agent's clerk who (in the draft) 'knows his way with women (and that's that!)'.[12] They owe more to Pope's second *Moral Essay* than to *The Rape of the Lock*, which is the ostensible object of the imitation; but they lack the range of feeling Pope displays—anger, banter, fascination—and certainly do not suggest a capacity to redress the scorn of women through a recognition of such qualities as Pope movingly celebrates in Martha Blount. It is not to Eliot's draft material that we will look for significant relationships between his work and Pope's.

Both *The Waste Land* and *The Dunciad* can make us feel what it would be to redeem the time by redeeming the heritage. But they do so by holding true creativity close to the prospect of its collapse, and close to what we might call its raw materials—the irritants in the oyster. In both poems, the redeeming creative act occurs, or seeks to occur, within the zone of what variously excites it, resists it, or is fundamentally hostile to it. We may feel, on balance, that Pope has the more ranging critical awareness of his time—its modes of behaviour, its cherished idioms, its currents of thought—and that Pope's teeming inventiveness, his alacrity, feels all the more valuable in the contrast with Eliot's more careworn and calculating creative economy. The languages of the past modulate into Pope's language, *become* it, pointedly invade it, with a governed zest and a self-delighting virtuosity that would be alien to much of Eliot. Obscenities in *The Dunciad*

[11] 'Sweeney Erect'.   [12] *Facsimile*, 45.

84

share in this general mischievous creativity; sexuality is not associated in it with deep revulsion or fear. Relatedly, we are not left to wonder whether some preoccupations that are not fully disclosed are in truth providing Pope's poem with its essential motive: on the contrary, we gain access to its profounder implications and sense its genesis through the readily available, if dense, play of meanings and tones. But what might look in such a light deficiencies in Eliot's poem are in another light the authentic expression—the expressive equivalents—of a different kind of awareness, with a different tonal range and different scope. In Pope, a witty allusiveness and comic verve holds the mirror up, at close range, to arts of servile imitation and mere sensational opportunism. In Eliot, a difficult but true coherence is won from, but still within, distracted and demoralized states of awareness. Custard, lavatory paper, dab chicks, pies, Lord Mayor's processions, John Locke, Virgil, Welsted, and Aphrodite; cardboard boxes, the Cannon Street Hotel, Lil's husband, Mrs Porter, Spenser, the gashouse, Dante, and a pocket full of currants.

'Fourmillante Cité':
Baudelaire and 'The Waste Land'

Nicole Ward

One does not often reflect, these days, on the relation between the word 'police' and the Greek 'polis', city—and such words as 'policy' and 'politics'. The French 'policer une nation' means to civilize and refine it. And in Montaigne the word 'police' still retains its etymological purity: it indicates the web of relationships which connect people as social beings and as citizens, as members of a great civic body. In an impassioned plea for the importance of speaking the truth, he says that whoever cheats with or misuses language destroys the basis of civil society, perverts men's knowledge of one another, and breaks all the springs of our 'police'.

Thus

> Words strain,
> Crack and sometimes break, under the burden,
> Under the tension, slip, slide, perish,
> Decay with imprecision, will not stay in place,
> Will not stay still. . . .

Words, to take a more worldly stance than Eliot's, follow the decay of institutions, of relations between men, of the quality of life. Other words become current, outside the pale of literature, it seems, but expressive of new forms of life. And one could argue that the poet is responsible to the 'police' in more senses than one: that the society to which he belongs is at stake in the quality of the language he uses; that, for instance, by resurrecting dead meanings of language, by discovering poetic dimensions in new forms of speech, he can create or recreate possibilities of feeling. Thus of Wordsworth's salesgirl whose cry 'thrills' the London streets, instead of feeling, as in Mrs Radcliffe, a 'kind of pleasing dread thrill her bosom'; thus of Baudelaire's *Ennui*, freed from its modern sense of boredom to recapture the barely endurable agony of soul which afflicted Racine's Antiochus, in *Bérénice*:

> Dans l'Orient désert quel devint mon ennui!

In Baudelaire too it lays the world waste:

> Il ferait volontiers de la terre un débris,
> Et dans un bâillement avalerait le monde.
> C'est l'Ennui! . . .
> Tu le connais, lecteur, ce monstre délicat,
> —Hypocrite lecteur,— mon semblable,— mon frère:[1]

Thus also, by an opposite process as it were, everyday platitudinous words can become 'poetic': like 'bric-à-brac', which in Baudelaire's 'Le Cygne' forms the milieu in which a stranded swan gradually achieves mythic stature, and which also forms the milieu where Prufrock's voice loses its impetus:

> My smile falls heavily among the bric-à-brac.

Given the preoccupation of the *Four Quartets* with the creative task of poetic language, given Eliot's attempt, in his early poems, to make poetry out of the language of modern, urban life, one is surely entitled to ask how well the language of *The Waste Land* succeeds in either typifying or revitalizing what it is about. Does it, in its truthfulness to experience, private and public, in the transmuting power of its song, promote the sense of 'police' which Montaigne defined, or does it simply 'do the Police in different voices', as in the original draft of the 'Burial of the Dead'? Does it merely, that is, record depressing or pointless facts to describe a disjointed civilization, one in which, according to Dr Leavis, there has occurred a 'breakdown of forms and the irrevocable loss of that sense of absoluteness which seems necessary to a robust culture',[2] or in which, according to Edmund Wilson, amidst the 'terrible dreariness of the great modern cities', 'nameless millions' perform 'barren office routines, wearing down their souls in interminable labours of which the products never bring them profit—people whose pleasures are

---

[1] *Œuvres complètes, texte établi et annoté par Y.-G. Le Dantec, édition révisée, complétée et présentée par Claude Pichois* (Paris, 1961), 6.
[2] *New Bearings in English Poetry* (London, 1932; Ann Arbor, 1960), xx.

so sordid and so feeble that they seem almost sadder than their pains'?[3]

> Get me a woman, I said; you're too drunk, she said,
> But she gave me a bed, and a bath, and ham and eggs,
> And now you go get a shave, she said; I had a good laugh,
> Myrtle was always a good sport"). treated me white.
> —We'd just gone up the alley, a fly cop came along,
> Looking for trouble; committing a nuisance, he said,
> You come on to the station. I'm sorry, I said,
> It's no use being sorry, he said; let me get my hat, I said.[4]

This passage was suppressed, but the Lil and Albert passage is not all that different (though its idiom is more distinctive); and the question remains: is the language of *The Waste Land* typical and creative enough to justify the claims which have been made for the greatness of the poem, that it focuses an 'inclusive human consciousness' (Leavis) or that it is an Orphic triumph over a state of emotional disturbance?

Perhaps one could explore the question both of the redemptive quality of its song, and of its inclusiveness, by using some of Baudelaire's poems as a term of comparison. One or two memories of Baudelaire flit across the verbal landscape of *The Waste Land*. But their meaning is much distorted, made, as it were, ghostly, and one cannot speak of any recognizable 'influence' of Baudelaire on Eliot. What makes the reference important is that Eliot felt such need to situate himself in relation to Baudelaire, that Baudelaire was in his eyes the major modern poet he had to come to terms with; that, as his two essays on Baudelaire reveal,[5] he recognized many of his own tendencies in him—interest in 'order', in similar moral and spiritual values, in using for his imagery the 'sordid life of a great metropolis'.[6] Also, even more importantly for our purpose, Eliot saw Baudelaire as having succeeded precisely in the way he himself has been described as having succeeded:

> One difference between Baudelaire and the later poets—
> Laforgue, Verlaine, Corbière, Rimbaud, Mallarmé—is that

---

[3] *Axel's Castle* (London, 1961, reprint of 1931), 90.

[4] *Facsimile*, 5. [N.B. revisions in the draft are not reproduced here.]

[5] 'Baudelaire', *Selected Essays* and 'Baudelaire in our Time', *For Lancelot Andrewes* (London, 1928).

[6] On Eliot's relation to Baudelaire, see E. J. H. Greene's useful *T. S. Eliot et la France* (Paris, 1951).

Baudelaire not only reveals the troubles of his own age and predicts those of the age to come, but also foreshadows some issue from these difficulties. . . .[7]

Let us start from the centre of *The Waste Land*, from Tiresias; and let us accept that Tiresias' vision of 'love' both reveals and 'objectifies' a state of emotional disturbance. Paralysis of feelings and energies, blasé coldness and disgust in the face of love, all contributed to Baudelaire's waste land, the land of Spleen, of *Ennui*, from which, at the end of *Les Fleurs du Mal*, there seems to be no escape but death. The poem which best compares with Tiresias' vision is perhaps 'Un Voyage à Cythère', where emotional sickness reaches a climax. The poet is sailing gaily under a free sky when the ship comes close to a 'sad and black island'; it is Cythera, Venus's island, which instead of idyllic landscapes reveals a 'rocky desert' troubled only by 'sour shrieks'. The ship sails closer to the shore, and the poet discovers that the 'singular object' which troubled him from a distance is a three-branched gibbet:

> De féroces oiseaux perchés sur leur pâture
> Détruisaient avec rage un pendu déjà mûr,
> Chacun plantant, comme un outil, son bec impur
> Dans tous les coins saignants de cette pourriture;
>
> Les yeux étaient deux trous, et du ventre effondré
> Les intestins pesants lui coulaient sur les cuisses,
> Et ses bourreaux, gorgés de hideuses délices,
> L'avaient à coups de bec absolument châtré. . . .
>
> Habitant de Cythère, enfant d'un ciel si beau,
> Silencieusement tu souffrais ces insultes
> En expiation de tes infâmes cultes
> Et des péchés qui t'ont interdit le tombeau.
>
> Ridicule pendu, tes douleurs sont les miennes!
> Je sentis, à l'aspect de tes membres flottants,
> Comme un vomissement, remonter vers mes dents
> Le long fleuve de fiel des douleurs anciennes;
>
> Devant toi, pauvre diable au souvenir si cher,
> J'ai senti tous les becs et toutes les mâchoires
> Des corbeaux lancinants et des panthères noires
> Qui jadis aimaient tant à triturer ma chair.

[7] Quoted by P. Quennell, 'Baudelaire and the Symbolists', *Criterion* (January 1930), 357–8.

— Le ciel était charmant, la mer était unie;
Pour moi tout était noir et sanglant désormais,
Hélas! et j'avais, comme en un suaire épais,
Le coeur enseveli dans cette allégorie.

Dans ton île, ô Vénus! je n'ai trouvé debout
Qu'un gibet symbolique où pendait mon image. . . .
— Ah! Seigneur! donnez-moi la force et le courage
De contempler mon coeur et mon corps sans dégoût![8]

It is difficult to feel the power and meaning of the imagery in this poem thus in isolation, as they depend upon effects grown through the whole volume.[9] This is an ultimate step in the descent into waste which the 'love' experience of the *Fleurs du Mal* has revealed: especially the executioner–victim relationship, in which having been in turns 'victime', then 'bourreau', then 'Héautontimo rouménos', self-torturer, the poet ends up all passion and energy spent, his substance bled away, a prey to rapacious elements, like Villon's hanged men, grotesquely crucified to Venus: 'Ridicule pendu'. But the redemptive movement of this poem is fully impressive in its own right. In the very description of the plucked corpse, the majesty and the wide-eyed impartiality of the voice fully contain the sickening vision. There is pleasure in the precision of the gestures mimed by the voice:

Chacun plantant, comme un outil, son bec impur

and in the cool craftsmanship, verging on irony under the strain, with which disgust is rendered:

Et ses boureaux, gorgés de hideuses délices

There is no estheticism in this, but a creative power fully equal both to the pressures of the subject-matter and to the demands of the poetic voice—so that there occurs this paradox which Baudelaire regards as central to poetry: 'C'est un des privilèges prodigieux de l'Art que l'horrible, artistement exprimé, devienne beauté, et que la *douleur* rythmée et cadencée remplisse l'esprit d'une joie calme.'[10] As the movement of increasing nearness of

[8] *Œuvres complètes*, 112–13.
[9] Like the heavy, ominous presence of animals, of a significance in Baudelaire's vision much too complicated to be dealt with here, but which appear as early as the 'ménagerie infâme de nos vices' in 'Au Lecteur' and constantly reappear in association with love.
[10] 'Théophile Gautier', *Œuvres complètes*, 695.

the poem proceeds, the perceiver identifies himself with the perceived, the poet discovers himself to be that repulsive, ludicrous hanged man:

> Ridicule pendu, tes douleurs sont les miennes!

Baudelaire here is doing what he demands of his reader— 'Hypocrite lecteur,— mon semblable,— mon frère!' He comes so inquisitively and passionately close to the unpalatable reality before him that he has to become it. The moment of recognition nearly kills him—it generates a terrible sense of darkness, of chasm:

> Le ciel était charmant, la mer était unie;
> Pour moi tout était noir et sanglant désormais

This is like Blake outstaring an ever-nearing Leviathan while the Angel flies out. Baudelaire asks his reader not to be that Angel, to remain *fraternally* there. For the staying brings its reward. It leads to an extreme splendour of song, the sustained magnificence of a state in which pain cadences itself:

> Je sentis, à l'aspect de tes membres flottants,
> Comme un vomissement remonter vers mes dents
> Le long fleuve de fiel des douleurs anciennes

And this itself leads to the total openness, the reversal of the final prayer, as much transcending the darkness morally as the song had translated it poetically:

> Ah! Seigneur, donnez-moi la force et le courage
> De contempler mon coeur et mon corps sans dégoût!

If we now turn to the Tiresias passage, it is rather striking that its movement is something like the opposite of this. While in 'Un Voyage à Cythère' shocked revulsion turns into gradual identification and acceptance, an enlargement of poetic powers, in *The Waste Land* a distinctly 'poetic' voice sheds its tension as it starts dealing with a distasteful experience:

> At the violet hour, when the eyes and back
> Turn upward from the desk, when the human engine waits
> Like a taxi throbbing waiting,
> I Tiresias, though blind, throbbing between two lives,
> Old man with wrinkled female breasts, can see
> At the violet hour, the evening hour that strives
> Homeward, and brings the sailor home from sea,
> The typist home at teatime, clears her breakfast. . . .

This is explored with syntactical brilliance. The 'throbbing between two lives' is masterfully mimicked by the suspense of the ends of the lines: for instance what is to follow the 'eyes and back' which could make them joint subjects in any situation? The 'waits' of the second line hangs in mid-air through not getting its 'for' but being instead represented in its state of waiting by the taxi—the open-endedness of the waiting itself represented by the bizarre image, which leads nowhere, is suspense itself. And it goes on, with fine inventiveness, prolonging then protracting itself till the voice tires of suspense (after the second 'At the violet hour') and strain creeps into it. So that when it finally alights on the typist uneasily made the object of the evening hour and the subject of the clearing of her breakfast, what was tension becomes confusion.[11] The disappointment thus inflicted upon the voice may act as an insight into the daily disillusionment of leaving the office all for nothing—what Edmund Wilson talks about. But more importantly perhaps, is it not also about the inability of the poet's voice to maintain its pitch in its encounter with the actual? For when the quatrain is established with the typist's experience at its centre, is it not full of (deliberately contrived, of course) shortcomings? 'Perilously' doesn't quite achieve humour, and the setting sun doesn't quite manage to touch the scene up with merciful romance in:

> Out of the window perilously spread
> Her drying combinations touched by the sun's last ray

nor do the combinations quite get to their verb. And the supercilious detachment with which the 'young man carbuncular' is portrayed:

> One of the low on whom assurance sits
> Like a silk hat on a Bradford millionaire

the reluctant voyeurism of:

> Endeavours to engage her in caresses

the deadpan quality of the quatrain:

> Flushed and decided, he assaults at once;
> Exploring hands encounter no defence;
> His vanity requires no response,
> And makes a welcome of indifference.

[11] What happens here is very similar syntactically speaking to the Cleopatra passage analysed by Empson.

which once (in Gray's *Elegy*, for instance) had ennobled humble experience:

> Far from the madding crowd's ignoble strife,
> Their sober wishes never learned to stray;
> Along the cool sequester'd vale of life
> They kept the noiseless tenor of their way.

all seem to record a fall, emotional and musical.

This is magisterially brought about and controlled, as the opening of 'Prufrock' is—the *elan* of the 'Let us go' exhausting itself through its encounter with mazes of streets and language, and later the inability of the 'Do I dare', 'Shall I say', 'would it have been worth while' ever to reach their actions, their pronouncements. But all that is at stake in Prufrock's voice is Prufrock himself; there is a perfect circularity about his song. What is perhaps worrying about Tiresias' vision is that he damns more than himself—that by recording his distaste of 'love' or 'the contemporary', that by failing to rise poetically to it, while he does write interesting poetry, may be he does actually fail to rise up to his subject-matter? It is rather striking that when the 'violet hour'—the 'violet air' or the 'violet light' of 'What the Thunder said'—is inhabited by prophetic undertones or mystery, however ominous, rather than by the 'actual', the poetry has an unimpeded fineness which puts into perspective the more dubious quality of the typist passage. The Prufrock-like prepositions ('after all . . . after the toast, the marmalade, the tea . . .') instead of biting the tail of time, create the possibility of a future: 'After the torchlight red on sweaty faces . . .' The questions are real questions ('Who is the third . . .' 'What is that sound . . .') instead of means of dallying. And the voice swells up under the impulse of its longing, cadencing it as it goes, instead of undergoing a loss of impetus:

> If there were water
> And no rock
> If there were rock
> And also water
> And water
> A spring
> A pool among the rock
> If there were the sound of water only . . .

But is it not true that the moments of flowing or expansive

music one finds in 'What the Thunder Said' have left behind the experience and vocabulary of the contemporary? Bats, derelict mountain chapels, hooded hordes and hermit-thrushes (and hyacinth girls for that matter) have, on the surface at least, little to do with Europe after the First World War. This may be a facile crack, but it points to an important change in Eliot's poetic enterprise, which one sees beginning to happen in *The Waste Land*. In that poem, the failure to achieve the finer sort of song when dealing with the obviously actual is never redeemed, and yields to a quite different sort of exploration. One may well argue that what is gained by this is well worth the change of direction, but one could equally suggest that a great deal is lost— half-deserted streets, men in shirt-sleeves, reading the newspaper in the park, emotional sickness and (as Laforgue would say) 'toute la misère des grands centres' do not retain or never reach the poetic status they seemed to be demanding in the earlier Eliot, which they still seem to be clamouring for in *The Waste Land*.

For there is more at stake than self in a poet's failure or success to make song out of his own waste. He damns or redeems with himself the language—the experience—of the actual. One could take other examples from Baudelaire than 'Un Voyage à Cythère' to show this. In 'Le Cygne', Virgil's and Racine's Andromaque:

> Andromaque, des bras d'un grand époux tombée,
> Vil bétail, sous la main du superbe Pyrrhus,
> Auprès d'un tombeau vide en extase courbée;
> Veuve d'Hector, hélas! et femme d'Hélénus!

breathes the 'immense majesté' of her pain, of her rhythm, into the loneliness of the black immigrant in a northern city:

> Je pense à la négresse, amaigrie et phtisique,
> Piétinant dans la boue, et cherchant, l'œil hagard,
> Les cocotiers absents de la superbe Afrique
> Derrière la muraille immense du brouillard[12]

so that words like 'boue' and 'brouillard' expand into a grand landscape of exile, and 'phtisique' attains the rhyming status of 'Afrique'. Similarly a new, foreign term like 'wagon' in 'Le Voyage' is fused with Gothic fiction, Roman gladiatorial games and Greek myth into a poetically *whole* exploration of flight (in

---

[12] *Œuvres complètes*, 82–3.

the face of Time, of oneself; Progress and drugs as flight):

> L'un court, et l'autre se tapit
> Pour tromper l'ennemi vigilant et funeste,
> Le Temps! Il est hélas! des coureurs sans répit,
>
> Comme le Juif errant et comme les apôtres,
> A qui rien ne suffit, ni wagon ni vaisseau,
> Pour fuir ce rétiaire infâme; il en est d'autres
> Qui savent le tuer sans quitter leur berceau.[13]

One could say that 'wagon' is so well integrated because its hard 'v' sound (in French) builds up with the 'v' of 'vaisseau' into alliterative counterpoint with the gentler 'f' of 'suffit . . . fuir . . . infâme', creating a compulsive flight, still goaded on by the 'ns' of 'ne . . . ni . . . ni . . .', threatened by the nets of the 'r': 'rien . . . Pour fuir . . . rétiaire . . .'. But it is more than a question of 'cuisine', as Baudelaire would have said. The word fits because the mood in which the predicament of flight is being explored in this poem—as the predicament of exile in 'Le Cygne'—is one of such passion and self-exposure that it gathers the impetus to embrace practically any source of images, of experience, of language.

But the opposite of this happens in the Tiresias passage. The taxi pares the 'human engine' down to urban size. The 'food in tins' and the stockings piled on the divan-bed doggedly refuse to be stirred into nobility. And on the other hand the cultural reminiscences, instead of magnifying the contemporary they are brought into touch with, reductively contrast with it or are sucked into its quicksands. Dante cannot help the 'unreal city' to reach a level of greatness any more than Baudelaire can introduce a sense of brotherhood between the speaker and Stetson; the splendour of Shakespeare's Cleopatra sinks into the cloying mannerism of the furniture, synthetic perfumes and pasty syntax; the Spenser cannot outlive the debris of the river-banks: the second 'The nymphs are departed' is as curtly ironic as the first was appropriately elegiac. And when Tiresias moves from:

> I who have sat by Thebes below the wall
> And walked among the lowest of the dead.

to:

> Bestows one final patronizing kiss

[13] *Œuvres complètes*, 126.

one's sense is: 'from what height fallen!' Indeed, the two lives between which Tiresias is throbbing are too barren for that throbbing not to waste its power upon itself. What will happen when they have sprung to rich significance one can see in the opening of 'Little Gidding':

> Midwinter spring is its own season
> Sempiternal though sodden towards sundown,
> Suspended in time, between pole and tropic.
> When the short day is brightest, with frost and fire,
> The brief sun flames the ice, on pond and ditches,
> In windless cold that is the heart's heat . . .
>   . . . Between melting and freezing
> The soul's sap quivers . . .

The tension here is not pure suspense, it is the contradictory pull of states which are being intently explored. But they are the states of what Huysmans, after Baudelaire, calls 'Là-Bas'. All the words of the modern 'polis' have been left behind. Where there is water, for Eliot, there are no bric-à-brac, trams, broken finger nails, gramophones and food in tins.

It is not only lack of poetic largesse which may make one feel some dissatisfaction with *The Waste Land*, but also its sameness. If the poem is about the disjointed nature of the contemporary world, do the fragments not confirm each other too much in their gloom? And if one looks at it as a consciousness's diseased view of life, is the disease sufficiently contained? Do the voices in the poem adequately place themselves in relation to each other? Or do they not reflect one another's pointlessness?

To make felt what this lack of contrasts entails, one could briefly evoke Baudelaire's 'Tableaux Parisiens', the second section of *Les Fleurs du Mal*. There, disjointed meetings, visions, memories, bespeak the haphazard, fragmentary quality of city life as well as the atomized nature of a modern consciousness. Poems are written in the first, second and third person (as the fragments of *The Waste Land*), about brief encounters, derelict old or blind people, gambling rooms, hospitals, prints seen in the stalls on the banks of the Seine, widows sitting in public gardens, Haussmann's demolition and rebuilding of Paris, opium-taking, childhood memories, day nightmares, sculpture, gay social life seen in the perspective of a medieval *danse macabre*, prostitutes, city dawns and twilights, attics from which one contemplates the sea of rooftops, workmen, scientists, theatres, thieves, cobble-stones. But they are not only crowded with life, with things. The experiences which they relate contradict each other—which the fragments of *The Waste Land* never do. Baudelaire said that his ideal had been to find a form that would be both faithful to the jaunty, multifarious life that 'enormous cities' have brought about, and to the peculiar quality of an individual perceiving consciousness. It was the 'crossings' of the 'innumerable relations' of a city that inspired him with this 'obsessive ideal'. And in 'Tableaux Parisiens' instead of confirming each other, the poems, the fragments, actually cross. They send the mind into varieties of directions, as the configuration of streets, the multiplicity of people in them, can do. And these crossings give more range to the imagination than the individual poems might do in isolation—Baudelaire talks of the repercussions of the cry of the 'vitrier', the glazier, through the streets, from top to bottom of the houses, as an image of that range which the poems, through their placing and interaction, can have.

Showing how he succeeds would take more than a short essay, but perhaps one can get an inkling of how this esthetics of the city works by looking at the last two poems in the section. The first, 'Rêve Parisien' is an opium-dream:

> De ce terrible paysage,
> Tel que jamais mortel n'en vit,
> Ce matin encore l'image,
> Vague et lointaine, me ravit.
>
> Le sommeil est plein de miracles!
> Par un caprice singulier
> J'avais banni de ces spectacles
> Le végétal irrégulier,
>
> Et, peintre fier de mon génie,
> Je savourais dans mon tableau
> L'enivrante monotonie
> Du métal, du marbre et de l'eau.

This world of mineral, geometrical perfection goes on being unravelled and culminates with this:

> Et tout, même la couleur noire,
> Semblait fourbi, clair, irisé;
> Le liquide enchâssait sa gloire
> Dans le rayon cristallisé.

98

Nul astre, d'ailleurs, nul vestiges
De soleil, même au bas du ciel,
Pour illuminer ces prodiges,
Qui brillaient d'un feu personnel!

Et sur ces mouvantes merveilles
Planait, (terrible nouveauté!
Tout pour l'oeil, rien pour les oreilles!)
Un silence d'éternité.

II

En rouvrant mes yeux pleins de flamme
J'ai vu l'horreur de mon taudis,
Et senti, rentrant dans mon âme,
La pointe des soucis maudits;

La pendule aux accents funèbres
Sonnait brutalement midi,
Et le ciel versait des ténèbres
Sur le triste monde engourdi.[14]

The real world, here, is so dreadful that only dream escape from it makes sense. But also, one is aware of a certain unreality in the vividness of the contrast between 'there' and 'here', of a suspicion that it is the extreme perfection of the dream which makes the 'taudis' horrible, the actual sky pour darkness upon the world. The poem reinforces this by the counterpoint between the airy radiance of the octosyllabic lines in the first part and their thudding dullness in the second; between the silence and light of the dreamworld and the brutal awareness of time and blackness in the waking world. Is the dream beautiful because life is hideous, or has life been made hideous because the dream was destructively beautiful?

This tension is given quite another dimension in the next and terminal poem, 'Le Crépuscule du Matin':

La diane chantait dans les cours des casernes,
Et le vent du matin soufflait sur les lanternes.

C'était l'heure où l'essaim des rêves malfaisants
Tord sur leurs oreillers les bruns adolescents;
Où, comme un œil sanglant qui palpite et qui bouge,
La lampe sur le jour fait une tache rouge;
Où l'âme, sous le poids du corps revêche et lourd,
Imite les combats de la lampe et du jour.

---

[14] Œuvres complètes, 96–8.

Comme un visage en pleurs que les brises essuient,
L'air est plein du frisson des choses qui s'enfuient,
Et l'homme est las d'écrire et la femme d'aimer.

Les maisons çà et là commençaient à fumer.
Les femmes de plaisir, la paupière livide,
Bouche ouverte, dormaient de leur sommeil stupide;
Les pauvresses, traînant leurs seins maigres et froids,
Soufflaient sur leurs tisons et soufflaient sur leurs doigts.
C'était l'heure où parmi le froid et la lésine
S'aggravent les douleurs des femmes en gésine;
Comme un sanglot coupé par un sang écumeux
Le chant du coq au loin déchirait l'air brumeux;
Une mer de brouillards baignait les édifices,
Et les agonisants dans le fond des hospices
Poussaient leur dernier râle en hoquets inégaux.
Les débauchés rentraient, brisés par leurs travaux.

L'aurore grelottante en robe rose et verte
S'avançait lentement sur la Seine déserte,
Et le sombre Paris, en se frottant les yeux,
Empoignait ses outils, vieillard laborieux.[15]

The first thing that strikes one in this poem, coming after the close intensity of 'Rêve Parisien', is its out-of-doors, large-breathing atmosphere. The alexandrines, heard after the eight-foot lines, give an amazing sense of space:

Comme un visage en pleurs que les brises essuient,
L'air est plein du frisson des choses qui s'enfuient . . .

The air is moving, making people shiver, the light of lamps turns sickly, sharpening pains; it can be smelt in the fog, in the pink and green of the dawn, tasted in the cry of the cock, which relates all the people waking in the city as the dawn does, as Baudelaire said the cry of the 'vitrier' did, as it relates us, readers, to that city. The sharpness with which the crowing occurs lands us, as it were, inside that voice which tears through the mist, as well as inside the cough of the dying consumptive. It wakens our imagination to an expansive compassion as the breaking of the dawn wakens and aggravates pain. The movement is from anguish felt internally:

Où, comme un œil sanglant qui palpite et qui bouge,
La lampe sur le jour fait une tache rouge;

---

[15] *Œuvres complètes*, 99.

> Où l'âme, sous le poids du corps revêche et lourd,
> Imite les combats de la lampe et du jour

to a penetrative sympathy with all who suffer that anguish. Imagination here acts as a power of ever-growing insight instead of cutting itself off from life as in 'Rêve Parisien'. This is a dawn full of poverty, hard labour, yearnings, fear, death. But it is also an everyday dawn, communal, regenerative, the dawn of life that goes on for everyone in the big city and also for oneself. And the large consciousness that it embodies makes the hard contrasts of bliss and damnation of 'Rêve Parisien' appear like a narrow schizophrenia: the dream there has gutted reality. And yet one can see how fear of all the anguish of this Parisian dawn would impel the dreamer to seek escape in opium.

No such contrasts mark *The Waste Land*. Its London is never allowed to assume a life of its own, but remains the 'nightmare mirage' which it is in Lawrence's *St Mawr*, an 'Unreal city'. There is either irony or imprecision in the reference which Eliot here makes to the Baudelaire. True, the Paris of 'Les Sept Vieillards', whence the quotation comes, is a 'cité pleine de rêves', where the poet, in a dirty yellow fog, like the brown fog of Eliot's London, keeps encountering the same spectral old man, as the speaker in *The Waste Land* meets Stetson amidst the crowd of dead. But Baudelaire's Paris is also a 'fourmillante cité', swarming not only with nightmares but with life, a life 'colossally' beyond the scope of the poet's ego, independent from the constructions which he tries to put upon it. It is the poet who *chooses* to see the fog as an image of his soul—'décor semblable à l'âme de l'acteur'—and as a result sees the old man endlessly reproduce himself 'Dégoûtant sosie, fils et père de lui-même'; it is through a sort of moral failure that the poet meets reflections of his sick brain all around him, and not, as Kenner says of *The Waste Land* passage, the fog, the soul and the city which form an indissociable Bradleyan whole. And Baudelaire's encounter with mystery is one of the many occurring in the city:

> Fourmillante cité, cité pleine de rêves,
> Où le spectre en plein jour raccroche le passant!
> Les mystères partout coulent comme des sèves
> Dans les canaux étroits du colosse puissant.[16]

[16] *Ibid.*, 83.

Baudelaire's city assumes the creative functions of the rural world. It is the new *organic* milieu. *Sap* here runs through the channels of the colossus; the 'sinuous folds' of old capital cities, in 'Les Petites Vieilles', are like the folds of a gigantic brain or womb; and their 'chaos' is not the chaos of mechanical debris, but of life itself, bewildering, maternal, exciting:

> Telle vous cheminez, stoïques et sans plaintes,
> A travers le chaos des vivantes cités[17]

germinating, like the seed of future riots, in 'Le Vin des Chiffoniers'

> Au cœur d'un vieux faubourg, labyrinthe fangeux
> Où l'humanité grouille en ferments orageux[18]

and also noisy, ruthless to the blind men who, with uplifted eyes

> . . . traversent . . . le noir illimité
> Ce frère du silence éternel. O cité!
> Pendant qu'autour de nous tu chantes, ris et beugles,
> Eprise du plaisir jusqu'à l'atrocité[19]

'Atrocity' comes from 'ater', black, in Latin. Love of pleasure drives the city to a worse state of blackness or of blindness than the blind have to move in. Baudelaire's city is cruel and evil, but no more so than nature, than life itself. It calls out the same eternal anguished questions. But in *The Waste Land* the suggestion that it hides a mystery ('inexplicable') to be probed is tied to the survival of a cultural ('mandoline', 'Ionian') and mythical ('fishmen') past:

> O City city, I can sometimes hear
> Beside a public bar in Lower Thames Street,
> The pleasant whining of a mandoline
> And a clatter and a chatter from within
> Where fishmen lounge at noon: where the walls
> Of Magnus Martyr hold
> Inexplicable splendour of Ionian white and gold.

The 'natural' dimension which Baudelaire discovers to the city makes the life in it, the debris in it, assume an almost mythical scope; whereas cultural echoes, in *The Waste Land*, only underline the absurdity or faint obscenity of the noisy streets:

> But at my back from time to time I hear
> The sound of horns and motors, which shall bring
> Sweeney to Mrs Porter in the spring

---

[17] *Œuvres complètes*, 87.   [18] *Ibid.*, 101.   [19] *Ibid.*, 88.

in 'Les Petites Vieilles', the omnibuses passing by the fragile old women are one of the elemental forces of the new age, mechanically fateful, casting out, with the ruthless indifference of the old Greek gods, those who cannot keep up with the pace of things:

> Sous des jupons troués et sous de froids tissus
> Ils rampent, flagellés par les bises iniques,
> Frémissant au fracas roulant des ominbus,
> Et serrant sur leur flanc, ainsi que des reliques,
> Un petit sac brodé de fleurs ou de rébus

And city life is as 'poetic' as the old nature imagery. Thus these old women

> . . . ont des yeux perçants comme une vrille,
> Luisants comme ces trous où l'eau dort dans la nuit[20]

The unexpectedness of the images renews one's powers of vision. Baudelaire makes one look into those puddles, those eyes, divested of prejudices, sensing a terrible dormant depth. How private and quaint, by contrast, Eliot's attitude to 'trivia', his 'They wash their feet in soda water', his listings:

> The river bears no empty bottles, sandwich papers,
> Silk handkerchiefs, cardboard boxes, cigarette ends
> Or other testimony of summer nights . . .

This is in fact the toning down of a vision which was much blacker in the original draft of the 'Fire Sermon'. There, the 'swarming' becomes nightmarish, the sense of an immense fate is shrunk to a derisive telescopic view:

> London, the swarming life you kill and breed,
> Huddled between the concrete and the sky . . .
> London, your people is bound upon the wheel!
> Phantasmal gnomes, burrowing in brick and stone and steel![21]

Even images of mechanical compulsion, images of how industrial life can damage the human body, which in 'Les Petites Vieilles' were suffused with passionate sympathy:

> Ils trottent, tout pareils à des marionnettes, . . .
> Ou dansent, sans vouloir danser, pauvres sonnettes
> Où se pend un démon sans pitié![22]

in Eliot become savagely reductive:

[20] *Ibid.*, 85. [21] *Facsimile*, 31. [22] *Œuvres complètes*, 85.

Phantasmal gnomes, burrowing in brick and stone and steel!
Some minds, aberrant from the normal equipoise . . .
Record the motions of these pavement toys
And trace the cryptogram that may be curled
Within these faint perceptions of the noise,
Of the movement, and the lights!

Not here, O Ademantus, but in another world.[23]

Thus ended the gnome-life city passage which I have just quoted, and which in the primitive version separated the Mr Eugenides passage from the Tiresias passage. 'Not here, O Ademantus, but in another world': a reference to discussions, in Plato's *Republic*, of the City of God, whose 'home is in the ideal; for . . . it can be found nowhere on earth'.

The more one looks at Eliot's urban poetry in the context of another, expansive, urban poet, the more one is convinced that it was indeed to another world that he had to turn from now on for inspiration. That other world is still deep in darkness, in 'What the Thunder Said', it speaks sounds, not meanings—onomatopoeia: the 'drip drop drip drop drop drop drop' of the hermit thrush, the 'coco rico coco rico' of the cock, the three 'Das' of the Thunder; or altogether foreign words: 'Shantih'. The world of the actual has no words which could rejuvenate it for the sensibility at work in *The Waste Land*. The poem ends with a struggle between the fragments and the foreign, the other-world, possibilities. Against the 'Hieronymo is mad againe', the strange sounds

Datta. Dayadhvam. Damyata.
Shantih shantih shantih

occur.

That Eliot should have begun here already to be concerned with 'another world' helps one understand, perhaps, why he will respond with such warmth to another aspect of Baudelaire's thought: his sense that the city of men cannot become 'civilized' without becoming the city of God:

Théorie de la vraie civilization.

Elle n'est pas dans le gaz, ni dans la vapeur, ni dans les tables tournantes, elle est dans la diminution des traces du péché originel.[24]

[23] *Facsimile,* 31.
[24] *Mon Cœur mis à Nu,* 1291.

'This music crept by me':
Shakespeare and Wagner

Bernard Harris

'Shantih shantih shantih', the word is repeated here as in a formal opening to an Upanishad. 'May peace and peace and peace be everywhere' is a powerful translation of the content of this word in the version offered by Shree Purohit Swāmi and W. B. Yeats.[1]

To prefer one's own note to that offered, however sceptically, by the poet himself, may seem to stretch the liberty of interpretation to the limit. Yet presumably every reader makes his own commentary on such a difficult poem as *The Waste Land* and is forced into premature generalization if he is to establish even a roughly defined context for his private remarks. Thus, I begin comment at the poem's conclusion not because I believe that somehow the poem's 'meaning' is to be found there, like a crock of gold at the rainbow's end, but simply to indicate that I reject the critical approach which would propose that we should read a work of art, in any genre, as though it presents an argument moving from a proposition to a conclusion. To have the 'experience' and yet miss the 'meaning', or to know the 'meaning' and still lose the 'experience' are possibilities so present to Eliot's consciousness that they must communicate an essential diffidence to his reader.

My eventual purpose is simply to observe certain aspects of the presence of Shakespeare and Wagner in *The Waste Land*, and to attempt to establish some relationship between those presences. However, it may be necessary to state some large generalizations about the form of the poem as a whole if such local observations are to be pertinent. Thus, the proposition that the formal ending

[1] *The Ten Principal Upanishads,* put into English by Shree Purohit Swāmi and W. B. Yeats (London, 1937).

of *The Waste Land* may provide, even unconsciously, the formal opening to another poem, or, in another phrase of Eliot's, may involve 'a return to origins', assists my own sense of the way in which the poem requires to be heard.

I say 'heard' rather than 'read' deliberately, since some of the early response to *The Waste Land* drew upon a musical sensitivity appropriate both to the state of critical comprehension about the relationship of the arts in that whole phase of 'modernism' and to the evident musicality of Eliot as a poet. This musicality is, of course, related to the whole system of symbolism, and is a subject much larger than the concerns of my own aim. But one may break into it by means of a passage from Hugh Kenner's chapter on 'Sweeney and the Voice', where he notes that

> The strategy of the poems is to coerce the reader by a hundred precise indirections into a kind of co-naturality with some moral phase. This phase the reader, who has arrived at familiarity with it, knows as he knows the air in his room, neither discursively nor explicitly but with the immediacy of an emotion intensely undergone. It is related (in the reader's mind) to sensuous experience, but not to sensations variously recollected: rather to the substantiality of words on the tongue, and of cadences invading the sensibility's obsure musculature. *The Waste Land* or *Gerontion* in this way approach the condition of music, that they evoke rather than create their constituent vignettes, evade rather than resist explication, and live in performance: verse to read rather than to have read to one. 'A master of miniature' wrote Nietzsche of Wagner, intuiting the method of the long Eliot poem.[2]

The method of the long Eliot poem is a subject which I hope to contribute to; but the form is of initial importance. The recent publication of a facsimile edition of *The Waste Land*, with transcripts of the original drafts, makes clear some of the tasks with which Pound was faced and disposes of speculation about the nature of his intervention. For my own limited purposes two decisions are crucial: first, negatively, Pound removed no material deriving from Shakespeare or Wagner (so that my sense of their importance in the poem is not reduced); second, positively, he may be said to have Europeanized the poem, editing away—or agreeing to Eliot's own cancellation of—the American bar opening (but not the London pub scene), reducing the rather

[2] Hugh Kenner, *The Invisible Poet: T. S. Eliot* (London, 1960), 198.

gauche undergraduate pastiche of eighteenth-century satirical verse, and ruthlessly cutting the long narrative of New England voyaging to leave only that part of 'Death by Water' which is essentially recovered from Eliot's French original. In fact, from the chaos of competing forms Pound wrought a structure which was to serve Eliot again in *Ash-Wednesday* and *Four Quartets*. That form is difficult to describe in any confident manner; its five-part structure suggests most obviously the five-act structure of drama, but it has become customary to describe the five sections as movements, and it has been found appropriate to extend the musical comparison invited by the later poetry back to the earliest work. So that Paul Chancellor sums up recent criticism, and proposes his own formula, in the following manner:

> Is the entire work cast in a form analogous to any form of music, such as the symphony or the symphonic poem? Miss Helen Gardner, one of Eliot's most sensitive and appreciative critics, has found that the five 'movements' of *The Waste Land*, along with certain structural patterns within each movement, give it a form similar to that of *Four Quartets*. No doubt such similarities may be seen, but stylistic and structural differences between the two poems are even more evident. *Four Quartets* has justifiably evoked comparison with the late string quartets of Beethoven; but Eliot's sensibility as it is felt in *The Waste Land* is not Beethoven's—early, middle, or late. It is as distinctly a twentieth-century sensibility as Stravinsky's or Schoenberg's and, in 1922 at least, as new and startling.

Chancellor concludes that

> To suggest a full analogy of the form of *The Waste Land* to some musical form is a bold venture, but its structure may be seen as that of a symphonic poem in sonata form using the chief symbols as its themes, and with a declaiming voice woven with it, partly to supply related but dissonant leitmotifs.[3]

He believes that 'tentative acceptance of such an analogy may be useful as a "musical" approach to the meaning of the poem'.

I am not here proposing such an approach, rather suggesting that so much evidence of Eliot's knowledge and use of musical form should cause us to approach the music in *The Waste Land* with high expectation of its importance. The basic musical form

[3] Paul Chancellor, 'The Music of *The Waste Land*', *Comparative Literature Studies* (1971), 21–32.

of the poem was not dependent on Pound's editorship (*Prufrock* was already in evidence), but it took Pound's genius to discern the essential pattern beneath the layers of script before him. The form is personal to Eliot, but there seems no cause why we should revere chronology to such an extent that we cannot see some relationship between the form of Eliot's long poems and Bartok's famous E-type quartet form, in which the first and the fifth, the second and the fourth movements are set in complex relationship to each other, and the third movement is both a pivot for and a summation of those relationships.

Indeed, Eliot so frequently sets beginnings against endings that one is prompted to look for 'meaning' at the centre. In part I have succumbed to that temptation. I believe that 'The Fire Sermon' contains and expresses the essential experience of the poem. The elements of earth, fire, water, and air which later preside specifically over the sections of *Four Quartets* are already evoked by the titles of the sections of *The Waste Land*—not neatly so, but powerfully implicit.

Shakespeare and Wagner dominate the means by which 'The Fire Sermon' achieves its ends, which seem to me nothing less than the transformation of human experience beyond the capacity of human utterance to express it, for which the language of music is necessary; just as, in attempting to define life in elemental terms, fire is recognized as the purest element because the other elements cannot live within it but are transformed.

Such a process of transformation seems to me to take place in 'The Fire Sermon', and to argue the case we must go first to Wagner, who is explicitly used by Eliot in this respect, and then to Shakespeare, who stands as an exemplar of that whole world of Renaissance conviction and confidence which Eliot despaired of, but desired, and to which he eventually returned.

The two direct quotations from Wagner (the allusion to Verlaine's *Parsifal* sonnet seems to me to be supporting a theme rather than extending it), derive from the two most extreme statements to be found in Wagner's music of the opposing possibilities of eroticism—the fearful death-wish of passion and the pleasurable gaiety of seduction. There is no sense, either in Wagner's work or in *The Waste Land*, of the fruitful effectiveness of married love; nor is there reason why we should look for it.

In 'The Burial of the Dead' two famous moments from *Tristan und Isolde* are quoted; despite their familiarity they must be set down:

Frisch weht der Wind
Der Heimat zu
Mein Irisch Kind,
Wo weilest du?

'You gave me hyacinths first a year ago;
'They called me the hyacinth girl.'
—Yet when we came back, late, from the hyacinth garden,
Your arms full, and your hair wet, I could not
Speak, and my eyes failed, I was neither
Living nor dead, and I knew nothing,
Looking into the heart of light, the silence.
Oed' und leer das Meer.

In commenting on this passage F. R. Leavis sets the tone for much further criticism; he quotes the preceding line

I will show you fear in a handful of dust

and sees the quotation from *Tristan und Isolde* as 'offering a positive in contrast—the romantic absolute, love'.[4] But if I am right in thinking that Eliot uses Wagner, as he does Shakespeare, to intensify or dilate the substance of his own text, then we should expect not contrast but development, in the musical sense. Helen Williams may be quoted in support of this opinion; she observes that

> [Eliot's] quotations from Wagner's libretto surely add too a purely lyrical sound effect to the poem. They frame the garden scene and pin-point the two moods of expectation undermined by fear and desperate yearning and desolation which mark his own love episode. Eliot seems here to be aspiring almost to 'poésie pure', to sound above sense, hence perhaps his willingness to leave the fragments in German.[5]

I support the first part of this comment, since I believe that Eliot quoted a libretto which he considered capable of summoning to his reader's ear the music itself; I am uncertain that 'poésie pure' can be translated as 'sound above sense', but convinced that Eliot left the fragments in German because there was no other way by which the necessary music could be recalled.

The facsimile edition reveals an interesting slip on Eliot's part. He began to quote the third and fourth lines of text as they

---

[4] F. R. Leavis, *New Bearings in English Poetry* (London, 1932), 109.
[5] Helen Williams, *T. S. Eliot: The Waste Land* (London, 1968), 70.

appear in his lineation, reverted to the two previous lines and misremembered 'weht' as 'schwebt'; since the alternative makes sense there is here recorded a tribute to Eliot's knowledge of German, but it is also surely evidence of an aural mistake, a mishearing by one who was working by ear; not reading the libretto but listening to the music. Should we not do the same?

If we listen to that music several consequences seem to follow. We recognize in the sailor's opening song (repeated again as an introduction to the second scene of the opera), a tone of warning, even menace; at hearing it Isolde breaks into immediate rage; the ship is heading in the wrong direction, she would rather it were wrecked than continue its course; at the second hearing of the sailor's song, at the beginning of the second scene, she is indifferent, she does not respond. I cannot agree when Helen Williams claims that

> It is the evocative musical setting of the songs, sung by a sailor and a piping shepherd and epitomizing the passionate mode of the opera, that is relevant rather than the intricacies of the situation at the precise moments when they are sung. These intricacies can indeed distract.

Indeed thay can, but surely they are invoked. The sailor's song calls up the whole drama, and the sardonic note which he strikes perpetuates that 'fear' already expressed; that 'romantic absolute, love' is undermined from the start by the knowingness of the ordinary sailor.

Some limit must be proposed for the range of evocations prompted by these quotations; it is difficult to restrain comment, however, when these very quotations open the text of *The Waste Land* to the immense possibilities afforded by the *Tristan* material. Elliott Zuckerman, after noting that

> The first lines are from the Sailor's song which opens the opera and angers Isolde; the concluding line is spoken by the Shepherd at the beginning of the third act, and is associated with the desolation of that scene—evoked by the English horn and the empty thirds and fourths of the strings

and that 'quotations from Acts I and III, that is, frame an allusion to Act II', further remarks that

> The studies of *The Waste Land* point out the relevance of the second quotation to the sea-imagery of the poem, but they

overlook the interesting reference to the sea in the first quotation. The Sailor sings these words to one of the few immediately memorable snatches of tune in the opera:

Frisch weht der Wind der Hei - mat zu: mein

I - risch Kind, wo weil - est du?

Any reader familiar with the opera will hear the music as he reads the lines, just as he would hear the tune that goes with the quoted words of a popular song. And he would recognize the music of these lines as the leitmotif that is unambiguously associated with the sea.[6]

Zuckerman subdues to a footnote the extraordinarily potent observation that Wagner's own source, a modernized version of Gottfried von Strassburg's poem, 'puns on the triple meaning of LAMIER: Love, Bitter, Sea'.

Some limit must be set to the possibilities of annotation, but before it is reached a comment seems appropriate on the Shepherd's role at the opening of Act III.[7] It is his voice which arouses Tristan from his slumber; so that the line

Oed' und leer das Meer

does not stand simply as descriptive of the desolate state in which Tristan lingers; it is the same line, the same song, which calls him back, fatally, to life. So that at this point Eliot's own poem, in arriving at the mysterious recollection of a moment of complete emotional stasis, is marvellously caught between the musical evocations which suggest so much of the traditional material of romantic love, the garden of Act II of *Tristan und Isolde*, the storm, the hunting scene, the horns, the empty sea. But Eliot closes the casement, or door, on these vast possibilities, as soon as he has evoked them. For the present we are returned to the world of

[6] Elliott Zuckerman, *The First Hundred Years of Wagner's Tristan* (Columbia, 1964), 188.

[7] Any purely literary reader who thinks such attention to detail is excessive should consider the degree of concern which Karl Böhm devotes to his reading of the score. See *Handlung in drei Aufzugen Mitschnitt der Bayreuther Festspiele 1966*: DGG 2713001, (London, 1967), 39.

Madame Sosostris, who rules the fallible fates. We cannot be long denied the expression of their potency; indeed, once released into the blood-stream of the poem the morbid, potentially lethal, view of love remains until an antidote to the love-potion can be found.

The erotic liaisons of *The Waste Land* are numerous; some derive from legend, as Tristan and Isolde, some from history, as Antony and Cleopatra, some from gossip, as Elizabeth and Leicester; others are anonymous, the typist and the clerk, the heirs of city directors. The glamour of one kind is reflected in the received rhetoric of literary and dramatic passion ('The barge she sat in', 'The chair she sat in', etc.); but what is more remarkable is the manner in which Eliot relates his fictional worlds, so that in 'A Game of Chess' he moves with complete confidence between the language of the sophisticated society in which he has placed his modern counterparts of Antony and Cleopatra and the language of the pub scene. There conversational, colloquial, random utterance are all gathered up into poetic unity by the 'voice' of the poem, that consciousness which summons up Ophelia's farewell to impose a formality on this recurrent social occasion, so that the random experience of ordinary life is brought under the control of art.

It is in 'The Fire Sermon', however, that Eliot centrally achieves his fusion of the metaphoric worlds of Shakespeare and Wagner. The means by which he does this are available to him in Spenser's 'Prothalamion'. What has been hinted at in 'The Burial of the Dead'

(Those are pearls that were his eyes. Look!)

repeated in 'A Game of Chess'

Those are pearls that were his eyes

and exultantly proclaimed there in

O O O O that Shakespeherian Rag—
It's so elegant
So intelligent

becomes identified as an overwhelming need to raise the voice into song—as in a play of Shakespeare, where the mundane reality is carried effortlessly into the realm of art.

In 'The Fire Sermon' Eliot is often considered to be making a comparison between the vanished world of Elizabethan London and the contemporary reality, as though there were an ideal world

posited in Spenser and corruptly inherited by us. But surely
Eliot's choice of Spenser's 'Prothalamion' is more complex:
he is, after all, a poet not an ecologist. The issues involved are
profound, and clear. Spenser postulates a future golden world,
in which he had reason to believe that he would play an influential
part; he deplores our vulgar use ('bricky towers') of that world.
The harmony achieved in 'Prothalamion' is owed entirely to art,
not nature, nor history. Just as Spenser realizes that the golden
world he dreamt of is imperilled, that the ideal future for Elizabethan society is probably unrealizable, but that the scheme is
still potent in imagination, so Eliot works his way from disgust
at the present state of the world towards insistence on the necessary future state of human feeling.

'Prothalamion' has a structure of willed redemption: all that has
happened is acknowledged; the metaphors of the desired ideal
life have failed, those of the future life—so different as to be
scarcely recognizable—must be, somehow, accommodated. 'The
Fire Sermon' surely derives its own strength, and structure, from
such basic realism. The rivers of life, Spenser's or Shakespeare's
Thames, Wagner's Rhine, merge and flow. Elizabethan nymphs
become Rhine maidens. Their seductive music begins after the
actual event of the seduction in Eliot's poem. But once commenced
that music plays on to the end of 'The Fire Sermon'. It starts up at

> This music crept by me upon the waters

and continues thereafter. The characters in the poem, the reader
of it, are alike caught up in the lyricism so generated; the language
of the poem responds to this impulse: a poem within the poem
results

> The river sweats
> Oil and tar
> The barges drift
> With the turning tide
> Red sails
> Wide
> To leeward, swing on the heavy spar.
> The barges wash
> Drifting logs
> Down Greenwich reach
> Past the Isle of Dogs.
> > Weialala leia
> > Wallala leialala

The song occasioned here seems central to the experience of
The Waste Land.

> Elizabeth and Leicester
> Beating oars

recovers history—but

> 'Trams and dusty trees.
> Highbury bore me. Richmond and Kew
> Undid me. By Richmond I raised my knees
> Supine on the floor of a narrow canoe.'

Where is that to be 'placed'?

> 'My feet are at Moorgate, and my heart
> Under my feet. After the event
> He wept. He promised "a new start".
> I made no comment. What should I resent?'

Shall we dare to go on?

> 'On Margate Sands.
> I can connect
> Nothing with nothing.
> The broken fingernails of dirty hands.
> My people humble people who expect
> Nothing.'
>   la la

The poem continues to the end, as the sweet Thames runs softly
till the song is done—

> To Carthage then I came

> Burning burning burning burning
> O Lord Thou pluckest me out
> O Lord Thou pluckest

> burning

There is nothing in modern poetry to equal the scale of what is
attempted here, where the cities of Augustine, Dante, Shakespeare and the London of everyday acquaintance are reconciled.
That they are so related is due to the power of the music here
specifically invoked, and which may be sufficiently recalled by
reference to two passages of quotation from Robert Donington's
study of Wagner's 'Ring':

As we settle into our seats for the third act, the glad sound of horns reminds us of what the day's business is to be. The hunt is up. The music rejoices our ears in spite of our sad knowledge (also reflected in the music) of what the main prey will be; and now it quietens down into a steady flow of harmony all on one chord (F major, this time) such as we have not heard for a long while. There is a little arpeggiation, at first singly, then in canon. We know it well enough; it is (1), the primary arpeggiation from which all the music in the *Ring* has ultimately unfolded, beginning with (2), which is the Rhine as the first slightly differentiated symbol of primary nature herself. There can be no doubt that this return to the beginnings is a deliberate reminder of what were the sources of all the subsequent development.

We are carried along now by the slow surge and eddy of the Rhine itself. And in a moment, still on a pedal F, we hear (31) the resolving dominant ninths of the Rhinemaidens' cry for their gold; another horn-call; then the lilting tunes (32, 33, 34) to which they weave their swaying dance and their seductive spell.

There is surely nothing written in literary criticism which comes so near to the essential concern of 'The Fire Sermon'; and by living out that experience of Götterdammerung Donington is able to conclude

In the opera-house, at any rate, we are held safely in our seats. Like Ulysses tied to his mast, we can hear the sirens' song, which is the most alluring in the world, but from the comparative security of our uninvolved role as audience. That is the advantage of an artistic experience; we pass through the gamut of human emotion, but not as literal participants. We learn from the experience without paying the heavy price which that lesson might cost us in a direct encounter.[8]

Does that perhaps explain why Ferdinand, Prince of Naples, is the admired exemplar in *The Waste Land*? He is, of course, a drowned man, recovered from the sea, and set upon a redemptive pattern of behaviour. He plays chess, and obeys his future father-in-law, but there must, one feels, be more to him than that. Perhaps he inherits his father's lost capacity for metamorphosis:

(Those are pearls that were his eyes. Look!)

Indeed, Shakespeare is used in *The Waste Land* not just as a provider of comparative literary types but as a creative source.

[8] Robert Donington, *Wagner's 'Ring' and its Symbols: the Music and the Myth* (London, 1963), 232–3.

He stands for an age which Eliot needs to invoke. Perhaps we all need to recover that sense of the possibilities of the transforming power of art which was so readily available in Shakespeare's world, was revived in Wagner's art, and has been so flatly denied to us.

In his description of the City of Westminster, after citing the inscription 'In the great and Royal Chappell of king *Henry* the seventh' Stow quotes some verses headed

> Vpon the remove of her body from
> Richmond (where she dyed) to
> White Hall, by water, these
> lines were written

> The Queene was brought
> by water to White Hall,
> At every stroke
> the Oares teares let fall.
> More clung about the Barge,
> Fish under water
> Wept out their eyes of Pearle,
> And swom blind after;
> I think the Barge-men
> might with easier thighes,
> Have row'd her thither
> in her peoples eyes,
> For howsoever, thus much
> my thoughts have scann'd
> Sh'ad come by water
> had she come by land.[9]

There is probably no end to the fruitful annotation of *The Waste Land*, and there, no doubt, its greatness lies. But if I am right in thinking that its 'meaning' is approached most certainly by reference to music, confirmation seems to come from the translation by Shree Purohit Swāmi and W. B. Yeats of a section of Book V in Chapter Ten of their version of the Upanishads: there the voice is given full recognition; indeed, what the Thunder said is that the voice, that self-sustaining music, is all:

Thunder is the honey of all beings; all beings the honey of thunder. The bright eternal Self that is in thunder, the bright eternal Self that lives in the voice, are one and the same; that is immortality, that is Spirit, that is all.[10]

[9] John Stow, *The Survey of London* (London, 1963), 511–12.
[10] *Ibid.*, 134.

T. S. Eliot:
The Dantean Recognitions

A. C. Charity

In 1950, in a talk at the Italian Institute in London on 'What Dante Means to Me', T. S. Eliot explained his choice of subject:

> I thought it not uninteresting to myself, and possibly to others, to try to record in what my own debt to Dante consists. I do not think I can explain everything, even to myself; but as I still, after forty years, regard his poetry as the most persistent and deepest influence upon my own verse, I should like to establish at least some of the reasons for it.[1]

The task was never satisfactorily done, as Eliot more or less confesses; and perhaps it never can be. But without disrespect to Eliot himself, or to Professors Praz, Matthiessen and Leavis, all of whom (either formally or in passing) have made substantial contributions to our understanding of the topic, there is still room for advance. Because the influence was central, the exercise is central too. It should be 'exercise'—pursued, I mean, more energetically. For generally the situation, still, is one in which most writers about Eliot treat the subject of the part that Dante played in his achievement (when they touch on it) in peculiarly limited and unadventurous ways; so that Dante is used chiefly, in Humanist or Christian polemics, as an archetypal Catholic; in exposition, as a treasury of symbols (rose, eagle, wild beasts, ditches, flames and gardens); in critical writing, as the legatee of Latinate 'lucidity' and master of 'clear visual images'; and also, naturally, by all in general, as the lover and exalter of Beatrice.

For these limited emphases the essay Eliot wrote on Dante in 1929 is no doubt largely responsible. That piece, both as Dante criticism and as an account of Eliot's understanding, has been

---

[1] *To Criticize the Critic*, 125.

rather overvalued. Seeing it referred to (by L. C. Knights and Frank Kermode respectively) as 'the little masterpiece of 1929' and 'one of the true masterpieces of modern criticism', one feels bound to make a slight demur. For it is, by not a little, not a masterpiece; nor is it, with regard to Dante, very 'true'. For all its virtues, it is on occasion disingenuous, misleading, muddled —too often and too much to deserve that extreme praise. It is subject to too many distractions—the same ones as come out quite often when Eliot's most suggestive abstract thinking is consorted with his most eccentric concrete judgements. So it is with the essay on *Hamlet*, sometimes also with those about Baudelaire or Donne (in the essay on Lancelot Andrewes), as well as here in the treatment of Dante. In these areas we are directed again and again to think about the finding of 'objects' which might be 'correlative' to an intense emotion which cannot otherwise be 'dragged to light',[2] so that we will be able to compose 'morbidity' into 'a larger whole of strength'.[3] Baudelaire was not 'the dupe of passions' (we are told); 'he was engaged in an attempt to explain, to justify, *to make something of them*, an enterprise which puts him almost on a level with the author of the "Vita Nuova".'[4]

'Make something of them.' If the difference from Dante is not extreme, it is still important. The *Vita Nuova* is not engaged in quite that exercise (which Eliot calls, in the Dante essay, 'sublimation'); but Eliot intimates repeatedly that for him that *is* its exercise and its significance. The physical Beatrice is deprecated as 'the lower carnal love'; the spiritual Beatrice is wrapped up in final causes till she almost disappears. We are told that the *Vita Nuova* teaches us 'to look to *death* for what life cannot give'; and that its 'philosophy is the Catholic philosophy of disillusion'.[5]

It is fundamentally the tone that one objects to, but because of it the meaning has gone wrong. To correct the meaning, let me just observe that it is evident enough that Dante's creative endeavour was almost the reverse of disillusion: not to let life's meaning, even in face of death, be sold short, but to praise God's giving of a Beatrice. To counter the tone, let me recall how once, faced with the pronouncement (by a professor of Italian) that 'Beatrice was just a girl', my Cambridge research supervisor,

---

[2] *Selected Essays*, 144.
[3] *Ibid*., 422.
[4] *For Lancelot Andrewes*, 71; italics mine.
[5] *Selected Essays*, 274–5.

Kenelm Foster, a Dominican, reacted with a smile and with a musing question: 'Just a girl? What *can* that *mean*? . . . Who *is* "just a girl"?' If it is right to say of this reaction that it expresses 'the Catholic philosophy of disillusion' then I suppose that one might also say it of the *Vita Nuova*; but not otherwise.

The suspicions that I find myself expressing here of Eliot's treatment of the *Vita Nuova* have of course been voiced before— notably by Dr Leavis, who connects them with a larger context in the poetry of Eliot. But Leavis's scattered remarks upon Dante in the work of Eliot, though they contain important truth, sometimes leave the impression that the only times when Eliot leans significantly upon Dante are the times when Eliot needs help in treating sex, or women, positively.[6] That implication, which is probably not intended, is certainly not true, and in the end of course does justice neither to Eliot nor to Dante. One should take Eliot's own testimony on this matter much more seriously, when he speaks of Dante as the most pervasive and most durable poetic influence of his whole life. Eliot's meaning in that statement has to do with 'craft'—which is another emphasis. But in the end 'significance' and 'craft' cannot be held apart. For we are dealing, fundamentally, with attitudes towards experience, which ultimately qualify both craft and significance in both the poets. Therefore, in the hope of supplementing Eliot's published indications of what Dante 'meant to him', I shall try as far as possible to deal with technique and significance together. And to do that some account will first be necessary of the art, and of the impulses behind the art, of Dante.

I

Let us begin where Eliot in 1929 virtually concludes his essay with the *Vita Nuova* and its cultural setting at the close of the thirteenth century. Much of Eliot's treatment is suggestive, but it is tendentious too. For he consistently implies an undervaluation of what Dante owed, not to widespread 'Latinity', but to the relatively esoteric traditions of vernacular love poetry in which he trained himself. It is a debt which the *Comedy* itself is still

---

[6] E.g. in *Lectures in America*, 42: 'The general truth about him is that he can contemplate the relations between men and women only with revulsion or disgust—unless with the aid of Dante.'

repaying, a tradition which the *Comedy* is still fulfilling. What Eliot either does not see or does not make apparent in his dealings as a critic is the importance of this training and this background in creating Dante's confidence—which Eliot surely did see and for which, perhaps, he sometimes envied him—in presenting the experience of love as something which is 'representative' and can be carried forward into reflection on and relation with a universal context. Eliot's account needs complementing, and in part correcting too. It is, as I shall try to show, a fundamental matter, both in Dante and in Eliot.

There is, of course (what Eliot commonly alluded to) a fully-formed metaphysical system in the Middle Ages, which permitted certain kinds of confidence. There are, indeed, a number of them: medieval culture never was all of a piece. But among all the enterprises which the filial systems of Aristotle or Augustine did or could inspire with confidence, they would not, under celibate dominion, readily have inspired it at quite this point: a confidence in human love, and consequently in encounter between persons, which allows love and encounter to become the major locus and occasion of release of meaning. In Dante's period such inspiration much more probably derived from the comparatively esoteric and elite lay culture which runs from the Provençal troubadours to Guido Guinizelli and the poets of the *dolce stil nuovo*—among whom is numbered the young Dante.

In outline then (which is all that we need here), the troubadours, as is well known, contributed a quasi-religious celebration of the lady and along with that a number of associated conceits, culminating in the *donna-angelo* which was to become practically a hallmark of 'stilnovist' poetry. On those foundations it was the achievement of the Bolognese poet, Guinizelli, to construct, in a few poems, the framework of a more elaborate metaphysical context, and of Cavalcanti, Dante, and a few other Tuscan poets to add a closer, subtler, psychological attentiveness; so that from being, as *amour courtois*, a vaguely heretical cult or witty dissipation in the courts and castles of Provence, Love came in Italy, now in the form of *amor gentile*, to be considered (at least within this circle) as the beginning of religious wisdom and efficient cause of moral rectitude: the intellectual centre, at any rate in Dante's case, of a comprehensive vision of the world and man.

This brief account may seem to some of purely theoretical interest, and is not of course original. But I spend time on it here for two substantial reasons. First, because it has not I think been generally appreciated how much the *Comedy*'s stylistic and dramatic character depends upon this history—particularly in connection with Eliot's own topics of 'allegory' and 'clear visual images'; and second, because it has some diagnostic usefulness in setting forth the kind of virtue Dante had for Eliot, but of which Eliot the critic hardly speaks.

For the coincidence or coalescence of these elements in Dante's literary background with his own experience of Beatrice led not only to the heightening (as a reading of the *Vita Nuova* amply illustrates) of the significance of encounters, but eventually also to a heightened sense of encounter in the literary narrative in general (for which, of course, one reads the *Comedy*). And it also led not only to 'clear visual images' but to an extraordinary clarity, variety and articulation in the description of the processes *of* vision, and sensation generally—of recognition, and ultimately of cognition too: the theme, we may recall, of Eliot's Harvard thesis. All of this is what I mean in speaking of 'the Dantean recognitions'; and in order to bring out the kind of potency they hold—and held, in some degree, I think, for Eliot—two or three examples will be necessary.

But first an illustration from another poet of the *dolce stil* (which to save space I offer only in an excerpt, and translated) will prove helpful; it is from Lapo Gianni's poem which begins by addressing the lady, characteristically, as 'Angelica figura':

Angelic form, newly from heaven come down to spread salvation —the mighty lord of love has concentrated all his powers in you!

Within your heart a little spirit moved and came out from your eyes and came to wound me as I was gazing on your lovely face; and it made its way through my eyes so quick and fiercely that it put heart and soul to sudden flight (sleeping, the one, and much afraid the other), and when they felt it make so proud an entry and the swift blow so strong, they feared that death that moment would exercise his power.

Then, when the soul had been restored a little, it called out to the heart, 'Are you dead, then? For I don't feel you in your proper place!' The heart, which had a little life left in it (that little was a lonesome wanderer, comfortless, trembling so much that it could scarcely speak), made its reply eventually, saying, 'Soul, help me up, and lead me back to the mind's citadel.' And in this way, together, they went back to the place they had been expelled from.

Naturally enough, as well as typically, the episode begins with sight. But that is only the beginning. The way in which the encounter is developed is much more distinctive of stilnovist practice. Much, plainly, is owed by all stilnovist poets to the elaborate analysis of psycho-physiological processes undertaken in the love poetry of Cavalcanti. The mercurial 'spirits' (*spiriti, spiritelli*) which communicate between the various faculties of the mind are specially associated with him. With the remainder of the cast (Heart, Soul, Mind, and Love personified, or brought to an apotheosis) the spirits are deployed as actors in a brief internal drama whose tendency is often as here, to highlight the disorder which Love's coming brings about. The action may be more or less developed within individual poems, and there are variations too in the seriousness or scrupulousness of the poet's investigation into an actual emotional morphology; but the tendency is fairly constant, to slow time down and study Love's effects. Slow time down: it is as well to note, for instance, as Maurice Valency does, that all that happens in the poem quoted (according to another way of looking) is that 'the sight of the beautiful lady causes the poet to gasp with admiration'[7]—his heart misses a beat, and then the spirits surge back to resume their functions, more or less, as best they can.

'I' mi son un,' says Dante in the encounter with the poet Bonagiunta (*Purg.* XXIV, 51–4), identifying himself and the *stil nuovo*, we may notice, very largely by this quality, 'che quando/ Amor mi spira, noto, e a quel modo/ch'e' ditta dentro vo significando.' 'I am one who when Love inspires [or 'breathes upon'] me, take note, and trace in that way what he speaks within.' We should not be misled by the word *spira*: it connects as much with exhalation as with inspiration—and, perhaps, as some would have it, with '*spiriti*' too. The key-word is *noto*, which in the context of *ditta* and of Love the *Dittator* (cf. l. 59) can be more or less precisely rendered as 'take notes'—and that which the 'dictator' points to (as the content of the average stilnovist lyric shows) is his effects upon the organization of the soul or sensibility. The verse is quite as analytics in its manners as it is 'romantic'.

We are sometimes told, Eliot remarks in a quite different place (his essay on the English 'metaphysicals'), 'to "look into our hearts and write". But that is not looking deep enough; Racine

[7] *In Praise of Love* (New York, 1958), 232–3.

or Donne looked into a good deal more than the heart. One must look into the cerebral cortex, the nervous system, and the digestive tracts.'[8] The comment is perhaps mischievously displaced. Witty and suggestive in the context that he gives it, it is scarcely more than literal truth, applied to poets of the *dolce stil*. It is practically certain they inspired it—wholly certain that the interest they had for him was of that kind. The boast of the stilnovists, that they had achieved a more delicate expressive means than their predecessors, together with a subtler and more philosophical psychological attentiveness, is closely paralleled by Eliot's remark on Racine and Baudelaire: 'The greatest two masters of diction are also the greatest two psychologists, the most curious explorers of the soul.'[9]

Now it is my contention (Eliot's too, we may assume) that the parallel development of the expressive and the psychological disciplines was not fortuitous. It is impossible to demonstrate this adequately in so short a space, but let me put beside Lapo's *ballata* a poem which in some ways complements it, Dante's early sonnet (from the *Vita Nuova*), *Tanto gentile*.

> Tanto gentile e tanto onesta pare
> la donna mia quand'ella altrui saluta,
> ch'ogne lingua deven tremando muta,
> e li occhi no l'ardiscon di guardare.
>   Ella si va, sentendosi laudare,
> benignamente d'umiltà vestuta;
> e par che sia una cosa venuta
> da cielo in terra a miracol mostrare.
>   Mostrasi sì piacente a chi la mira,
> che dà per li occhi una dolcezza al core,
> che 'ntender no la può chi no la prova:
>   e par che de la sua labbia si mova
> un spirito soave pien d'amore,
> che va dicendo a l'anima: 'Sospira.'

(So gentle and so full of dignity appears my lady when she greets anyone that all tongues tremble and fall silent and eyes dare not look at her.

She goes on her way, hearing herself praised, graciously clothed with humility; and seems a creature come down from heaven to earth to make the miraculous known.

She appears so beautiful to those who gaze at her that

---

[8] *Selected Essays*, 290.   [9] *Ibid*.

through the eyes she sends a sweetness into the heart such as none can understand but he who experiences it; and from her lips seems to come a spirit, gentle and full of love, that says to the soul: 'Sigh.')[10]

The feeling is, of course, intensely personal, but Eliot was right (in speaking of the *Vita Nuova* generally) to stress the representative value which Dante attaches to it. The suggestion (similar to that of Lapo's opening, but more sustained) of the lady's heavenly origin is one sign of it. The cult behind this may be esoteric, but the 'miracle' is public: Dante's wonder is a thing to share, and is shared. One feels the wonder prompts the poem as a whole, and beyond that the *Vita Nuova* and the *Comedy* as well. The miracle may also be a stilnovist commonplace; but the apparent modesty of the initial assertions ('*pare* la donna mia'; '*par* che sia') is so unexceptionable, the welcome that he gives to her saluting others ('altrui') so disarming, and the breathless spell so absolute, that even as the poem contrives our assent it also seems to gain, for its experience, authority and authenticity.

Unlike Lapo's poem, Dante's does not work to a clear chronological, or even logical, programme; and we who are more used to the direct assault upon the last line of so many English sonnets may not readily appreciate, or assent (in the octave especially) to an organization which, in Italian sonnets typically, invests heavily in tidal balance between stanzas, and the ebb and flow of waves within them. Nevertheless, if we set this poem by the side of Cavalcanti's analogous sonnet, with its glorious beginning

> Chi è questa che vèn, ch'ogn'om la mira,
> che fa tremar di chiaritate l'âre
> e mena seco Amor, sì che parlare
> null'omo pote, ma ciascun sospira?

(Who is this coming, upon whom all gaze, who makes the air tremble with brightness, and leads Love with her, so that no man can speak, but each one sighs?)[11]

—we must notice how successfully the Dante sonnet has delayed and supported its main climax through the awed, subdued trance and tone that it maintains throughout the minor and prefigurative

[10] Text and translation from *Dante's Lyric Poetry*, ed. K. Foster and P. Boyde (London, 1967), vol. I.

[11] Text from *Poeti del Duecento*, ed. G. Contini (Milan and Naples, 1960), vol. II, 495.

ones that end each stanza—until that final word 'sospira', in direct speech, breaks the spell and so releases us—while Cavalcanti, having reached his not dissimilar peak too soon, trails off into relatively vapid anticlimax.

Dante's control and ordering of the sestet, especially, is only to be wondered at. The corresponding prose description which immediately precedes the poem in the *Vita Nuova* (XXVI) is beautiful in its own right;[12] but at this point there can be no competition; and the reflection imposes itself that the superior dramatic urgency—that which holds us, in the poem, *there*—is owed in no small measure to the very commonplaces of stilnovist articulation which we glanced at in the case of Lapo. As well as the common vocabulary of interior biography (*spirito*, *cor*, etc.), which may well be what alerts us, we should note the favoured syntax—the almost pedantically graphic prepositional phrases ('dà *per* li occhi una dolcezza *al* core'; '*de* la sua labbia si mova'; 'va dicendo *al* anima'), almost as if a map were being drawn, or followed; and the predilection for consecutive clauses with *si* + adjective . . . *che*, or *tanto* + adjective . . . *che*—a syntactic process which makes succession and results depend on the *intensity* of a particular stimulus rather than on other types of emotional or logical causation. Also stilnovist, of course, is the sweet exclusiveness of the cult of the 'gentle heart' ('intender no la può chi no la prova'), which here as elsewhere by its very charm invites, and finally the way by which this particular *spirito*, 'pien d'amore', can be poised equivocally between the usual personified messenger of the charmed circle (rather like a sylph in Pope) and a real exhalation from the lips of Beatrice: a breath that whispers, 'sigh!' The simultaneous unfolding of the sonnet's most sensuous moment with its poet's largest and most obvious drafts on the conventional resources of the 'school' does not strike as a coincidence. The stilnovist documentary (in moving X-ray, as it were) turns to drama partly by its own internal logic and along the lines of its own discipline. 'I note', says Dante to Bonagiunta in a fictitious AD 1300. The processes of meeting, recognition and response, through such notation, turn eventually to the reader, and involve him in the seeing and its consequences, too.

[12] 'Io dico ch'ella si mostrava sì gentile e sì piena di tutti li piaceri, che quelli che la miravano comprendeano in loro una dolcezza onesta e soave, tanto che ridicere non sapeano; nè alcuno era lo quale potesse mirare lei, che nel principio nol convenisse sospirare.'

The relevance of this to the *Divine Comedy* and to Eliot can be made clear if we turn next to the episode involving Dante's meeting with Brunetto Latini, his dead 'master', in *Inferno* XV. The scene here is specific.[13] There is a dike, along which Dante and Virgil, having left the wood of suicides behind them, are now proceeding through a torrid desert where a rain of fire continually falls. The wood is out of sight now:

> Già eravam della selva rimossi
> tanto, ch'i'non avrei visto dov'era

(Already the wood was so far behind that I could not have seen where it was) (*Inf.* XV, 13 f.).

And once again we start, not just with 'clear visual images', but with an elaborately-constructed description of a process which begins with meeting and still more, of course, with vision.

> . . . incontrammo d'anime una schiera
> che venìan lungo l'argine, e ciascuna
> ci riguardava come suol da sera
> guardare uno altro sotto nuova luna;
> e sì ver noi aguzzavan le ciglia
> come il vecchio sartor fa nella cruna.
> Così adocchiato da cotal famiglia,
> fui conosciuto da un, che mi prese
> per lo lembo e gridò:—Qual maraviglia!—

(We met a troop of souls coming along the bank, and each one looked at us as one tends to look at someone in the evening under a new moon; and they peered towards us as intently as an old tailor at his needle's eye. Thus eyed by that family, I was recognized by one who caught me by the skirt and cried out, 'What a miracle!') (*Inf.* XV, 16-24)

The insistence on the visual process is, to say the least, quite marked. If we include the phrase *aguzzavan le ciglia*, there are in seven lines five words or phrases to denote looking. But more important is the way that they control the pace and progress. From the pure indifference of the conditional *non avrei visto* which helps establish the passivity, the almost idle undertaking of the temporal clause which follows (*quando incontrammo*), we pass to a meeting which at first has nothing but indifference

---

[13] A text and translation of the main part of the episode will be found in the appendix to this essay, pp. 157 ff.

still: *d'anime una schiera*—a troop of souls (another one). Then, through what at first appears the similarly neutral looking of the souls (*ci riguardava come suol . . . guardare*—'they looked at us as one is wont to look') we pass to what begins to seem attentive, even curious, after all (*aguzzavan le ciglia*—literally, 'they sharpened their brows').

And then the recognition. 'Eyed thus' (*adocchiato*, too, suggests attentiveness) by that family, 'I was recognized by one who took me by the skirt and cried, "*Qual maraviglia!*" ' Encounter, looking, peering, recognizing, reflex, and sensation. The gradations are articulated wonderfully—and familiarly. The cast has changed. The old cast of *spiriti* and the rest of the personified faculties has been replaced by spirits of another sort, more external and more palpable—but still, like Beatrice herself, 'significant' and 'representative' for what they are, and do. And for all the changes in the context, the articulated processes have not essentially changed at all. It hardly needs to be said, surely, that the training in the peculiar stilnovist rhetoric is what accounts for the peculiarly heightened drama of the scene.

And Dante in his turn is jolted by the words and gesture of the one before him into a looking and discovering that is once more minutely, almost pedantically, analysed in terms of individual faculties—one of them, the *intelletto*, seeming still to bear the traces of the old personifications with it, while another, the 'gentle heart' itself perhaps, is altogether unnamed but comprehended in an act of bending and a sigh as like and unlike to the old sort (*sospira*) as Brunetto's wonder at the sight of Dante may be like or unlike Dante's everlasting wonder at the 'miracle' of Beatrice.

> E io, quando 'l suo braccio a me distese,
>   ficca' li occhi per lo cotto aspetto,
>   sì che 'l viso abbruciato non difese
> la conoscenza sua al mio intelletto;
>   e chinando la mia alla sua faccia,
>   rispuosi:— Siete voi qui, ser Brunetto? —

(And I, when he reached out his arm to me, fixed my eyes on the baked features so that the scorched face did not prevent my mind from recognizing him; and bending my face down to his I answered, 'Are you here, Ser Brunetto?') (*Inf.* XV, 25–30)

And if the process of recognition and the sigh descend legitimately from the poetry of the *stil nuovo*, so surely do the processes
whereby 'meaning' is discovered. Dante's so-called 'allegoric'
practice, too, can best be accounted for by this peculiar congruity
between tradition and experience.

For here again, as in the *Comedy* at large, encounter between
persons is the chief occasion of released significance; and the
'meaning' so released depends still, mainly, on the quality of an
emotional and intellectual engagement with an 'other'—an
engagement that is scrupulously watched and then dramatically
(and poetically) represented. 'Meaning', as with Beatrice so
with Brunetto, is felt to be not imposed but discovered: the
'allegory' moves out of 'occasion'.

The historical occasion of their meeting is, admittedly, impossible to ascertain in detail or with accuracy. In any case, the
episode itself is the occasion that now matters. Still, what is
discoverable from history is worth relating briefly, not to force
particular interpretation, but to help assess the canto's underlying
tensions and explain the poet's deep respect.

Brunetto Latino (or Latini) must have been about forty-five
when Dante was born (1265), and, dying in 1294 (that is to say
some four years after the death of Beatrice, some six before the
fictitious date of the action of the *Commedia*, and some seven and
a half before Dante's exile from Florence), left behind him a high
and widespread reputation for his services to Florence as notary,
prior, diplomat and statesman. Incidentally, when Brunetto
speaks in the *Comedy* of his dying too soon (*per tempo*, *Inf.* XV,
58) he cannot be speaking of an early death but with regard to the
time in Dante's life at which death had divided them. His greatest
European reputation, however, was as an author. For the five
years of Ghibelline rule over Florence after the battle of Monta-
perti in 1260, he was himself, as if prefiguring Dante, in exile
and compiling his main literary work, the encyclopedic *Trésor*
(in French) and the allegorical poem, *Il Tesoretto* (in Italian). His
poetry is specifically rebuked by Dante in the *De Vulgare Elo-
quentia* (I, xiii) on the grounds that it does nothing to purify the
dialect of its own region (its language, says Dante, is *municipalia*
not *curiala*); and, indeed, it leans towards doggerel. To his
Italian epistolary prose, on the other hand, must go some credit
(even for curial purity) since here Brunetto was among the first to
establish a dignified and cadenced 'high style' in the vernacular.

The *Trésor*, however, is the *chef d'œuvre* and provides the surest sign of what kind of debt Dante is acknowledging in the *Inferno*. The work is a vast compendium of the knowledge which should inform political man. Its subject was 'rhetoric' in the broad sense which a confused medieval etymology encouraged: the art of persuasion (the skill of the *rhetor*) leading to mastery of the art of governing (the skill of the *rector*); so that the *opera* (*Inf.* XV, 60) in which Brunetto would wish to have supported Dante would refer, in all probability, like the *ben far* of line 64, to political and not to poetic activity. Of the connection between these two areas, however, Dante the poet is by now fully aware, and it may be one aspect of the canto's tension which would also be of interest to the Eliot of 'Little Gidding'. At any rate we note how there, in the 'imitation' of Dante, and possibly also in the 1950 essay on 'What Dante Means to Me',[14] Eliot's musings on the connection between language and the moral life occur in a context more heavily indebted to this episode than to any other in the *Commedia*. (I shall return to 'Little Gidding' in section III.)

But another kind of tension, which is certainly more central, derives of course from the sodomy for which Brunetto is apparently punished—damnable, in the Dantean scheme of things, as a form of violence against nature. For shame, and out of tact, the conversation cannot touch on it; but the pathetic disparity between a public (but none the less real) devotion to public affairs and the private enslavement to a secret vice can be already recognized in Dante's anguished greeting, 'Siete voi qui, ser Brunetto?' ('Are *you here*, ser Brunetto?') (l. 30), and in the other's answer, with its apologetic and appealing prayer that he be allowed to reassume the temporal relation ('figliuol mio') in temporary forgetfulness of the eternal one (that which relates him to 'the family' or 'troop' of those 'who go bewailing their eternal pains'—ll. 41-2):

> 'O figliuol mio, non ti dispiaccia
> se Brunetto Latino un poco teco
> ritorna in dietro e lascia andar la traccia'

(My son, be not displeased if Brunetto Latino go back a little way with you, and lets the rest go on)   (ll. 31-3)

[14] Remembering that Brunetto seems to offer himself as a guide in the *mastery* of language (in his literary work), compare the paragraph in Eliot's essay on the poet as the *servant* of the language (*To Criticize the Critic*, 132-3).

The judgement cannot be forgotten, of course. To miss that would be to miss much of the feeling—the sad contrast between affectionate reverence and afflicted compassion, between nostalgia for a 'dear and good paternal image' (l. 83) which remains in the mind from old days and the appalled recognition of a new reality, which the changed encrusted features that peer up at Dante from the burning sand somehow disclose. The positive judgements and positive feelings, the respect and the affection, are clearly distinguished from the negative ones, the horror toward the sin, and the regret, and they reinforce and clarify each other, not only in the understanding but in the sensations which the drama of the canto forces on us. The final image of Brunetto chasing after the little band of his companions 'rather like one who wins than one who loses' in the race for the green cloth at Verona sums up these distinctions almost visually. And another kind of help to orientate us in these matters is given in the lines immediately before. There are the awful imperatives of the place and the condition. A dust cloud tells of the approach of a group of sinners 'with whom I must not be'. There is time for a few words only, to express Brunetto's dearest concern—that the life of the work may (in Dante's memory at least) make up for the wasted life of the soul:

> sietí raccomandato il mio Tesoro
> nel qual io vivo ancora, e più non cheggio

(let my *Trésor*, in which I still live, be commended to you; I ask nothing more) (ll. 119–20).

> Poi si rivolse, e parve di coloro
> che corrono a Verona il drappo verde
> per la campagna; e parve di costoro
> quelli che vince, non colui che perde.

(Then he turned away, and seemed like one of those who at Verona run for the green cloth through the fields; and among them he seemed the one who wins, not he who loses.) (ll. 21–4)

It is a fitting climax. The headnote to this canto in the Temple Classics edition has a nice phrase about Dante and his old master parting here 'under the pressure of separate eternities'. But it is not only 'separate eternities'—a matter of their separate destinations, hell and heaven; there are separate *notions* of eternity at work here too. Brunetto's final reference to his *Trésor*, 'in which I am alive still', hints accurately at the way we should interpret Dante's (the character's) previous testimony to the master's teaching:

> ché 'n la mente m'e fitta, e or m'accora,
>   la cara e buona imagine paterna
>   di voi quando nel mondo ad ora ad ora
>   m'insegnavate come l'uom s'etterna

(For in my memory is fixed, and goes to my heart now, the dear and kind paternal image of you when hour by hour up in the world you taught me how man makes himself eternal) (ll. 82–5)

The *Trésor* itself provides a similar clue to the meaning, for Brunetto, of *s'etterna*—where he seeks to show how fame or glory gives to the 'man of prowess' a kind of 'second life' because 'after he is dead the renown which stays behind of his good works shows him alive still'.[15] But it is the *Comedy* which gives the fuller commentary on the idea in general—implicitly within this episode. Brunetto '*seems* like one who wins', but in the sense that matters for this poem we must notice he has lost, pathetically. The notion of eternity which here prevails is governed by the journey of the poet, winning his salvation, so to speak, not by his own works or 'prowess', but through his faith in Beatrice, in Virgil, and in God.

Now it is obvious, I hope, already that the topics of this canto are of a kind that Eliot would be likely to find interesting; and we have, besides the second section of 'Little Gidding', abundant testimony in his published work (some six or seven references at least in the critical prose) to its hold on him. And surely the communicative methods, which this canto illustrates effectively, would be of interest to him too. One in particular needs stating. It is this: *the allegorical significance or meaning* (the 'separation of eternities', for instance) *moves out of an occasion which inspires or embodies it*. Surely it is in the highest degree unlikely that Eliot was impervious to this kind of truth about the *Comedy*. Careful reading of the poem as a whole makes it practically inescapable, and Eliot evidently at times read the poem carefully. Moreover, his sensitivity to this kind of truth can I think be inferred with

---

[15] N. Sapegno's edition of the *Divina Commedia* (Milan and Naples, 1967), *ad loc.*

certainty in several places—notably in the middle of the 1929 essay, from his expression of a similar, if different, perception:

> The experience of a poem . . . is very much like our intenser experience of other human beings. There is a first, or an early moment which is unique, of shock and surprise, even of terror (*Ego dominus tuus*); a moment which can never be forgotten, but which is never repeated integrally; and yet which would become destitute of significance if it did not survive in a larger whole of experience; which survives inside a deeper and a calmer feeling.[16]

But the context of this is a general one (about our growing response to the poem), and perhaps enfeebling too; at any rate it would have had more special and local significance if he had noted that Dante has so arranged that our experience of *his* poem is not only 'very like', but the very reflex of, *his* intenser experience of other persons and of events. And it is curious that the remark is in fact almost totally isolated from the discussion where it was most wanted and in which it would have had that sort of extra definitive force—the discussion, near the beginning of the same essay, in which 'allegory', 'lucidity' and 'clear visual images' are connected in noticeably confusing ways: ways which appear to imply the exact opposite of the general, capable, truth.

Allegory, Eliot says there (excusably if it is noticed that his eye is almost wholly absorbed by the atypical episode of the three beasts in *Inferno* I), can best be understood if we consider 'not so much the meaning of the images, but the reverse process', i.e. what it was that 'led a man having an idea to express it in images'.[17] This is, of course, a legitimate enquiry, but with reference to Dante it seems oddly perverse. For by Dante's own account (in the *Vita Nuova* and, a little less directly, in the *Comedy*) it was usually experience itself which did the leading; experience of the phenomenal, of Beatrice and of her effects upon him, for example (*Ego dominus tuus* may again be aptly quoted), was what prompted the idea and is what stays as image of it in the poetry. 'Idea' or 'meaning' did not go in search of 'images', but 'images' and, still more, 'events' inspired and energized the search for 'meanings'—significance, that is, in a 'larger whole of experience' —a larger context of intellectual and existential value. In that sense events and not ideas seem primary—which is why one feels

---

[16] *Selected Essays*, 250–51.   [17] *Ibid.*, 242.

it apt to say of Dante that the experience of Beatrice prompted both his understanding of the world and the finding of his method as a poet: in a sense she taught him poetry—the way experience will be located and significance elicited within the *Divine Comedy*. For in the *Comedy*, as in the *Vita Nuova*, the clarity of those particular visual images which stand out as 'characters' within the literal narrative springs repeatedly from an intense reflection on an encounter—whether biographical (as with Brunetto, Belacqua and Beatrice), literary (as with Ulysses, Geryon, Charon), or through tradition (Justinian, Cato, Farinata) or their written work (Virgil, Bertran de Born and Sordello).

Again this point is one which Eliot might have been expected to take, and again he does not—at least publicly. In connection with Beatrice and the *Vita Nuova* he comes quite close to it, indeed—as when remarking in that context how

> Dante, I believe, had experiences which seemed to him of some importance; not of importance because they had happened to him and because he, Dante Alighieri, was an important person . . . , but important in themselves; and therefore they seemed to him to have some philosophical and impersonal value.[18]

But the further point is not made—that happening in the thirteenth century they had revolutionary literary value too. Thus Pirandello notices (and of course he is assuming reference to the same 'experiences'): 'It is not Grace which becomes Beatrice; it is Beatrice who lives in her essential form of divine Grace.' And he adds: 'It is clear that we have here an absolute reversal of the concept of allegory.'[19] And it is clear too that we have here the first supreme sign of the new ascendancy of the *human* drama in European literature and the European imagination: a drama in which human beings and the human order are the main repositories of value and significance, and in which the significances that are sought predominately have to do with finding values in and for that order. But of all this, Eliot writing in 1929, and writing about Dante, says nothing.

That there are reasons—in their way good reasons—for this

[18] *Ibid.*, 272–3.
[19] 'The Poetry of Dante', in *Dante: A Collection of Critical Essays* ('Twentieth Century Views'), ed. J. Freccero (Englewood Cliffs, New Jersey, 1965), 22.

silence I will hope to suggest later. But in the meantime, with regard to Dante, let me note that the isolated, atomistic, even random character of Eliot's insights in my view partially disqualifies them. The integral principle which Eliot's earlier essay, in *The Sacred Wood*, had once invoked, which too (as I believe) much of the poetry inspired by Dante earlier and later than 1929 indirectly recognizes, and which might have helped his truths support each other, is here generally distinguished by its absence. This is why I think it is regrettable—though also symptomatic—that Eliot, in speaking of the *Comedy*, makes virtually no reference to Beatrice, and in speaking, in connection with the *Vita Nuova*, of Beatrice makes little or no link with poetic practice. In the latter place he would almost persuade us that Love is not Love (it is true, 'love' changes meaning; but there is a counter-truth); in the former, that an idea, not experience, was primary. In both places the subject comes to seem quite oddly, and unnecessarily, rarefied. The point begins to seem excessively and frighteningly occult. It is comparatively rarely hinted (what our argument and analysis by now begin to make plain) that another fairly simple fact concerning 'meanings' in the *Comedy* is this: that almost every meaning it encourages is climaxed as a 'judgement'; and because it *is* a judgement moves both from and to the individually represented case.

True it is, as we shall see, that the judgements offered can be more or less complex in the individual context and the individual case; they are, after all, a matter of quite fine discriminations. Indeed, that fact is plain already, in Brunetto's case. But this is not the same as saying that they are mysterious. And the more important truth is this—that they are not finally dependent on the poet's discursive intellectual assertion, but as far as possible on our responding with emotional and intellectual assent to what we sense inheres in the poetic interplay—of character and situation, structure, style, imagery, feeling *and* assertion—in a narrative that scarcely ever offers (for I think we must admit there are exceptions) mysteries arcane or cabalistic to search out or re-search in—which Eliot's repeated (gnostic or agnostic?) references to 'further depths' and 'deeper meanings' would apparently imply.

Once again then, let me urge a fresh consideration of the canto of Brunetto—this time remarking not only what Eliot in an early essay ("Tradition and the Individual Talent') called the 'working up of the emotion evident in the situation'—of which perhaps another reference to those 'separate eternities' will suffice as memorandum—but also (what he there also refers to) the 'considerable complexity of detail' upon which the singleness of its effect depends. The canto is not specially ambiguous or controversial, and the few remaining comments that I offer are intended mainly as a check-list illustrating on the one hand the poetic interplay, which (I said) tends to find its meanings in the act of judgement, and on the other the complex responsibility towards the human life of which the poetry is witness. It is worth spelling out how much there is—how very much—within the episode for the reader (Eliot especially) to respond to. 'Complexity of detail' is no doubt an understatement.

There is first, then, its extraordinary range of themes or moral interests, and the extraordinary responsibility towards them all which the poetry implies or, in some cases, fully discovers: filial and religious *pietas* (the shade of Virgil is there, of course, in more senses than one); the public life, the private sin; the claims that different notions of success, fame, immortality, can make, or seem to make, upon us; the threat of exile (ll. 61–78) and the threat which that foreshadows, death (cf. ll. 80–1, 'dell'umana natura posto in bando'); hence, 'aftersight' and 'foresight'. It is worth noticing how much of the focused interest is engaged with Florence, the community, and with the poet's precarious association with that people's order and disorders. And one could dwell too on the varied kinds of confidence inspired by the dike, by Virgil, by Fortune, by the work, the self, and God—each of which the canto touches on, and tests, or lightly questions.

And because, beneath the assurance of the narration and the consistent *gravitas* of tone, all the materials seem to preserve their own life, their own forms and own voices, there is (next) the variety and personality of the *voices* in the language to be noticed— not just the varied voices of the characters and of Dante the narrator, but the voices in the very medium of the language used. It is a language that can pass with apparent ease from understated or unstated, hinted, judgement and a tactful self-effacement, to tough, urgent, acrimonious tirade; from an approximation to the poet's early 'sweet new style' to the harsh *stil aspro* of certain others of his great *canzoni*; from courtly compliment (l. 70: 'La tua fortuna tanto onor ti serba') to the plebeian and proverbial invective ('Faccian le bestie fiesolane strame/di lor medesme', ll. 72–3; and 'lungi fia dal becco l'erba' l. 72). One might mention also Virgil's laconic interjection of another proverb, just after Dante the character has with some complacency predicted his own fortitude: *Bene ascolta chi la nota* (which might plausibly be translated as, 'Here Virgil dryly emphasized "N.B." ') (l. 99). More to the point here, though, would be the remark that the language can contain not only separately but together both analytical clarity and physical immediacy (besides the opening sequence, to which I shall shortly return, look at ll. 73–87), both courteous control and a kind of shamefaced diffidence (ll. 31–3), both the cultivated and superior distaste (even slight malevolence?—for the *maligno* of l. 61 may cut both ways) of Ser Brunetto, and the incorrigible ruggedness (*macigno*) of the hill-town, Fiesole, and its natives. *Una somma stilistica* is what the *Comedy* has been called by a noted critic (Contini); but it is a *summa* which seems to preserve the echo of voices still spontaneous, urgent, primitive, untouched or unretouched by 'style'. Attentiveness to canto after canto of the *Comedy* confirms and reconfirms the presence of these qualities.

Now it is incredible to me that Eliot, the poet of *The Waste Land* and of *Prufrock*, should have been generally insensitive and unaware of this sort of power and virtue in the supreme work of his Italian master. The essay in *The Sacred Wood* shows pretty clearly, in my judgement, that he was not. Why then, in 1929, did Eliot choose (if that is the right word) to speak of meaning and of allegory in such a different context and with such a different and misleading emphasis? Why the curious silences, within that later essay, and the no less curious indirections?

One part of the answer may be made clear by recollecting that at this time Eliot was most actively engaged in the composing of *Ash-Wednesday*. And the inference that strikes one who puts the poem and the Dante essay alongside each other is that Eliot was not then interested in devoting to the *Comedy* a very full or passionate attention—except in a limited but suggestive way. For in the poem too he shows a special interest in the sort of 'provisional' images—definite in feature, reserved in the disclosure of their 'meaning'—which the three beasts of *Inferno* I and some few other isolated passages of Dante's allegory also exemplify. Thus Mario Praz remarks of the images in *Ash-Wednesday*: 'It is as if Eliot had been reading Dante without giving much heed to the meaning, but letting himself be impressed by a few clear visual images'; and he goes on to apply Matthiessen's description of the 'paradoxical precision in vagueness' to the images of Eliot's poem with the comment that the production of such images was probably the 'principal influence of Dante's allegory on Eliot'.[20]

Perhaps another clue to Eliot's thinking about this same facet of *Ash-Wednesday* and his concurrent use of Dante can be found in the 'Conclusion' of the lectures of some two or three years later, *The Use of Poetry and the Use of Criticism*:

> The chief use of the 'meaning' of a poem, in the ordinary sense, may be (for here again I am speaking of some kinds of poetry and not all) to satisfy one habit of the reader, to keep his mind diverted and quiet, while the poem does its work upon him: much as the imaginary burglar is always provided with a bit of nice meat for the house-dog. This is a normal situation of which I approve. But the minds of all poets do not work that way; some of them, assuming that there are other minds like their own, become impatient of this 'meaning' which seems superfluous, and perceive possibilities of intensity through its elimination.[21]

But Eliot's interest in Dante or in Dante's 'meaning' was not always of this special and, I would say, limited kind. The poetry reveals a little more than Eliot's criticism, and what it does reveal, I think, explains a lot about the reticences and resistances within the criticism. But to make that point, it will be useful first to summarize a few of the conclusions, with regard to Dante, reached so far.

II

The effects of his experience of love is 'noted' by a poet who believes somehow in love's transcendent possibilities. The noting, and the confidence apparently integrally associated, for Dante, in the love-experience, extend to other areas of experience, to other meetings, other occasions—in the end to that extraordinary range of moral interests and responsible responses which makes up the poem's universe. But the root is always there, in love, and in encounter generally. Hence the importance of the recogni-

[20] Mario Praz, *The Flaming Heart* (New York, Doubleday Anchor edition, 1958), 369.
[21] *The Use of Poetry and the Use of Criticism*, 151.

tion scenes and processes in Dante: they are essential and constitutive.

For in Dante the concern for articulating and distinguishing
and even judging in the end is not the product either of the
scientific passion for investigation, or of theories of final causes,
or Latinity, or the inflation of self-righteous zeal but of the need
to order and discover that 'just solicitude for things' which is the
ordering of love. Beatrice, Dante would say, inspired the whole.
The experience of her, by its own weight and profundity, required
both scrupulous attention and religiously devout expression.
One may speak here of a discipline of feeling; but the feeling
demands discipline not to check it but to do it justice, to express
it with responsibility in a context which the feeling itself alters,
makes potentially momentous. *All* things come to require a just
solicitude.

And so with words, with language—the concern for right
words ('Sì che dal fatto il dir non sia diverso', *Inf*. xxxii, 12)
is the reflection of this need. 'Let your care for words', said
Quintilian, 'be one with your solicitude for things'. The affective
aspect of this phrase, when we associate it with Dante, demands
emphasis. Because of love, the universe becomes momentous, its
components more or less of moment; hence it *becomes* a universe,
bound together by love in one volume (*Par*. XXXIII, 86):
no part of it is now inconsequential or a neutral matter. All things
(one refers these days habitually, to ecology, insecticides, and
plankton) come to require a just solicitude; and if we care for
anyone we ought to care, implicitly, for all things. The poet's
care for words reflects that kind of care—the particular passion
of the felt relationship and interaction—and is called upon to do
so. In a world that matters—and which therefore cannot stay
objectively or neutrally 'out there' where live pure mathematics
and sometimes the learned journals—knowledge, even speculation has appropriate emotions, and the poet's language should
convey them. That is, I think, a fair reflection of the task which
Dante set himself.

How much of this Eliot understood I do not pretend to know.
His expressed views on Dante seem to me too isolated and
infirm—infirm in part because they are so isolated. One notices,
for instance, that for all his correct references (or deferences) to
the 'unity' of the *Divine Comedy*, he does very little to establish
it—little more than saying, 'we shall understand *this* better after

we have read *that*'. His comments on 'lucidity' are almost frankly sentimental and nostalgic. They do not relate to Dante's '*noto*' (*Purg.* XXIV, 53). His comments on Beatrice (partly true, like nearly everything) do not appear to have in his mind any necessary connection with his thinking on the subject of 'clear visual images'. His truths, when truths they are, are offered piecemeal. And the fact may have its consequences—and its causes.

For a universe which *is* a universe was not in Eliot's grasp. As with most of us, the necessary confidence was lacking. There may have been besides (for such an enterprise) a more individually disabling factor—experience which left him in some ways unconfident *about* experience. That would account, doubtless, for the surprising poverty of themes—the sometimes unnerving slightness of the moral interests. Obviously it was not a matter of his having no experience, or of having experience of no very profound kind. But sometimes (as he knew well) the freedom *from* experience is as important as experience itself. The poetry he made deals greatly (that is, as great poetry) with the experience of distrust of experience—of apparent isolation from what had been springs of life. That could perhaps be put another way. The poetry he made deals often and deals greatly with the experience of existential insecurity. For over ten years, perhaps twenty, Eliot's poetry is filled with it. And there, in marked contrast to the Dante essay, he makes no attempt to hide the fact that Dante stood, in this respect, as the portentous opposite of his poetic world and its protagonists. Prufrock, Tiresias, Gerontion and the hollow men really make no bones of knowing that Dante was the poet who, above all, had dared to 'disturb the universe', had squeezed it up, as if 'into a ball' (*in un volume*, *Par.* XXXIII, 86), so as to 'roll it towards an overwhelming question'. For if it is not in their power to do likewise, it is still, obliquely, *vis-à-vis* the Dantean model that they measure themselves and are found, representatively, somehow wanting. Thus Professor Rajan remarks how, in *Gerontion*, 'The confrontation of reality cannot be endured; the images twist away into rites of expiation and anxiety, surrogates for the truth that will not be faced.' And he adds: 'It is this falling short, this failure of metaphysical nerve, that makes the difference between dying and dying into life.'[22]

[22] B. Rajan, 'The Overwhelming Question', in *T. S. Eliot: The Man and his Work*, ed. Allen Tate (Harmondsworth, Pelican edition, 1971), 369.

And where not only the allusions but the poetic manners recall Dante, we find that situation rendered with peculiar intensity and pathos. This means, of course, no disrespect to Eliot; it is not to his discredit. There can be no form nor comeliness in Limbo ('Shape without form, shade without colour,/ Paralysed force, gesture without motion' is the condition of the hollow men); and Eliot's *Waste Land* cannot well have fortresses or citadels for hope: there is no water.

> If there were water
>   And no rock
>   If there were rock
>   And also water
>   And water
>   A spring
>   A pool among the rock
>   If there were the sound of water only
>   Not the cicada
>   And dry grass singing
>   But sound of water over a rock
>   Where the hermit-thrush sings in the pine trees
>   Drip drop drip drop drop drop drop
>   But there is no water
> ('What the Thunder Said')

And yet here in its very desolation and insubordinable, unsubmissive life, the passage stands up well beside a passage, also in its way unequalled, in the Inferno proper.

> — O voi che sanz'alcuna pena sete,
>   e non so io perché, nel mondo gramo,—
>   diss'elli a noi — guardate e attendete
> alla miseria del maestro Adamo:
>   io ebbi vivo assai di quel ch'i' volli,
>   e ora, lasso!, un gocciol d'acqua bramo.

('Oh you who from all punishment are free, and I do not know why, in this grim world,' he said to us, 'look and attend to Maestro Adamo's misery: alive, I had in plenty what I wanted: now, alas, I crave one drop of water.')

> Li ruscelletti che de' verdi colli
>   del Casentin discendon giuso in Arno,
>   facendo i lor canali freddi e molli,
> sempre mi stanno innanzi, e non indarno . . .

(The little brooks which from the green hills of the Casentino fall down to the Arno, so that their channels are kept cool and soft, are always in my mind and not in vain . . .) (*Inf.* XXX, 58–67).

For Eliot's *Waste Land* has been made to resound with at least the echo of the hermit-thrush's 'water-dripping song'. The poignancies are equal.

III

Before, however, we proceed to Eliot's *Waste Land* and the related 'Limbo' poetry, it is worth our while to glance at 'Little Gidding' —which of course comes from a later period and is of a different kind. I begin there—more specifically, with its second movement —for two reasons. One, because it is the clearest, most acknow-ledged 'imitation' of the style of the Florentine poet in the whole of Eliot's works, and has some claim, therefore, to be a kind of touchstone for our inquiry. Two, because the problems it presents seem useful diagnostically. The dialogue or tension that it holds with Dante is not the same as in the earlier poetry—nor should we expect it; but it touches on the same concerns and dramatizes issues not indeed identical to those in Limbo but still intimately related.

*

'Twenty years after writing *The Waste Land*, I wrote,' says Eliot, 'in Little Gidding, a passage which is intended to be the nearest equivalent to a canto of the Inferno or the Purgatorio, in style as well as content, that I could achieve.'[23] It was impos-sible of course for any reader who was likely to be reading 'Little Gidding' to miss the Dantean character of the episode in question. The similarities were manifest: not only in the several clear allusions to the *Comedy* (Brunetto is the chief but not the sole source of them), but in more general qualities. The adaptation of Dante's *terzina* is one, obviously. Another is the recreation (a genuine triumph of the passage—though a triumph shared, perhaps, with Shelley's)[24] of that eminently Dantean stylistic elevation—quite unlike the 'high' style of the classical tradition—

[23] *To Criticize the Critic,* 128.
[24] See the same essay ('What Dante Means to Me') for Eliot's appreciation of Shelley's Dantesque style, *Selected Essays,* 130–2.

which lies in mobilizing spacious paragraphic units through a syntax formal and rhetorically sophisticated enough to allow sharp, individual, unstylized voices ('What! are *you* here?') and 'low' diction ('tin', 'asphalt', 'pail') to be incorporated with no loss of tonal gravity. There are stylistic parallels of a more minute kind too, including the use of some of Dante's own clear 'images of vision'—but these need not concern us at the moment. And finally (that which accounts most, one supposes, for the undertaking as a whole) there is the general situation: an encounter (it is, of course, the only dramatized encounter in the *Four Quartets*), which is not of this world wholly, and whose very unexpectedness and 'unreality' releases the expression of generally unspoken but entirely urgent cares.

Of course there are dissimilarities as well. Some of these I take to be quite simply flaws. For instance the clause 'yet the words sufficed/To compel the recognition they preceded' (ll. 101-2), though plainly framed on Dantean models (compare it, for example, with ll. 27-8 of the Brunetto canto) is surely somewhat lame here. The trace of stilnovistic psychological pedantry which I noticed in the Dante serves there as a curb and resistance, to impress on us the difficulty of the recognition as the verse slows momentarily down. But here the metre practically loses heart, allowing us to muse why 'they preceded' needs be there at all. Nor does there seem to be good reason for the ghost's abrupt explosion into would-be proverb:

> Last season's fruit is eaten
> And the fullfed beast shall kick the empty pail   (ll. 116-17).

It may be dutifully 'after Dante' (imitated), but the vehemence seems to my ear out of place.[25] Brunetto's similar acerbities (ll. 65-6, 72, 73-4), like Dante's own (*Lascia pur grattar dov'è la rogna*,[26] *Par.* XVII, 129), are evidently occasioned by the matter contemplated, and one assents to the imperious manner out of a kind of sympathy that is not, by Eliot's compound ghost, quite earned.

---

[25] 'Full' may be intended to add vigour; but the temporary disturbance of the metre lends to the first solidly iambic foot a 'kick' of extra virulence; which, in an immediate context where the tone has hovered between cool, remote, phlegmatic and flat, is at any rate a little disconcerting.

[26] 'Let them scratch where they itch!'

Lest such criticisms seem pernickety, let me say that I believe these flaws do point beyond themselves, to some arbitrariness in the selection of stylistic details to be imitated, and perhaps also to an unexpectedly limited understanding of the organic *function* of such details as are borrowed (piecemeal). We have already, in discussing Eliot's 1929 Dante essay, seen some evidence of a failure to relate his separate insights satisfactorily. It is a question whether in the poetry—where instinct and sensitivity tend to operate more critically than in the prose—the same disorders still prevail.

But other dissimilarities between the 'Little Gidding' passage and its Italian model are quite plainly intentional and valid. That the ghost is 'compound' is but one of these, the plainest, possibly. That when one speaks (as properly one may) of the intended heightening of the sense of encounter in the episode one says it meaning, 'relative to other (to all other) episodes in the *Four Quartets*, and even in Eliot generally,' and not 'relative to Dante'— this, too, is surely consonant with Eliot's intention.

What, though, do we make of certain other marked departures? There is, in the first half especially, a persistent failure to achieve the kinds of minor climax which the working up would lead us to expect. The recognition, heralded by manifest allusions to the passage of *Inferno* XV that we looked at earlier, does not turn out to be so unequivocal. The face, intensely scrutinized in l. 90 and 'still forming' in l. 101, never *will* form. The meeting, advertised by no less than five adverbial clauses of time and one of place, is also 'nowhere' and has 'no before and after'. Consistently with that, the cry of Dante, 'What! are *you* here?' is immediately countered by 'although we were not', which has not I think so much to do with logic (paradox or contradiction) as with cooling off the salient intensity. In a word, the meeting never *is* a meeting in the ordinary, still less the Dantean, sense—as between a 'one' and an 'other'. (It is, of course, not just because the 'ghost' is 'compound' and the 'I' 'double', but because the 'double part' may or may not include the 'ghost'.)

This, in itself, seems plain enough. But the reasons for it are not. Undoubtedly the 'hallucinated' quality of the scene, which Eliot said that he was after, is genuinely, by these means and others, created. But it still leaves questions, one of which of course is this: 'Why Dante?' And on that, a sentence which I just referred to must now be fully quoted:

The intention, of course, was the same as with my allusions to Dante in *The Waste Land*: to present to the mind of the reader a parallel, by means of contrast, between the Inferno and the Purgatorio, which Dante visited and a hallucinated scene after an air-raid.[27]

It does not get us far; but it helps to frame the question with a little more precision. One can understand the sense of 'contrast', but why 'parallel', and 'parallel' with what? If it really does not matter whether it is with the *Inferno* or the *Purgatorio*, then what is the parallel for? If the question seems to some irrelevant, I can only answer that it does not seem so to me—and point out that even on Eliot's showing the purpose cannot have been quite 'the same as with my allusions to Dante in *The Waste Land*', for there, as higher up this same page he again confirms, his use of Dantean allusion in the vision of the crowd on London Bridge was unequivocally 'to establish a relationship between the medieval inferno and modern life'. There, a judgement, even a moral judgement, was apparently implied. Can we say for sure that here it is not?

The problem basically arises out of the emotional unevenness obtaining in the various sections of the dialogue—arises in particular, in the ghost's speech, out of the contrast between the generally innocuous drift of the opening ten or fifteen lines and the tense mordancy of the Yeatsian disclosures towards the end. Admittedly this disequilibrium may be seen, in one way, as a thing the author may have willed and needed. Such factors, in the speech's opening, as lead us in the first place to take note of it—the references to forgiveness, for example, which despite their liturgical origin have here no certain grace to borrow or to give, and which, like the musings upon 'last year's language', begin to feel habitual merely—such factors may be calculated to suggest the presence of precisely that indifference which the next movement of the Quartet will identify as something growing between attachment and detachment and resembling both 'as death resembles life'—they are like, but radically different, 'unflowering'. On the other hand, it may also be felt that (whatever the calculation) the apathy here is too little, too faintly, identified as such—so that one wonders, how 'intimate' is it, or how much understood? As with the reference to purgatorial fires at the end,

[27] *To Criticize the Critic*, 128.

the references to 'language' and 'forgiveness' here, near the beginning, perhaps tilt the balance of our responses unfairly, and lend to the figure too much of a specious authority when we come to the heart of his speech.

And when we do come there, it is clear surely that the words which most betray the nature of the ghost's own 'spirit' ('spirit unappeased' and 'exasperated spirit') are not allowed in context literally to apply to it, or not to it alone. Their force hides under, or is blunted by, a syntax that looks elsewhere.

Yet they do apply, or could. Beneath the assumed apathy, beneath the whole hallucinated episode (the trance that slightly dulls the moral sensibility), something quite possibly malignant develops, something that has plainly the note of confession in it, and the impulse to confession, but which (cast as it is in the form of morbid, hopeless prophecy) may not be designed to make a clean breast, but to torture.

> . . . Let me disclose the gifts reserved for age
> To set a crown upon your lifetime's effort.
> First, the cold friction of expiring sense
> Without enchantment, offering no promise
> But bitter tastelessness of shadow fruit
> As body and soul begin to fall asunder.
> Second, the conscious impotence of rage
> At human folly, and the laceration
> Of laughter at what ceases to amuse.
> And last, the rending pain of re-enactment
> Of all that you have done, and been; the shame
> Of motives late revealed, and the awareness
> Of things ill done and done to others' harm
> Which once you took for exercise of virtue.
> Then fools' approval stings, and honour stains.

There is nothing of equivocation about the force or the directness of these lines—in themselves. Alvarez says of the passage that 'it has more direct power than anything else in the *Four Quartets*', and notes that it is this 'sense of the desolation of life which remains', when the poem is done.[28] Kenner says that 'no other voice in Eliot's repertoire articulates with such authority'[29] (I have already given reasons for suggesting, however, that the authority rests in the articulation here, not in the ghost's 'moral'

[28] A. Alvarez, *The Shaping Spirit* (London, 1958), 27.
[29] *The Invisible Poet: T. S. Eliot*, 274.

authority). And Harding notes, I think rightly, that 'the motive power of this passage . . . is repulsion'.[30] In isolation from its context, the tone and tenor of the passage seem quite unambiguous.

Nevertheless, even though they cannot be wholly contained or countered by their context, that context seems strangely intent on concealing or muffling their intransigence. The working up, as I have implied, is slow and suspiciously aimless—as if the verse, like the ghost, loitered, for all its hurry. The lines quoted are introduced by a clause which, in the light of what follows, looks bland and disingenuous in its dwelling on 'theory':

> Since our concern was speech, and speech impelled us
> To purify the dialect of the tribe
> And urge the mind to aftersight and foresight,
> Let me disclose the gifts. . . .

And they are followed by a sentence which appears to withdraw too easily (unless ironically) from the hopelessness and laceration which has just been so vividly enacted:

> From wrong to wrong the exasperated spirit
> Proceeds, unless restored by that refining fire
> Where you must move in measure, like a dancer.

Put beside Prospero's epilogue,

> (And my ending is Despair,
> Unless I be reliev'd by prayer,
> Which pierces so that it assaults
> Mercy itself and frees all faults),

the relative perfunctoriness of the ghost's final clause seems plain. To put it sharply: we cannot, on this ghost's simple say-so, turn Hell into Purgatory. The moral attitude is as irresolute or shifting as the distance of the ghost from Eliot is undefined.

For on that, to my mind anyway, the whole thing turns. That is why Harding's assertions that the section is 'the *logical* starting-point of the whole poem', that 'the passage amounts to a shuddering "There but for the grace of God go I"', and that 'the other parts of the poem can be viewed as working out an alternative

---

[30] D. W. Harding's *Scrutiny* review of 'Little Gidding', cited from the reprint of it in *T. S. Eliot, The Four Quartets: A Selection of Critical Essays*, ed. B. Bergonzi (London, 1969), 65.

to the prospect of life presented in this narrative',[31] are not so fully realized in poetic practice as perhaps they should have been if that were Eliot's intention. For if 'Little Gidding' as a whole depends upon the laying of this ghost—and of the negativeness of his role there is little doubt—the ghost should have been better exorcized. If this ghost's function is to offer an alternative ('the dreary bitterness in which a life of literary culture can end if it has brought no sense of spiritual values'),[32] then it ought to be more clearly *alter*, 'other'. Instead, the passage proffers a confession (where confession is still urgent) which still falters in a partial incognito, an irresolute alibi.

This much is clear as well: that the contrasts with the Dante are quite radical. In Dante the 'eternities' (in nearly every sense) do 'separate', and here they do not. In Dante, though the judgements may be complex and, in certain cases (like Ulysses' or Brunetto's), be distinct, according to which aspect of the man is being thought of, we always know which way the poet's judgements go, and on the whole corroborate them in our sympathies. In this episode of 'Little Gidding' our sympathies and judgements are at best uncertain; we do not know for sure what sympathies to lend, what kind of judgement to apply: which is especially surprising in a passage otherwise so Dantean as this; for Eliot is on record, after all, for disapproving what he sees as moral ambiguity in Milton, and specifically contrasting Dante:

> About none of Dante's characters is there that ambiguity which affects Milton's Lucifer. The damned preserve any degree of beauty or grandeur that ever rightly pertained to them, and this intensifies and also justifies their damnation.[33]

And if one asks again, *why* the recourse to Dante? one begins to wonder if it is not partly out of weakness here, and not of strength; partly to assist the poet disavow that which, another way, he would acknowledge; both to help him form, and to evade, a judgement. One finds, beneath the first, another question rising therefore. Does Eliot's 'heaven', on this showing, really understand (as I think Dante's does) his 'hell'? To ask that is not to doubt that Eliot's heaven has force,[34] but to indicate what kind

[31] *Ibid.*   [32] *Ibid.*

[33] 'Dante', in *The Sacred Wood* (London, 1920), 167.

[34] To read 'Little Gidding' sensitively, as a whole, or to hear Eliot read it ('Quick, now, here, now, *al*ways!') is the best way to dispel doubts of that kind.

of force it may or may not have. It is not Dante's kind. For Dante's
Paradiso (understanding his *Inferno*) offers us the hope that a
'heaven' need not be based on ignorance or incomprehension
('fugitive and cloistered'), still less on fastidiousness and fear.
It is a hope that we can do with, and the important matter for the
reader of the *Comedy* is not that which Eliot so taxed himself
about, whether it requires faith; but rather whether it creates
hope and sustains it. Maybe it is 'of our time' that Eliot's poetry
creates no more in that direction than the wish for hope.
But in that form, where hope is so intensely wished for, this
creation in itself deserves all honour.

> In this last of meeting places
> We grope together
> And avoid speech
> Gathered on this beach of the tumid river
>
> Sightless, unless
> The eyes reappear
> As the perpetual star
> Multifoliate rose
> Of death's twilight kingdom
> The hope only
> Of empty men.
>
> (*The Hollow Men*)

IV

The other passage that I mean to treat in detail is the passage in
The Waste Land at the end of 'The Burial of the Dead': the flood
of bank-clerks. Here once more, the Dantean allusions seem to
point to something deeper than allusion, if not quite to imitation.
Here once again the impulse seems to me in part confessional;
and here once again the pressure which brings Dante into it has
to do with the externalizing, in a recognition and encounter
more dramatic and more bitter and incisive possibly than any
that surround it in the poem as a whole, of intransigent inner
tension.

> Unreal City,
> Under the brown fog of a winter dawn,
> A crowd flowed over London Bridge, so many,
> I had not thought death had undone so many.

Sighs, short and infrequent, were exhaled,
And each man fixed his eyes before his feet.
Flowed up the hill and down King William Street,
To where Saint Mary Woolnoth kept the hours
With a dead sound on the final stroke of nine.
There I saw one I knew, and stopped him, crying: 'Stetson!'
'You who were with me in the ships at Mylae!
'That corpse you planted last year in your garden,
'Has it begun to sprout? Will it bloom this year?
'Or has the sudden frost disturbed its bed?
'O keep the Dog far hence, that's friend to men,
'Or with his nails he'll dig it up again!
'You! hypocrite lecteur! — mon semblable, — mon frère!'

Here, as I remarked before, the reference to Hell (or the
Inferno) is unambiguous:[35] it *is* a 'hell' that is implied. But to
catch that implication only provides us with a start in understanding why, and how, the *Comedy* is drawn on in the passage,
To press further, we must look harder both at Eliot's references
in the Dantean context and at the passage as a whole.

There are, of course, two references to Dante in the author's
notes. One I think can readily be disposed of, for it is true to say
that the infernal context of the 'Sighs, short and infrequent' is
established, insofar as it *is* established, in the verse, not by the
particular reference in the note to a passage from *Inferno*, canto IV
(which has the word *sospiri*, 'sighs', in common with the line of
Eliot, and nothing more), but by emanation from the line before:

I had not thought death had undone so many.

Sighs after that are likely to be thought of as the sighs one hears
among the muted, saddened shades in Limbo and the upper
spheres of Hell.

But the reference in that previous line is more noteworthy.
Three kinds of significance are possible in the allusion. First,
that this is a modern Hell. For that, the reference '*Inferno*' would
suffice. The second needs '*Inferno* III', for it assumes the reference
is more specifically to Dante's Limbo, where the *ignavi* (listless,
indecisive, uncommitted) find enternal anonymity. They include
the angels who were on the side of neither God nor Lucifer, and
one whom Dante sees and recognizes as 'the shade of him who

[35] Cf. the passage from 'What Dante Means to Me' quoted on p. 144
above.

out of cowardice made the great refusal'. (The commentators are themselves forced into indecision here: among the possibilities are Pontius Pilate and Celestine V, whose resignation from the Papal Chair led to the election of a Pope whom Dante much abhorred, Boniface VIII.) And the third interpretation asks of us that we also put *Inferno* III back into context. The general condition of *viltà* (cowardice), though it be 'there', outside the self, for Dante the traveller to look at, has also particular and inescapable significance for him: it is one of those occasions where the tag already quoted, 'There but for the grace of God go I', is most pressing. In the previous canto Dante the traveller came close to making his own 'great refusal'. Why must *I* go down through Hell? 'I'm not Aeneas; I'm not Paul,' Why me? (*Inf.* II, 31–3) Viltà was actually ascribed to him, by Virgil (*Inf.* II, 45, 123; and, more fugitively, *Inf.* III, 15; cf. 19–21). Having set his hand to the plough he practically drew back from the ploughing—preferring, it seems, security with anonymity. (For over sixty cantos, by the way, that is until *Purgatorio* XXX, the *Comedy*'s protagonist never *is* named). A failure of nerve (*ardezza*) is only recently behind him. The reason for my thinking that this matter has its relevance to Eliot will be clear if we remember Prufrock and Gerontion. Its relevance to this particular section of *The Waste Land* will emerge more clearly soon.

But whatever our decision on these points of 'commentary', we must as critics register a further Dantean echo, and another kind of Dantean presence, in what shortly follows:

> There I saw one I knew, and stopped him, crying . . .

The phrase, I say at once, is not exactly paralleled in Dante—so far at least as my researches have discovered; and it would be difficult to argue with a reader who supposed it ordinary enough to make the search for sources futile. But in context it is far from ordinary; it's arresting; and it seems to me that it distils and borrows from a number (a large number) of such moments of encounter in the *Comedy*, and the accompanying syntax of 'arrest'. In this it has an extreme Dantean potency. One such moment was (precisely) under Eliot's eye when he attended to the line he has just quoted: 'I had not thought death had undone so many' (*Inf.* III, 56–7)—I have referred to it already, for another purpose:

> Poscia ch'io v' ebbi alcun riconosciuto

vidi e conobbi l'ombra di colui
che fece per viltà il gran rifiuto

(After I had recognized some of them there I saw and knew
the shade of him who out of cowardice made the great refusal)
(*Inf.* III, 58–60)

Vidi e conobbi—part of the quality which one identifies is the
way the seeing and the knowing are persistently, insistently,
distinguished—the way the cognitive and sensational chronologies
of peering, recognizing, grasping, crying out, are maintained
equally in the elaborate forms (Brunetto) and the compressed
(Stetson), in instances both relatively direct—

Mentr'io andava, li occhi miei in uno
furo scontrati; e io sì tosto dissi:
— Già di veder costui non son digiuno —;
per ch'io a figurarlo i piedi affissi

(As I went on my eyes were met by someone; and straight away
I said, 'This one I've seen before'—so that I stayed my feet to
make him out more clearly) (*Inf.* XVIII, 40–43)

and oblique—perhaps this, for example:

La molta gente e le diverse piaghe
avean le luci mie sì inebriate,
che dello stare a piangere eran vaghe;
ma Virgilio mi disse: — Che pur guate?
perché la vista tua pur si soffolge
là giù tra l'ombre triste smozzicate?

(The many people and the diverse wounds had made my eyes
so drunken that they longed to stay and weep; but Virgil
asked, 'Why are you gazing still? Why does your sight rest
still down there among the dismal mutilated shades?')
(*Inf.* XXIX, 1–6)

And with these instances before us we may ask whether Dante
has not given Eliot another kind of prompting in the speeches
they precede—speeches combining pungent sarcasm and acri-
mony ('That corpse you planted last year in your garden—has it
begun to sprout?') with the politer formulae of old acquaintance
and a common interest ('You who were with me in the ships at
Mylae'). The *ombre triste smozzicate* were the souls of those who
had sown discord ('warmongers' and 'troublemakers' in compara-

tively feeble current patois), and include, besides Mahomet and Bertran de Born, the shade of one who cries out, 'You, whom guilt condemns not and I saw before, up there upon Italian ground . . . remember Pier da Medicina if you ever go back again to see the gentle plain that from Vercelli slopes to Marcabò. And let the worthiest pair in Fano know' (the treacherous death that is in store for them) (*Inf.* XXVIII, 70–90). (The attitude of Pier to the troubles that he forecasts is not clear.) And in *Inferno* XVIII he whom Dante's eyes encounter was a man who had delivered up his sister to the lust of his Marchese (Azzo, or Obizzo, d'Este), and who now lowers his face in shame until the traveller, with a mordant colloquialism which reminds him of the world above (ll. 53–4), brings him to declare himself, and others there:

> io dissi: — O tu che l'occhio a terra gette,
> se le fazion che porti non son false,
> Venedico se' tu Caccianemico:
> ma che ti mena a sì pungenti salse? —

(I said, 'O you who cast your eyes to the ground—if the features that you bear do not deceive, Venedico Caccianemico's your name. But what brings you to such a biting pickle?')
(ll. 485–1)

Such passages as these are not to be identified as Eliot's specific sources but as representing the generic background of the passage as a whole: they confirm the radically Dantean inspiration, and, to some extent, define its limits.

Of course, it still is not a question of a simple 'imitation'. Eliot is attempting something different and, one may say, something more: at any rate more fitting to his poem as a whole. The truculence, one may well say, is Dante's (or has Dantean parallels), and so with the particular forms it takes: beneath the chatter, accusation and derision; beneath them, suspicions of complicity.[36] But ' "Stetson! . . . in the ships at Mylae" ' that is different. Stetson, who had promised at his introduction, through a single Dantesque line, to be more clearly polarized as 'other' possibly than anyone in the whole *Waste Land*, is once again a 'compound ghost'. A Westerner, the name suggests, and yet also, because

[36] Obviously Webster is here too, beyond the single quoted line— Webster ('much possessed by death') showing through the layer of cellophane of a gardening conversation. And Baudelaire: this garden grows 'les Fleurs du Mal'.

of Mylae, a figure in an ancient epic or an ancient history; an acquaintance; Homeric, and eventually (but the eventuality is quick) anti-Homeric; a secret murderer, and one whose secret may come out. The compound situation here is quite impossible in Dante.

Nor is this compound, any more than 'Little Gidding's', exclusive of Eliot (or of, at any rate, *The Waste Land*'s fugitive 'I'). For one thing, the shared secret that the speaker threatens to reveal brings him and Stetson into fearful accomplicity, like that of blackmailer and victim. For another, there is an unaccustomed stridency ('The horror! The horror!') about the passage which Eliot's note about Tiresias does not fully comprehend. It is more painful than the note brings out, and perhaps more genuinely personal. Beneath the taunts and innuendoes is a feverishness which scarcely offers anything by way of an 'objective correlative' to account for it.

So this, too, brings an altogether different kind of self, a different kind of situation, and a different kind of pathos, to the one we find in Dante. In Dante, what we see and know is always felt to be *there*, 'other', if not wholly 'alien'. The Latin tag, *Nil humanum a me alienum puto*, may stand as a short explanation of the reason for my qualifying phrase; but there is nothing pat or cliché about the urgency it would have had for Dante. The idea is fully occupied and justified in the Florentine poet by the profound effect that the notion of the central and constitutive inhabitation of Love in all things has upon his sensibility. Thus, in a passage from *Purgatorio* XVII which Eliot quotes in his Dante essay, Virgil instructs Dante:

> —Né creator né creatura mai,—
> cominciò el—figliuol, fu sanza amore . . .

and he concludes,

> ch'esser conven
> amor sementa in voi d'ogni virtute
> e d'ogne operazion che merta pene—

('Neither creator nor creature,' he began, 'my son, was ever without love'. . . 'so that love must be the seed of every virtue and of each deed that deserves punishment')
(*Purg.* XVII, 91–2; 103–5)

This explains perhaps in one way how, in Dante's universe, even

Hell is made by Love—as the inscription over Hell-gate testifies—
made by the Love that pervades the universe, and dominates and
moves both cosmos ('the sun and the other stars') and the micro-
cosmos, man. It is Love that binds the universe's scattered leaves
into one volume (*Par.* XXXIII, 86). It is no less by Love's
operation that souls interact, give, sympathize, control, 'move'
one another, even though, because they are responsible, they are
also finally distinct—and so have 'real' encounters. Very different,
then, is Dante's (the poet's or the traveller's) sympathy or horror,
pity or fear, responding to the sinners whom he meets, from
Eliot's or Tiresias' uneasy acquiescence in the experience of
almost solipsistic sin, which the investigation of this episode
within 'The Burial of the Dead' brings out.

And here or hereabouts, to recapitulate, the crucial difference
between the poets I think lies in their very different engagements
with the idea or the experience of love. I have already quoted
Leavis: 'The general truth about [Eliot] is that he can contemplate the relations between men and women only with revulsion or
disgust—unless with the aid of Dante.'[37] That, by concentrating
on the sexual, is too overstated and too partial: Dante's aid, as
the analyses of 'Little Gidding' and the Stetson passages have
now indicated, is called up almost whenever an encounter with
an 'other' is required by pressure of an urgently confessional
horror.

Of course, the sexual may have been, and may have seemed to
Eliot's own mind, primary: remembering the distractions of the
Vita Nuova section of his essay—on the 'coupling of animals',
and 'final causes', on 'indiscretion' and 'confessions'; and remembering too how in 'Dans le Restaurant' the infantile experience of sex is treated, by a kind of anti-Dante summoned up to
do it, as obscene. But whether sexual disgust, or other kinds, are
in view it is worth recalling Eliot's earliest Dante essay (1920):

> The contemplation of the horrid or sordid or disgusting, by
> an artist, is the necessary and negative aspect of the impulse
> toward the pursuit of beauty. But not all succeed as did Dante
> in expressing the complete scale from negative to positive.
> The negative is the more importunate.[38]

'The negative is the more importunate': it is a sad little sentence,

[37] *Lectures in America*, 42.
[38] *The Sacred Wood*, 169.

one which the Dante of *Tanto gentile* or the *Vita Nuova* or even of the *Inferno* never could have written—all along for him, I think one feels it ultimately, the praise of Beatrice is what was importunate: beatitude lies 'in those words that praise my lady' (*Vita Nuova* xviii); and 'I hope to write of her what has never been written of any woman' (xliii).

Of course one could elaborate the comparison—reflecting, for example, on the similarities and differences between the time when Dante's eyes fail (as in life they often had) on re-encountering the shade of Beatrice in the Earthly Paradise, and the time when

> We came back, late, from the hyacinth garden,
> Your arms full, and your hair wet, [and] I could not
> Speak, and my eyes failed, I was neither
> Living nor dead. . . .

but the point is plain enough, I think, already.

More important is it at the end to say that I have not of course gone all this way about in order to confirm (what no one qualified and in their right mind could have ever doubted) a point about the relative stature of these poets. Instead, it ought to be affirmed that Eliot's poetry has another kind of success—in its way as difficult and as original as Dante's. And it seems to me that the use of Dante that he makes here, in 'The Burial of the Dead', and in what I have called the Limbo poetry generally, is subject neither to the point that Dr Leavis makes nor to the suspicions, that the 'use' in part is 'abuse', which arise in 'Little Gidding'.

With 'Little Gidding' there is of course still some similarity, at which we have glanced already: a confession which, at its most climactic moments, is thrust off into an 'alias' or 'alibi' with Dante's help, until the alibi breaks down, perhaps from its own strenuousness. ('The lady', we remember, 'doth protest too much.') The importunate negative emotion starts to look like Eliot's own.

But if, in the 'Little Gidding' passage, we are sometimes led to suspect trickery, in 'The Burial of the Dead' there is only the most appropriate kind of shuffling, and the action (since it must lie) 'lies, *in its true nature*'. There is no pretence within the poetry that the author has achieved a Dantean vantage-point from which to utter Dantean judgements: to suggest that the juxtapositions, in *The Waste Land*, between 'sordidness' and 'echoes of great literature' mean anything of that kind would be to make Eliot *hypocrite lecteur* of that same literature in a sense much more disparaging than the phrase intends or Eliot deserves (for, to my ear anyway. *Hypocrite lecteur!* soon loses its belligerence, becomes regret and anguish and confession: *mon semblable,—mon frère!*). The poetry has its own kind of sincerity, and it is difficult to see how Eliot's sense of his, and his world's, complicity in the covert murder of a God, or of a Beatrice,—for this, surely, is what 'The Burial of the Dead' tries to express—could have been conveyed more honestly or powerfully.

Here then, as elsewhere in the poetry of two decades, the state of Limbo is anatomized—typically, at the point of sharpest pressure, with a decisive turning to the modes and recognitions of the Dantean model or the Dantean poem—anatomized so finely and courageously that it ceases to be fully Limbo after all. For the fact is that the neutral, indecisive, radically discouraged, virtual nonentities who speak out of poem after poem justly earn for their creator or their spokesman the identity they lack themselves. He is, of course, not Dante, any more than Dante was or could have been Aeneas or St Paul. But he has won a salient position for himself as poet: he is one of 'those who have crossed/with direct eyes, to death's other Kingdom' where the hollow men exist; and he has remembered them, and made them be remembered, in ourselves.

Appendix: from *Inferno XV*

Già eravam dalla selva rimossi   13
   tanto, ch'i' non avrei visto dov'era,
   perch'io in dietro rivolto mi fossi,
quando incontrammo d'anime una schiera   16
   che venìan lungo l'argine, e ciascuna
   ci riguardava come suol da sera
guardare uno altro sotto nuova luna;   19
   e sì ver noi aguzzavan le ciglia
   come 'l vecchio sartor fa nella cruna.
Così adocchiato da cotal famiglia,   22
   fui conosciuto da un, che mi prese
   per lo lembo e gridò:—Qual maraviglia!—
E io, quando 'l suo braccio a me distese,   25
   ficca' li occhi per lo cotto aspetto,
   sì che 'l viso abbruciato non difese
la conoscenza sua al mio intelletto;   28
   e chinando la mia alla sua faccia,
   rispuosi:—Siete voi qui, ser Brunetto?—

Already the wood was so far behind that I could not have seen where it was even had I turned round, [15] when we met a troop of souls who were coming beside the dike; and each looked at us as one tends at dusk to look at someone under a new moon—[19] all screwing up their brows intently at us, as an old tailor does at the eye of his needle. [21] Being eyed so by that company I was recognized by one, who caught me by the hem and cried, 'What a miracle!' [24]

And I, when he reached out his arm to me, scrutinized the charred figure until the scorched face did not stop my mind from recognizing him in turn; and bending down my face to his I answered, 'Are you here, Ser Brunetto.'[30]

E quelli:—O figliuol mio, non ti dispiaccia   31
  se Brunetto Latino un poco teco
  ritorna in dietro e lascia andar la traccia.

I' dissi lui:—Quanto posso, ven preco;   34
  e se volete che con voi m'asseggia,
  faròl, se piace a costui che vo seco.

—O figliuol,—disse—qual di questa greggia   37
  s'arresta punto, giace poi cent'anni
  sanz'arrostarsi quando 'l foco il feggia.

Però va oltre: i' ti verrò a' panni;   40
  e poi rigiugnerò la mia masnada,
  che va piangendo i suoi etterni danni.—

I' non osava scender della strada   43
  per andar par di lui; ma 'l capo chino
  tenea com'uom che reverente vada.

El cominciò:—Qual fortuna o destino   46
  anzi l'ultimo dì qua giù ti mena?
  e chi è questi che mostra 'l cammino?

—Là su di sopra, in la vita serena,—   49
  rispuos'io lui—mi smarri' in una valle,
  avanti che l'età mia fosse piena.

And he: 'O my son, don't be displeased if Brunetto Latino turns back a little way with you, and lets the rest go on.' [33]

I said to him, 'With all my heart, I beg you to; and if you would have me to sit down with you here, I will, so long as it contents him whom I go with.' [36]

'O son,' said he, 'whoever of this flock stops for a moment lies for a hundred years without fanning himself when the fire strikes him. [39] Therefore move on; I shall come at your skirts, and afterwards go to rejoin my band, who go lamenting all they have lost for ever.' [42]

I did not dare to get down off the path to go along on the same level with him, but kept my head bowed as one walks in prayer. [45] And he began: 'What fortune or what destiny brings you down here before the end of life? And who is this who's showing you the way?' [48]

'Up there above, in the bright world,' I answered, 'I lost my way in a valley before my years were at the prime. [51] Just

Pur ier mattina le volsi le spalle: 52
  questi m'apparve, tornand'io in quella,
  e reducemi a ca per questo calle.—

Ed elli a me:—Se tu segui tua stella,   55
  non puoi fallire a glorioso porto,
  se ben m'accorsi nella vita bella;

e s'io non fossi sì per tempo morto,   58
  veggendo il cielo a te così benigno,
  dato t'avrei all'opera conforto.

Ma quello ingrato popolo maligno   61
  che discese di Fiesole ab antico,
  e tiene ancor del monte e del macigno,

ti si farà, per tua ben far, nemico: 64
  ed è region, ché tra li lazzi sorbi
  si disconvien fruttar lo dolce fico.

Vecchia fama nel mondo li chiama orbi;   67
  gent'è avara, invidiosa e superba:
  dai lor costumi fa che tu ti forbi.

La tua fortuna tanto onor ti serba,   70
  che l'una parte e l'altra avranno fame
  di te; ma lungi fia dal becco l'erba.

---

yesterday I turned my back on that; but as I still slipped down this man appeared, and he leads me by this route to my home.' [54]

And he to me: 'So long as you follow your star you cannot fail to reach a glorious haven, if I discerned well in fair life; [57] and had I not died too soon, seeing heaven so gracious to you I should have given encouragement to your work. [60] But that incorrigible and malignant tribe who came down from Fiesole long since, but still retain something of mountain and rock, [63] will be your enemy, for your good work. And naturally; for a sweet fig is out of place among the bitter sorbs. [66] By old repute on earth they are called 'blind'—an avaricious folk, envious and proud: see that you cleanse yourself of all their ways. [69] Your future saves up so much honour for you that both factions one day will crave after you—but the grass shall be well out of the goat's reach [72] Let the beasts of Fiesole make fodder

Faccian le bestie fiesolane strame   73
    di lor medesme, e non tocchin la pianta,
    s'alcuna surge ancora in lor letame,
in cui riviva la sementa santa   76
    di que' Roman che vi rimaser quando
    fu fatto il nido di malizia tanta.
—Se fosse tutto pieno il mio dimando,—   79
    rispuosi lui—voi non sareste ancora
    dell'umana natura posto in bando;
ché 'n la mente m'è fitta, e or m'accora,   82
    la cara e buona imagine paterna
    di voi quando nel mondo ad ora ad ora
m'insegnavate come l'uom s'etterna: 85
    e quant'io l'abbia in grado, mentr'io vivo
    convien che nella mia lingua si scerna.
Ciò che narrate di mio corso scrivo,   88
    e serbolo a chiosar con altro testo
    a donna che saprà, s'a lei arrivo.
Tanto vogl'io che vi sia manifesto,   91
    pur che mia coscienza non mi garra,
    che alla Fortuna, come vuol, son presto.

---

of themselves, and not touch the plant (if any in their dung-heap still survive) in which may live again the holy seed of those Romans who stayed there when the nest of so much wickedness was first made.' [78]

'Were my desires fulfilled entirely,' I responded, 'you would not yet be banished from our life; [81] for your dear, kind, paternal image stays, fixed in the mind, and breaking now the heart, just as it was when, up in the world above, hour after hour you taught me how man makes himself eternal: [85] how grateful I am for that so long as I live my tongue must testify. [87] What you have told me of my future course, I take note of it, and preserve with another text for a Lady to gloss; she will be able, should I arrive where she is. [90] This much I want, though, to make clear to you: so long as conscience does not rebuke me I am ready for whatever Fortune wills. [93] Such omens are no

Non è nuova alli orecchi miei tal arra: 94
   però giri Fortuna la sua rota
   come le piace, e'l villan la sua marra.—

Lo mio maestro allora in su la gota   97
   destra si volse in dietro, e riguardommi;
   poi disse:—Bene ascolta chi la nota.—

Né per tanto di men parlando vommi   100
   con ser Brunetto, e dimando chi sono
   li suoi compagni più noti e più sommi.

Ed elli a me:—Saper d'alcuno è bono;   103
   delli altri fia laudabile tacerci,
   ché 'l tempo sarìa corto a tanto sòno.

In somma sappi che tutti fur cherci   106
   e litterati grandi e di gran fama,
   d'un peccato medesmo al mondo lerci. . . .

Di più direi; ma 'l venire e 'l sermone   115
   più lungo esser non può, però ch'i' veggio
   là surger novo fummo del sabbione.

Gente vien con la quale esser non deggio: 118
   sieti raccomandato il mio Tesoro
   nel qual io vivo ancora, e più non cheggio.—

---

new thing to my ears. Therefore let Fortune turn her wheel as she likes—and the peasant his mattock too!' [96]

At that my master (Virgil) turned his head and looked at me over his shoulder; then he said, 'He's a good listener who takes note of it.' [99]

None the less I keep talking with Ser Brunetto, asking him who among his companions are the greatest in fame or rank. [102] And he to me: 'To know of a few is good; for the rest it will be best to keep our silence, since for so long a list our time is short. [105] In brief, know that all here were clerks and great and famous scholars, by one and the same crime defiled on earth. . . . [108] I would say more; but now I can walk and talk no longer with you, for I see there another cloud of dust rise from the sand. [117] People are coming whom I must not be with. Let me commend my *Trésor* to you, in which I still live: I ask nothing more.' [120]

Poi si rivolse, e parve di coloro   121
    che corrono a Verona il drappo verde
    per la campagna; e parve di costoro
quelli che vince, non colui che perde.   124

Then he turned back, and seemed like one of those who at
Verona run for the green cloth through the fields; and among
them he seemed the one who wins, not he who loses. [124]

'Broken images':
T. S. Eliot and Modern Painting

John Dixon Hunt

'the tangle or complex of the inrooted ideas of any period. . . .
The Paideuma is not the Zeitgeist. . . . At any rate for my own
use . . . I shall use Paideuma for the gristly roots of ideas that
are in action.' Ezra Pound, *Guide to Kulchur*

I

T. S. Eliot himself offers no ready encouragement for such an
inquiry as this.[1] His writings, unlike those of Yeats or Pound, do
not suggest that the visual arts were at all important to him as
a poet: after all, 'I gotta use *words* when I talk to you.' Only at
rare moments do the verbal configurations of his poetry provoke
thoughts of visual analogues. We might perhaps suspect Paul
Klee's *Twittering Machine* in the underground darkness of the
'twittering world' of 'Burnt Norton'. Although Eliot has himself
invoked his recollections of Bosch, there is equally a sensation of
Dali when the woman

> drew her long black hair out tight
And fiddled whisper music on those strings
And bats with baby faces in the violet light
Whistled . . .

---

[1] There have been, correspondingly, only a few attempts to relate
Eliot to modern art: Jacob Korg, 'Modern Art Techniques in *The
Waste Land*', *Journal of Aesthetics and Art Criticism* XVIII (1960),
456–63; Wylie Sypher, *Rococo to Cubism in Art and Literature* (New
York, 1960), 265–6, 283–5, 313–7; Mario Praz, *Mnemosyne, The Parallel
Between Literature and the Visual Arts* (Princeton, 1970), 201–7 and
passim.

There are equally several intimations of expressionism—notably Edvard Munch—in Prufrock's lonely evening or the grey and smoky solitudes at the end of 'Portrait of a Lady'; while Kirchner's *Five Women* of 1913 provides some visual equivalent for Prufrock's nervous obsession with the women talking of Michelangelo who are poised, like Kirchner's, in the uneasy spaces of his mind. So that, just as Eliot seems to have been innocent of interdisciplinary intention, his critic would seem to advance little, for example, by invoking Gauguin's *Sous les Palmiers* simply because in *Sweeney Agonistes* the libretto of the song by Wauchope and Horsfall contans the lines

> Where the Gauguin maids
> In the banyan shades
> Wear palmleaf drapery
> Under the bam
> Under the boo
> Under the bamboo tree.

Yet we might give ourselves pause for thought precisely over this quite unimportant allusion to Gauguin. For that very painting was exhibited in Boston[2] during Eliot's time at Harvard Graduate School, when he was preparing the dissertation on F. H. Bradley, upon which his literary commentators draw so thankfully. Cousin Harriet, eagerly devouring her *Evening Transcript*, could not have failed to notice that the paper found this and other Gauguins unexpectedly interesting. In the same exhibition were works by Munch and Kirchner, whom I have already invoked alongside Eliot's early poetry, as well as a wide and exciting range of other European modernists, including Kandinsky, Brancusi, Cézanne and Picasso. The exhibition, as it appeared in Boston from April to May 1913, consisted of roughly one third of the items from the famous Armory Show held earlier that year in New York.[3]

Eliot's precise encounters with the exhibition we cannot know. It was not until two years later that Pound tried to arrange for Eliot to meet the lawyer and art collector, John Quinn, who had been legal adviser as well as guiding genius of the Armory Show

[2] The picture is now in the Ralph M. Coe Collection, Cleveland, Ohio.

[3] For information on the Armory Show I am largely indebted to M. W. Brown, *The Story of the Armory Show* (New York, 1963).

Plate 1 Marcel Duchamp, *Nude Descending a Staircase No. 2*, 1912. The Louise and Walter Arensberg Collection, Philadelphia Museum of Art.

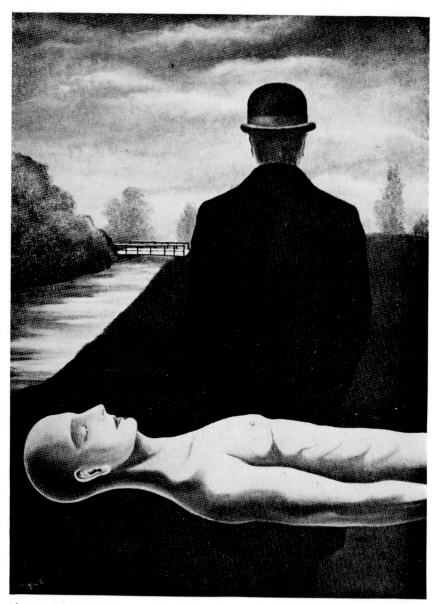

Plate 2 René Magritte, *Les rêveries du promeneur solitaire*, 1926 or 1927. Collection E. L. T. Mesens, Brussels.

Plate 3a (*top*) René Magritte, *Les objets familiers*, 1927 or 1928. Collection E. L. T. Mesens, Brussels.

Plate 3b René Magritte, *Le chef d'œuvre ou Les mystères de l'horizon*, 1955. Collection L. Arnold Weissberger, New York.

Plate 4a (top) René Magritte, *Le fils d'homme*, 1964. Collection Harry Torczyner, Green Castle, New York.

Plate 4b René Magritte, *Le bouquet tout fait*, 1957. Collection Mr and Mrs Barnet Hodes, Chicago.

Plate 5a (top) Giorgio di Chirico, *The Dream Transformed*, 1913. The City Art Museum, St Louis.

Plate 5b Giorgio di Chirico, *The Uncertainty of the Poet*, 1913. Private collection, London.

Plate 6 Giorgio di Chirico, *The Soothsayer's Recompense*, 1913. The Louise and Walter Arensber Collection, Philadelphia Museum of Art.

Plate 7 Juan Gris, *Still Life Before an Open Window: Place Ravignan*, 1915. The Louise and Walter Arensberg Collection, Philadelphia Museum of Art.

Plate 8   Georges Braque, *Violin and Palette*, 1910. The Solomon R.
Guggenheim Museum, New York.

and who had ended by being the largest purchaser of items from it. Whether Eliot might have seen the exhibition in New York or Boston and whether he bought any of the fifty-seven postcard reproductions or four booklets (including one on Cézanne, one on Odilon Redon, one that printed extracts from Gauguin's *Noa-Noa*) we cannot tell. Yet it would seem astonishing if he were not aware of the furore that the Armory Show provoked. This was America's first opportunity to see modern European art collected on such a scale, and it might surely be supposed to have attracted the attention of a man setting himself to be so adept a European.

If the popular press jibed with meagre wit and little comprehension, there were more thoughtful reactions: especially in those that stressed the show's intelligent refusal to work in outmoded forms Eliot would have recognized ideas that chimed with his own philosophic and poetic interests. Thus, Harriet Monroe celebrated 'the revolt of the imagination against nineteenth-century realism . . . disgust with the camera, outrage over superficial smoothness'. The Professor of Philosophy at Columbia, Joel E. Spingarn, found art at last 'recapturing its own essential madness'. Other critics recognized the emergence of an exciting yet strenuous subjectivity—the 'expressions of subjective experience', as the *Tribune* saw it. For Charles Caffin, Brancusi had 'stripped away the partial disguise of natural accident and revealed . . . the naked, essential facts of structure'.

We may begin to define what is interesting in the conjunction of Eliot and the Armory Show by recalling that a year afterwards Eliot attended the seminar of Josiah Royce on 'A Comparative Study of Various Types of Method'. During the course of a paper read to the seminar Eliot argued that each new interpretation adds to the facts by introducing a new point of view. He could have sought no more exciting artistic support for such a thesis nor encountered more insights into the amusements and anxieties of 'point of view' than in the work of Matisse or the Cubists, whom the Boston *Transcript* had recently dismissed for 'playing a game of mystification'. For among the mysteries that Cubism sets itself to reveal is exactly the process by which an object is fundamentally altered and augmented by the variety of our opinions and views of it.

The most notable, if not notorious, example of this in the exhibition was Marcel Duchamp's *Nude Descending a Staircase*

(Plate 1). It was a painting that represented for a large public everything that was startling or absurd or profound about the whole show. Even the crudest journalism managed to respond to its disequilibrium in phrases—'pack of brown cards in a nightmare' or 'orderly heap of violins'—that oddly recall 'Rhapsody on a Windy Night', written when Eliot was in Paris in 1911. Few of those who saw the painting could claim for it the lunar *synthesis* that Eliot discovered along the reaches of the street. But Duchamp's use of light controls the divisions and precisions of our memories of movement and their representation in painting. Among the many poetasters who sang Duchamp's achievement was one who expressed (perhaps ironically) his absorption and delight:

> O lady fair,
> As down the stair
> You trip, your air
> Enthralls my being!
> Ah, could you wis
> The sense of mys-
> Tery, the bliss
> With which I'm seeing.

A similar delight in the mystery of seeing from various perspectives is at the centre of a poem Eliot wrote just before the Armory Show, 'La Figlia Che Piange'. Eliot's lady, standing on the highest pavement of her stair, offers to the speaker of the poem, as Duchamp's nude does to its spectator, an opportunity for aesthetic adventure. The spectator in each case wavers between self-sufficiency and involvement, between delight at 'a gesture and a pose' and the inability to evade the customary adjudications we make in our treaties with reality in art. In each case the completion of movement—'She turned away': the nude at the bottom of her staircase—is complicated by recollections and recreations of its process.

While this essay will not attend to any influences, one upon the other, of Eliot's poetry and modern painting, its concern is to exemplify Wallace Stevens's claim that 'it would be possible to study poetry by studying painting'.[4] We may use Duchamp's *Nude*, which draws us to the limits of painterly coherence while

---

[4] 'The Relations between Poetry and Painting', *The Necessary Angel* (London, 1960), 160.

still preserving an interest in representation, to recall that *The Waste Land* brings us to the limits of verbal coherence, as the *Times Literary Supplement* perceived (not altogether wrongly) in its original review of the poem. The uncertainties and stimulating difficulties we continue, I believe, to experience in front of much modern painting may perhaps help us to recover some of the equally striking and unnerving manoeuvres of Eliot's verse. We may not still share the distaste of the *Boston Evening Transcript* for the 'offensive presentations of human form divine' in Cubist art; but our actual experience of and involvement with visual images on canvas still enforces our participation in reading the art and counters any instinct to 'explain' visual meaning, whereas Eliot's critics often seem to metamorphose their experience of insecurities in his poetry into the confident explanation of their own coherent prose. Cubist art consists of the marvellously uneasy 'interaction of many unknowns and variables'[5] that are generally too forceful a visual presence to allow the mind to reconcile them. *The Waste Land*, too, is a structure of such interactions; yet the poet himself—doubtless with some wry mockery—is too ready to provide lucid explanations of verses that should continue to disturb us:

> The Hanged Man, a member of the traditional [Tarot] pack . . . is associated in my mind with the Hanged God of Frazer, and . . . with the hooded figure in the passage of the disciples to Emmaus. . . .

It is the voice of Chardin explaining a Picasso still life. The appeal to Eliot's commentators of such calm deliberation in the face of the poetic ambiguities is, while understandable, nonetheless alarming.

The temptation to 'explain' his images springs perhaps from some confusion as to the proper weight to be given to the visual in his poetry. In the disturbing cross-currents of the *Four Quartets* there often lurk visual images; but to be told that the movement of the first section of 'Burnt Norton' progresses 'easily and

---

[5] Quoted by John Berger in *The Moment of Cubism and other essays* (London, 1969), 25. On similar effects in Eliot that we have tended to lose through familiarity, see Helen Gardner, 'Explorer of Moral Distress', *New Statesman* (28 November 1969), 760.

excitedly . . . towards *a definite image*'[6] is a wilful neglect of the mingling of mental space and visual delight in

> Footfalls echo in the memory
> Down the passage which we did not take
> Towards the door we never opened
> Into the rose-garden. My words echo
> Thus, in your mind.

The reiteration of 'mind' as the territory of action—as in Eliot's gloss on the Emmaus allusion—is crucial. Whatever the strength of visual insistence in poetry, it is in the mind, in the creative intelligence, that the visual reference is considered. Whereas in painting the visual shapes are ineluctably *there* and the mental encounter with them is mediated by their visible presence. However, in modern poetry and painting such distinctions are, arguably, less clear. In painting on the one hand, the shapes and images have often a less immediate insistence—and Picasso, as we shall see later, locates the organizing, creative process in the mind rather than the senses. In poetry, on the other hand, like Eliot's early verse, there is a firmer recognition of the visual, not just as material for mental assimilation, but somehow as an absolute counter in its own right. The Emmaus passage deploys the third distinct shape on the white road, hooded in its brown mantle, as a visual item not readily assimilated to the mental process of Eliot's note. It is perhaps only by the *Four Quartets* that the visual elements assume a more usual literary role.

The consequences of the stronger visual presence in early Eliot endorses an approach which tries to read him in the light of modern painting; this is not to blur the limits of either art, but to note where the distinctive attention that each demands may assist the other. The suave lucidity of much Eliot criticism, taught not only by the poet himself but by the discourse of F. H. Bradley as well, often denies the experience of the poems themselves. Eliot's explanation in his thesis on Bradley that the 'real and unreal develop side by side' could be just as apt as a comment upon Picasso or Duchamp. And since such developments also constitute a major activity in Eliot's poetry, we may try to perceive them by recalling how frequently in modern art the real and the unreal have fruitfully if disturbingly cohabited.

[6] C. O. Gardner, 'Some Reflections on the Opening of "Burnt Norton"', *The Critical Quarterly* XII (1970), 329.

It must be postcards from the Armory Show, not the conventional views of Oxford colleges, that will illuminate the daring perspectives of Pipit and Madame Blavatsky; not the traditional art above some antique mantel—'As though a window gave upon the sylvan scene'—but some startling image, like Magritte's *Le domaine d'Arnheim*, where we face the shattered pane of glass on which *and* through which are seen the eagles, trumpets and snow-deep Alps.

II

René Magritte shares with his fellow Surrealists and with the Cubists a boredom with the illusionist space of post-Renaissance painting. Similarly, it seems to me, Eliot is at pains to evade the temporal exigencies of words in sequence. The 'fractured atoms' of 'Gerontion' are to be registered among 'windy spaces' that disarm any simple and conventional connections between them, like the fresh discoveries of space in modern painting:

> In depraved May, dogwood and chestnut, flowering judas,
> To be eaten, to be divided, to be drunk
> Among whispers; by Mr Silvero
> With caressing hands, at Limoges
> Who walked all night in the next room;
> By Hakagawa, bowing among the Titians;
> By Madame de Tornquist, in the dark room
> Shifting the candles; Fräulein von Kulp
> Who turned in the hall, one hand on the door.

Though we necessarily experience these images in sequence, it is their ambiguous interaction, their simultaneity, that is striking. And surely this is one reason why the usual invocation of the cinema as an analogy for Eliot's techniques won't do—in the cinema we have visual succession, while in the poetry we have a contrivance of instaneity. The names of shrubs that *at the same time* signify the betrayal of Christ and the education of Henry Adams merge with the aliens or patrials that hover in boarding house or museum gallery. At its most anarchic such techniques merely obfuscate; at their best, as in some Magritte paintings, they disorientate our accustomed perspectives and eliminate the connections even of juxtaposition.

The encounter of the sacramental Host across apparently vast geographical distances with items of seedy cosmopolitan culture recalls the notion of Lautréamont that there was 'beauty' in the 'chance meeting of a sewing-machine and an umbrella upon a dissecting-table.' This apophthegm on the excitements of random encounters has haunted modern artists and one of them, Max Ernst, in *Au-delà de la Peinture* explains his fascination in a way that is helpful when we come to Eliot's own dissecting-table at the beginning of 'Prufrock'. Ernst writes:

A ready-made reality, whose naïve destiny would seem to have been fixed once and for all (an umbrella), finding itself in the presence of another reality which is very remote from it and no less absurd (a sewing-machine), in a place where both of them must feel disorientated (on a dissecting-table), will escape by this very fact from its own naïve destiny and from its identity; and will pass from a false absolute, by detour of the relative, to a new absolute which is true and poetic.[7]

Prufrock, too, escapes momentarily from his own naïve destiny and identity in the face of a dissecting-table:

Let us go then, you and I,
When the evening is spread out against the sky
Like a patient etherised upon a table.

The relativist experiment that Eliot, encouraged perhaps by Lautréamont, practises here has a curious counterpart in Magritte's painting, *Les rêveries du promeneur solitaire* (Plate 2).[8] The visual images of Magritte prevent any easy verbalizing about Eliot's lines, which have themselves displaced a motto from Dante and the preposterous congruence of Love with a Mid-Western name in the title. We cannot in the picture reconcile the two images of walker and anesthetized patient; we cannot adjudicate their relationship except as two shapes upon the same canvas that question each other's 'false absolute'. Similarly, readers of the poem must hold the two images uneasily in their

[7] Quoted by Suzi Gablik in *Magritte* (London, 1970), 45. All the paintings by Magritte discussed here are illustrated either in Suzi Gablik's study or in the Arts Council catalogue by David Sylvester (3rd corrected edition, London 1969).

[8] The influence can only be of Eliot upon Magritte; but see Eliot's remark in *The Frontiers of Criticism* that 'When the poem has been made, something new has happened, something that cannot be wholly explained by *anything that went before*' (my italics).

minds and refuse any critical tactics that impose upon them a false logic of reconciliation: it just will not do to say (my willing victim is Grover Smith):

> The opening image symbolizes through bathos the helpless Prufrock's subjective impression of the evening, which is like an anesthetized patient because he himself is one.[9]

The 'symbolism' cannot displace in our minds the 'ready-made' realities that Eliot invokes. The obtrusiveness of this strategy makes the image unique in Eliot; its relativist, Surrealist manoeuvre does not. I find, for example, the bland acknowledgement of Rochefoucauld in a Boston street as upsetting as Magritte's picture of a glass of water firmly perched upon an umbrella and titled *Les vacances de Hegel*.

Magritte's illustrations for Lautréamont's *Les Chants de Maldoror* reveal his fascination with any alarming revision of our normal expectations. They help in their turn to illustrate Eliot's juxtapositions:

> His laughter was submarine and profound
> Like the old man of the sea's
> Hidden under coral islands
> Where worried bodies of drowned men drift down
> in the green silence,
> Dropping from fingers of surf.

> I looked for the head of Mr Appollinax rolling
> under a chair
> Or grinning over a screen
> With seaweed in its hair.

Eliot's lines assert both the startling clarity of objects and their unexpected contiguities in the reaches of the mind. We can recognize in them a sinister apotheosis of ordinary detail in the light of Magritte's works like *Le musée d'une nuit* or *Les objets familiers* (Plate 3a), where insignificant carbuncular clerks are hypnotized with the unique yet fortuitous visitation of some item from their domestic paraphernalia. Similarly, in 'Rhapsody on a Windy Night' there are the toothbrush hanging ready on the wall, the woman hesitating in the light of a door that has changed into a grin and other items of his nocturnal museum:

[9] *T. S. Eliot's Poetry and Plays. A study in sources and meaning* (Chicago, 1956), 18.

> The memory throws up high and dry
> A crowd of twisted things;
> A twisted branch upon the beach
> Eaten smooth, and polished
> As if the world gave up
> The secret of its skeleton,
> Stiff and white.
> A broken spring in a factory yard. . . .

Magritte is at his best when he illustrates the panic of lost connections, especially the connections of logic and sequential explanation. Eliot, too, dissolves 'the floors of memory/And all its clear relations' as

> Every street lamp that I pass
> Beats like a fatalistic drum,
> And through the spaces of the dark
> Midnight shakes the memory
> As a madman shakes a dead geranium.

The 'Rhapsody' ends with an ominous, Magritte-like, phrase— 'The last twist of the knife'—as the lamp coolly admonishes us to return to life after the lunar synthesis. Like Magritte's *Le jockey perdu* series of paintings, Eliot's *personae* present the spectacle of recognizable forces discovered in equally familiar topography, yet the connection either we or they would normally make between their reality and that of their context has been mysteriously removed. The bowler-hatted figures in Magritte, faced with vast metaphysical abstractions in the trivia of everyday circumstance (Plate 3b) remind me constantly of J. Alfred Prufrock shifting uneasily in face of the 'overwhelming question'.

Such revisions and reductions of experience preoccupy Eliot's characters as they do us as readers, disturbing the 'elaborate compromise that exists between the mind and life'.[10] The fog that is also a cat in Prufrock's evening consciousness is not just a cosy metaphor, but every bit as alarming a metamorphosis as 'Morning at the Window':

> The brown waves of fog toss up to me
> Twisted faces from the bottom of the street,
> And tear from a passer-by with muddy skirts
> An aimless smile that hovers in the air
> And vanishes along the level of the roofs

[10] Gablik, *Magritte*, 122.

—and hovers, too, like the disembodied face of Magritte's *Tous les Jours*. Eliot shares with Magritte what we can learn again to experience in his poetry after attending to the pictures—a subtly controlled sense of panic, dread, fear. The young man of 'Portrait of a Lady' loses his self-possession when confronted with the illusionist reality of a Magritte-like mirror image. Dread and fear are focused in the ordinary and so unexpected fabric of everyday life: fear in a handful of dust or in drowning, the dread of women's cultural small-talk or of silent men in mocha brown. What distinguishes Eliot from Magritte in these manoeuvres is his allowance for tenderness and delicacy. After the fractured anatomy of 'His soul stretched tight across the skies' and the rush hour in 'Preludes', we are told

> I am moved by fancies that are curled
> Around these images, and cling:
> The notion of some infinitely gentle
> Infinitely suffering thing.

But just as rapidly those conventional, because sentimental, perspectives dissolve into a nervous mirth (upon which Magritte, unlike Eliot, rather single-mindedly relies) and into the surreal 'the worlds revolve like ancient women/Gathering fuel in vacant lots'.

III

These speculations may be extended into a discussion of *The Waste Land*. And this is encouraged by Eliot's first thoughts for a motto for the poem—a motto, he told Pound (who objected to it), that 'is much the most appropriate I can find, and somewhat elucidative'.[11] The motto was from Conrad: 'Did he live his life again in every detail of desire, temptation, and surrender during that *supreme moment* of complete knowledge? He cried in a whisper at *some image*. . . .' It elucidates among other things, I suggest, Eliot's frequent need to focus a 'supreme moment' in some image, to organize his fractured atoms into the simultaneity of a painterly structure. Among the unpublished fragments of *The Waste Land* are the lines:

[11] *Facsimile*, 125. The motto (the italics are mine) is on p. 3.

I am the Resurrection and the Life
I am the things that stay, and those that flow.
I am the husband and the wife
And the victim and the sacrificial knife
I am the fire, and the butter also.[12]

This particular striving after simultaneous presence of various images was—rightly—abandoned. There were other more successful moments in which the multiplicity of image occurs— the road to Emmaus merging with Shackleton's expedition; the drowned Phoenician sailor of Madame Sosostris' Tarot pack melting into the drowned passengers of Alonso's ship in *The Tempest*; Ariel's music creeping up Queen Victoria Street.

Although, as we shall see, we need to invoke more complex structures than Magritte provides to organize the broken images of *The Waste Land*, it is still in Magritte that we may seek illuminating analogies for Eliot's continued and deliberate disruptions of our planned adjudications of reality. A lyrical return from the hyacinth garden—'Your arms full, and your hair wet'— barely consorts with the failure of speech and nerve—'I knew nothing/Looking into the heart of light, the silence'. We are not allowed to resolve those elements any more than we can reconcile the elements of the ironically entitled *L'aimable verité*. The sudden invocation of the 'Son of man' in 'The Burial of the Dead' arrives portentously after the international scene at the archduke's and elsewhere; it resounds like Magritte's own *Le fils d'Homme* (Plate 4a), where the apple, pregnant with *felix culpa*, baffles its clerk carbuncular—'Son of Man/You cannot say, or guess'. Eliot's conflation of Dante's inferno with the metropolis—'A crowd flowed over London Bridge, so many,/ I had not thought death had undone so many'—achieves a simultaneous presence of external and internal, of fact and dream, of conscious and unconscious, like Magritte's *Golconde*, where the wealth of the fabulous city in Hyderabad showers down like a rush-hour rain of clerks.

The mock-heroic possibilities of allowing Dante or Golconda to coexist with modern urban life further suggest a way in which Magritte's simultaneity of image comes closer to our experience of Eliot's verse than much critical explication. We have met in an earlier poem, 'Conversation Galante', the undercutting of

12 *Facsimile*, 111.

momentous event, where madam is the eternal humorist—'The eternal enemy of the absolute'. In *The Waste Land* we encounter absolutes rediscovered through what Max Ernst called a 'detour of the relative': the Marvellian 'at my back I always hear' meets both the scepticism of 'from time to time' and Sweeney motoring to Mrs Porter; the Rhine Maiden raises her knees at Richmond; Goldsmith's lady stoops to folly in a bedsitter. What we might have anticipated would have a fixed reality in literary history meets its revision among new and present realities, achieving an uneasy, even horrifying, new absolute upon the dissecting table of this encounter. If we recall Magritte's *Le bouquet tout fait* (Plate 4b), we may properly attend to the awkwardness of Eliot's bifocal strategy: the lonely and anonymous figure of Magritte (not yet grown a little bald behind) stares into a tangled wood, while Botticelli's conceptual account of spring hovers behind him. Past artifact (in Eliot's case, Marvell or Goldsmith) is forced to coexist with present actualities (Sweeney or the typist) and win some new recognition from the uneasy juxtaposition.

But it may register a sense of the advance that *The Waste Land* marks in Eliot's technique and vision that Magritte seems less than sufficient. We need to look to the richer visual poetry of his master, Giorgio di Chirico, and to the Cubist art which Magritte deserted very early in his career.[13] In formal terms there is little to relate Magritte, Chirico and the Cubists: but they have in common a fascination with fresh discoveries of reality and accordingly with ways of looking at it. And they share with Eliot a mischievous as well as a daunting sense of the pressures of history upon their endeavours. The head of a broken Coriolanus and the paraphernalia of still life (or *nature morte*?) in *The Dream Transformed* (Plate 5a) represent perhaps the burden of history upon Chirico; it is a burden, like Eliot's, that comprises both the accumulation of previous artifacts and the variety of achieved idioms. In place of some Titian or Poussin that represents the change of Philomel in some sylvan scene, the modern artist is forced to evade either illusionist traditions or narrative connections and simulate mythic event with inchoate and rudimentary atoms:

13 On Magritte's Cubist endeavours, all dating from 1922, see Gablik, *Magritte,* Plates 12–14. On Giorgio di Chirico, see Massimo Carra, *Metaphysical Art* (Milan, 1968; English translation London, 1971).

> Twit twit twit
> Jug jug jug jug jug jug
> So rudely forc'd.
> Tereu

Chirico celebrates the *Unquiet Muses* not with some traditional Parnassian idyll in the manner of a Venetian master, but by the scattered sculpture of dressmakers' mannequins mysteriously discovered in the open spaces of the unreal city.

Chirico, though he often preserves a scrupulous illusion of space, is more radical and adventurous a painter than his disciple. For Magritte deploys photographically 'real' objects in situations that call into question their distinct, careful and dull realities. But Chirico invokes the traditions of still life and classical sculpture, in such a picture as *The Uncertainty of the Poet* (Plate 5b), yet sets them down in the eloquent vacuum of a city square that deprives them of their habitual roles. Or, alternatively, he subjects an odd assortment of items—the brush, glove and ball of *The Song of Love*—to the mysterious discomforts of a *recognizable* sense of space: compare 'Of dowager Mrs Phlaccus, and Professor and Mrs Cheetah/I remember a slice of lemon, and a bitten macaroon'. Chirico also manifests, like Eliot, a delight in the metamorphosis of city streets. Paintings like *The Mystery and Melancholy of a Street*, or *The Soothsayer's Recompense* (Plate 6) single out various fragments—a girl running beside a hoop, his favourite image of a deserted colonnade—which are then marooned in the intense and rather eerie spaces of the canvas. Again, compare what happens 'round behind the gashouse', or, 'The wind/Crosses the brown land, unheard. The nymphs are departed.' The inquietude of these metaphysical (it is Chirico's word) images depends in part upon the mysterious collocation of their fragments.

IV

But the Cubist revision of traditional perspectives and connections is more radical than these images of Chirico, and depends less upon the *disjunction* of relationships than upon the *creation* of new ones. I find in this more constructive vision of Cubism an analogy for the progress of Eliot's own development, both in the revisions of *The Waste Land* and in the movement forward towards *Four Quartets*.

back into our mental notion of the motif. So Eliot (under Pound's guidance) emancipates some few ingredients from their usual explanatory context—not, like Magritte or Chirico, to undermine their confidence, though fear is still a strong presence in Eliot—but so as to create fresh patterns which are for the mind to understand. Gris's *Still Life with Bottles* seems to rescue the motif and allow it space to resolve its own geometric identity, a space that is no longer controlled, as it would have been in a Courbet still life, by other irrelevant contingencies, by both narrative or circumstantial and illusionist needs.

Eliot similarly works to create 'space around the words'.[15] He deprives them first of a space narratively completed—so he eliminates scene-setting like

> A bright kimono wraps her as she sprawls
> In nerveless torpor on the window seat;
> A touch of art is given by the false
> Japanese print, purchased in Oxford Street.

And he cuts psychological explanations:

> He munches with the same persistent stare,
> He knows his way with women and that's that!
> Impertinently tilting back his chair
> And dropping cigarette ash on the mat.[16]

Such elements are expendable in 'Cubist' poetry where the idea of waste and sterility rather than narrative vision controls the poem's movement. And it is surely significant that the most straightforward narrative section of the poem, that of the typist and her clerk, is framed by Tiresias. His concluding parenthesis insists upon the idea that informs such scenes, upon the shape that the mind must give to what is seen:

> (And I Tiresias have foresuffered all
> Enacted on this same divan or bed;
> I who have sat by Thebes below the wall
> And walked among the lowest of the dead.)

In his efforts to discover a more than anecdotal space around his images, Eliot deliberately breaks connections. The Thames Maiden on Margate Sands who can connect nothing with nothing had, in an early draft, explained:

[15] Harold Rosenberg, *The Tradition of the New* (London, 1970), 86.
[16] *Facsimile*, 45, 33.

> I was to be grateful. On Margate Sands
> There were many others. I can connect
> Nothing with nothing.
> I still feel the pressure of dirty hand

In the revision the circumstances of her seduction are removed from around her words and what remains, though it may still have such reference, inhabits a larger space in which more possibilities than before are present:

> On Margate Sands
> I can connect
> Nothing with nothing.
> The broken finger nails of dirty hands.[17]

'All is possible,' wrote the Cubist poet, André Salmon, 'everything is realizable everywhere and with everything.' In Cubist art, we have been told,[18] man extends himself indefinitely beyond the immediate. Eliot clears space around a modern girl where Rhine Maiden and *nymph*, as well as the arrival of St Augustine at Carthage, can claim our attention. Fishing by a dull canal, offered simply, by itself, can extend into the similar space surrounding Ferdinand's meditations upon a magic island. The new combinations may often seem to be realized—Eliot admits as much himself in the notes to *The Waste Land*—'quite arbitrarily'. The space that the fragments shored against ruin at the end of the poem clear for themselves seems to me sometimes so vast that I can connect nothing with nothing:

> London Bridge is falling down falling down falling down
> *Poi s'ascose nel foco che gli affina*
> *Quando fiam uti chelidon*—O swallow swallow
> *Le Prince d'Aquitaine à la tour abolie*
> These fragments I have shored against my ruins
> Why then Ile fit you. Hieronymo's mad againe.
> Datta. Dayadhvam. Damyata.
>   Shantih shantih shantih

But the perspectives of the mind allow more radical possibilities than those of the senses, including the senses that register Cubist paintings. So that Mr Eugenides can become the one-eyed merchant and Tiresias. And when the violet hour starts the

---

[17] *Ibid.*, 53. (N.B. revisions in the draft are not shown here.)
[18] By John Berger, *The Moment of Cubism*, 7: Berger quotes Salmon on p. 11.

human engine, the simultaneous presence of humans and the machinery of their culture is a richer configuration in Eliot than in Fernand Léger.

The technical revolutions that sustain these fresh visions were also urged upon Eliot by Pound, who disliked the regular expectations of the pentameter. Its absence at moments of high density in *The Waste Land* certainly allows more radical connections between its elements. In the same way Cubism neglects the syntax and metrics of illusionist perspectives and adopts what John Berger calls its diagrams:

> The metaphorical model of cubism is the *diagram*: the diagram being a visible, symbolic representation of invisible processes, forces, structures. A diagram need not eschew certain aspects of appearances; but these too will be treated symbolically as *signs*, not as imitations or re-creations.[19]

Such an explanation sorts well with some of Eliot's methods in *The Waste Land*, notably with the diagrammatic opening section. Appearance is not merely re-created, but rather its meaning as sign is stressed. The two portraits of the women in 'A Game of Chess' are not, by conventional standards, fully realized. Though there is some debt to appearances, they exist as diagrams to organize ideas of sterility and boredom in the poem. And, like shapes in a Cubist painting, they only assert their full meaning by taking their place among all the others.

V

In their book *On Cubism*, the artists Gleizes and Metzinger explained:

> Formerly the fresco incited the artist to represent distinct objects, evoking a simple rhythm, on which the light was spread at the limit of a synchronic vision, rendered necessary by the amplitude of the surfaces; today painting in oils allows us to express notions of depth, density and duration supposed to be inexpressible, and incites us to represent, in terms of a complex rhythm, a veritable fusion of objects, within a limited space.[20]

[19] *Ibid.*, 20.
[20] Quoted by Douglas Cooper in *The Cubist Epoch* (London and Los Angeles, 1971), 72. For a most useful collection of further documents on cubism see Edward F. Fry, *Cubism* (London, 1966).

The terms of their analysis refer aptly enough to Eliot's major poetry: the complex rhythms, the fusion of objects, the concentrated space. And I suggest that we may describe the progress in Eliot's poetry from *The Waste Land* to *Four Quartets* by saying that it is marked by a concentration upon precisely these 'Cubist' strategies.

Various elements, it may be argued, marred the Cubist endeavours in *The Waste Land* that are absent from *Four Quartets*. There is, firstly, what we might call (borrowing from the history of Cubism) the device of *collage*. From 1912 onwards Picasso and Braque decided to incorporate into their paintings elements of ready-made reality: these pasted fragments both attacked the idea that fine art was inseparable from fine materials and stressed the fresh realities of art by including in its new geometry unregenerate elements of the real world. Thus *collage* contributes to the emancipation of Cubism from any comfortable illusion that what we face on the canvas is like what we see. Eliot, too, involves in *The Waste Land* elements picked directly from the world of appearances: the language of the pub scene, songs from Australia, 'C.i.f. London', and others. There is also the quality of *collage*, I feel, about some of the literary allusions, although at their best they are revised in a fresh context. One major literary allusion by way of pastiche—the imitation of Pope at the start of 'The Fire Sermon'—never survived the drafts.[21] But the published version still hovers close to such *collage* in the opening moments of 'A Game of Chess', or the passages that have to do with Spenser or *The Tempest* in 'The Fire Sermon'.

Eliot has written how the poet's mind 'is in fact a receptacle for seizing and storing up numberless feelings, phrases, images, which remain there until all the particles which can unite to form a new compound are present together'.[22] And his account of Swinburne's poetry notes how language struggles to form new compounds and to 'digest and express new objects, new groups of objects, new feelings, new aspects'. Sometimes the language of *The Waste Land* fails to find these compounds and then the *collage* elements from earlier literatures are not mediated by their new context. They survive, in fact—and the end of the poem, already cited, is an example—as *papier collé*, using the literary fragments as the material to be pasted.

[21] See *Facsimile*, 23 ff.
[22] 'Tradition and the Individual Talent' in *Selected Essays*, 19. For the remark on Swinburne see *Selected Essays*, 327.

Four Quartets succeeds in absorbing these restless elements. The opening sections of 'East Coker' sustain a poetry that is assured of those best 'Cubist' elements I have tried to point to in *The Waste Land*. The phrases of Tudor English take their place happily in the larger meditative rhythms. The second paragraph moves from fractured items of a scenery that nevertheless we all recognize towards larger forms and patterns less immediately consonant with seen things, and then finally into still more abstract shapes. The subtle dialogue here between the time of a country dance and a larger time, between appearance and abstraction, is typical of most of the *Quartets*; and it is a type that we see frequently in the modern visual arts.[23] However, it is in Cubism that the shifting frontier between objects and our thoughts about them is most excitingly available and where we have to adjust, as Harry says in *The Family Reunion*, to the twilight zones of shifting visions.

The passage that ends with 'Dung and death' never allows us to lose either the real items or the notions and abstractions (ideas) that the artist's mind makes of them. In this we are close to the task set in reading Braque's images of a mandolin, or a still life with fish. With both Braque and Eliot we are aware constantly of the speculative possibilities of their perspectives: 'What might have been and what has been/Point to one end, which is always present.' The poem and the painting are each alert to the worlds of creative speculation. The door that we never opened into the rose-garden which we yet know so well also exists with the footfalls down the passage as if it *had* been explored; for the poetry's creation of the possibility, like the experience of incorporating another angle of vision into a Cubist synthesis, gives it being. As Braque says, the painter never tries to reconstruct an anecdote but to establish a pictorial fact. *Four Quartets* makes raids on the inarticulate, as Braque upon the invisible, to establish its own verbal diagram.

VI

These speculations on Eliot and modern art, like all analogies,

[23] A fascinating example of a modern artist's interest in the interplay of abstraction and appearance may be found in *The Graphic Work of M. C. Escher* (London, 1967).

may illustrate but not establish truths. They have been offered as an exercise in cultural history—a search for interesting contiguities and continuities between the arts, a quest for what Pound engagingly calls the 'Paideuma'. So it will be best to end by borrowing the scepticism that Herbert Read rehearses:

> I rarely discussed contemporary art with him (Eliot), and though I once or twice tried to establish some personal contact between him and artists like Henry Moore and Ben Nicholson, my efforts came to little or nothing. If pressed he would no doubt have admitted that the tradition that led from Poe and Baudelaire to Laforgue and Rimbaud and his own poetry could not be entirely divorced from the tradition that lead from Delacroix and Cézanne to Matisse and Picasso, but he would not himself have made much of the comparison.[24]

[24] *T. S. Eliot: The Man and his Work*, ed. Tate, 37–8.

'The Word within a Word'

Denis Donoghue

The publication of the first drafts of The Waste Land[1] has not greatly eased the difficulty of reading the poem. We now know that the poem issued, however circuitously, from the unhappiness of Eliot's first marriage—though certain lines and passages in the first drafts were written before 1915—but we hardly know what to make of that fact, unless it prompts us to say that the dominant feeling in the poem is not universal despair but particular guilt, and that the specific movement of feeling through the words corresponds, however obscurely, to the act of penance. Some readers of The Waste Land feel that Eliot is saying: 'God, I thank thee that I am not as the rest of men, extortioners, unjust, adulterers, or even as this small house-agent's clerk.' But this sense of the poem is unworthy, false to its spirit as a whole, though there are a few passages which support it. The area of feeling which the poem inhabits is the general provenance of guilt, fear, dread; the presence of disgust, including self-disgust, is not surprising. The first drafts show, and this is more to the point, that the poet's original sense of his poem made it, even more than the final version, a medley. Pound's criticism tightened the poem, but did not otherwise alter its movement. One characteristic of the poetry remains. Eliot's poems often try to escape from the emotional condition which incited them, not by willing its opposite but by working through a wide range of alternative conditions. The poems find safety and relief in numbers. One mood is answered not by another, equal and opposite, but by a diversity of moods. It is the diversity that saves. The medley of poems which eventually became The Waste Land was designed, it appears, with this diversity in view. To the charge that Eliot's poem is the work of a Pharisee, therefore, I would not reply that on the contrary it is the work of a publican, but rather that it effects a move-

[1] Facsimile, 31.

ment of feeling to make penance possible. Diversity, number and allusion are the auspices under which the poem moves.

I want to suggest now that this sense of the poem is related to our recognition of its character as a distinctively American work. Specifically, the poem is, in Hawthorne's terminology, a romance. In the Preface to *The House of the Seven Gables*, Hawthorne distinguished between romance and novel. The novel aims at minute fidelity to the probable, but the romance, claiming 'a certain latitude', proposes to present 'the truth of the human heart' under circumstances 'to a great extent of the writer's own choosing or creation'.[2] There has always been an implication, in later comments on the romance, that it is the form of fiction most congenial to those feelings for which social correlatives are not available; or, if available, seriously inadequate. It is a commonplace that the romance, in Hawthorne's sense, holds a special position in America literature and that it is particularly serviceable to the writer who feels his imagination driven back upon its own resources. One of the tenable generalizations we continue to make about English literature is that its position is not desperate in this regard. The English writer generally thinks himself ready to establish his feeling in a particular setting and to let it develop and take its chance there. He declares a certain confidence in representing the life of feeling in terms of man, Nature, and society. Nearly everything is allowed to depend upon the relation of man to the society in which he lives, the relation of person to person and to place. We say that English literature is personal, meaning that it is social, historical, and political. We do not say this of American literature. The question of locality is important to American writers, not least to Hawthorne in *The House of the Seven Gables*, but in American literature generally, and especially in the literature of the nineteenth-century a shadow falls between person and place. The feelings in the case are rarely entrusted to that relation, or indeed to any other: there is an impression that such feelings cannot hope to be fulfilled in such relations. There is a remainder of feeling which cries for release in dream, nightmare and fantasy. I want to pursue the notion that *The Waste Land* is best understood as an American romance.

It may be useful to recall Eliot's sense of American literature. He rejected the assertion that there is an American language

[2] Nathaniel Hawthorne, *The House of the Seven Gables* (Centenary edition, Ohio State University Press, 1965), vol. II, 1.

distinct from English: in his view, both languages use the same notes, even if the fingering is sometimes different. He was not of Mencken's party in that argument. As for the literature, he registered New England as a moral presence, a regiment in the army of unalterable law, but he was not intimidated by it. He reflected upon the complex fate of being an American when he read Hawthorne and, still more, Henry James, who embodied one of the great possibilities consistent with that fate. In an essay on James he wrote that 'it is the final perfection, the consummation of an American to become, not an Englishman, but a European—something which no born European, no person of any European nationality, can become.'[3] Of the relation between Eliot and Whitman it is enough to say that Whitman is audible, for some good but more ill, in the third section of 'The Dry Salvages', providing Eliot with a somewhat insecure tone. Of Mark Twain Eliot is on record as saying in praise that he was one of those writers who discover 'a new way of writing, valid not only for themselves but for others',[4] but I cannot recall any occasion on which Eliot moved in Twain's direction, despite 'the river with its cargo of dead negroes' in 'The Dry Salvages'. The question of his relation to Poe is far more interesting, because it is strange that he should have had any interest in such a writer. In fact, he did not admire Poe's poems, he thought them adolescent things; Poe had never grown up. But there were two aspects of the matter which he could not ignore. The first concerned Poe's style of incantation which, Eliot said, 'because of its very crudity, stirs the feelings at a deep and almost primitive level'.[5] Eliot had his own style of incantation, and he was greatly taken by Poe as a master in the singing style. The second consideration was that Poe's work, fruitless in the English and American traditions, had entered the sensibilities of the great French poets and especially of Baudelaire, Mallarmé and Valéry. Eliot was interested in this event, and he pondered it. There is almost a suggestion that Poe had somehow achieved the final perfection of an American by becoming a European, reincarnated in Baudelaire, Mallarmé and Valéry. Eliot was strongly engaged by

[3] 'Henry James', reprinted in *The Shock of Recognition*, ed. Edmund Wilson (New York, 1955), vol. II, 855.
[4] 'American Literature and the American Language', reprinted in *To Criticize the Critic*.
[5] 'From Poe to Valéry', reprinted in *To Criticize the Critic*.

Poe, as by Swinburne, for a similar reason, the call of one verbalist to another.

The great interest of American literature arises, it is commonly agreed, from the sense of American feeling as making a new start, every day, with little or nothing regarded as capital saved from yesterday. The world is all before the American writers. So these writers naturally think of making everything new, they do not feel overwhelmed by the weight of previous achievement. American writers burn their bridges behind them, relegating the previous, as James said of his compatriots generally in *The American Scene*, to the category of wan misery. If *The Waste Land* is written by an American who has set out to make himself a European, its chief labour toward that perfection is the assumption of the burden of history. The allusions in Eliot's poem show not the extent of his learning but the gravity of the whole enterprise, the range of those responsibilities he is ready to accept in such a cause. What most of the allusions say is: 'there have been other times, not utterly lost or forgotten; we ourselves were not born this morning.'

We may press the argument a little further. If English literature is devoted to the relation between person, place, and time, it acts by a corresponding syntax of prescribed relations. The first result is that the chief function of one word is to lead the mind to the next. No detail in *Middlemarch* is as important as the entire network of relations, word by word, sentence by sentence: the reader's mind is not encouraged to sink into the recesses of a word, but to move forward until the prescribed affiliations are complete. The modesty with which a word sends the reader's mind running to the next is the verbal equivalent of dependency in a given society, as one person accepts his enabling relation to another. But the modern revolution in such American poems as *The Waste Land* and *Hugh Selwyn Mauberley* depends upon a different sense of life and therefore upon a different syntax. One's first reading of these poems leaves an impression of their poetic quality as residing in their diction: the animation of the verse arises from the incalculable force of certain individual words or phrases which stay in the mind without necessarily attracting to their orbit the words before or after. The memorable quality of those phrases seems to require a clear space on all sides, and it has little need of before and after. I take this to mean that the relations to which the words of an American poem refer are not prescribed or predictive but experimental. Around each word there is a space or a void in which nothing is anticipated, nothing enforced. Every relation must be invented, as if the world had just begun. Harold Rosenberg has argued that this is the chief characteristic of modern French poetry, though he offers a different explanation. 'Lifting up a word and putting a space around it has been the conscious enterprise of serious French poetry since Baudelaire and Rimbaud'; and a little later he speaks of 'the space around words necessary for consciousness'.[6] In Eliot's early poems an American is trying to make himself a Frenchman, perfecting himself in the creation of Jules Laforgue; an enterprise capable of producing, in the longer run, the magisterial achievement of making himself a European. The space around the words is necessary for consciousness, and it puts at risk the continuity of relations, as between one person and another. In Eliot, consciousness is the most available form of virtue, to be conscious is to be holy: an equation which causes great difficulty in the later plays, and especially in *The Cocktail Party*. But the words thus surrounded by empty space receive a corresponding halo of significance, they compel the imagination not by their relation but by their isolation. Such words take unto themselves a force of radiance, an exceptional power which Eliot in the later plays ascribes to saints and martyrs. Martyrdom is Eliot's favourite version of the Sublime.

There is a passage in *Writing Degree Zero* where Roland Barthes offers virtually the same distinction between what he calls classical language and modern language. In classical language the meaning is continuous, linear, it is always deferred until the end. So the mind, like the eye, runs along beside the words, and the movement is gratifying. But in modern poetry it is the word 'which gratifies and fulfills like the sudden revelation of a truth'. The word has lost its prescribed relations, but for that very reason it has acquired a magical power, it has become complete in itself, a revelation in its own recesses. Giving up its old dependency, the word acquires Sibylline presence; it stands there like Rilke's archaic torso of Apollo. It is a mark of such words that we cannot read them, but they read us, they affront us by presenting their significance in relation to themselves. Barthes says of such words that they 'initiate a discourse full of gaps and full of lights, filled

[6] Harold Rosenberg, *The Tradition of the New* (London, 1970 reprint), 86, 89.

with absences and over-nourishing signs, without foresight or stability of intention, and thereby so opposed to the social function of language that merely to have recourse to a discontinuous speech is to open the door to all that stands above Nature'. Classical language 'establishes a universe in which men are not alone, where words never have the terrible weight of things, where speech is always a meeting with the others'. Modern language presupposes a discontinuous Nature, 'a fragmented space, made of objects solitary and terrible because the links between them are only potential'. I would say that the links between them must be invented and are then fictive rather than prescribed or agreed: they have the freedom of fiction and, paying the price, the loneliness of being arbitrary. Such words, since they cannot be continuous with Nature, must be above or below it, two conditions about equally lonely. They are exceptions deprived of a rule. These words become names because of their oracular power, but what they name cannot be defined; they are like Stetson in *The Waste Land*, whose chief character is that he does not answer, though he instigates, the questions addressed to him. Stetson is the name for the interrogation, but he is under no obligation to reply. *The Waste Land* is the name of another interrogation, and its words are less answers than hints and guesses. Barthes says of these modern words generally— 'words adorned with all the violence of their irruption, the vibration of which, though wholly mechanical, strangely affects the next word, only to die out immediately'—that they 'exclude men: there is no humanism of modern poetry'.[7] Stetson is not related to his interrogator or to London or even to Mylae, he is an oracle who stirs a nervous quiver of interrogation, and dies out in a line from Baudelaire.

Classical language, then, is a system organized on the assumption that Nature is continuous; hence the primacy of syntax. Classical poems stand in apposition to a seamless web of relations which we agree to call Nature: when the web is domestic we call it Society. The poems testify to those webs by enacting them in miniature. The long poem is valued as an extended ritual, offered to Nature in the grandest terms, a celebration of prescribed relations. The reader may still be surprised, because he does not know at any moment which of the indefinitely large number of

[7] Roland Barthes, *Writing Degree Zero*, translated by Annette Lavers and Colin Smith (London, 1967), 54–5.

relations the writer will enact, but he knows that one of them will be invoked. Each word is faithful to the others. But in modern poems, according to this distinction, the words are independent and therefore lonely. In *The Waste Land* we respond most deeply to the individual words and phrases with a sense of their exposure. The words are not obscure, because we know what the dictionary says of them and, mostly, we know where they come from. But they are Sibylline because of the darkness between them: they challenge us to provide them with a continuous syntax and they mock our efforts to do so; that was not what they meant at all. The whole poem looks like the sub-plot of a lost play; what is lost is the main plot, Nature as a significant action. The attempt to specify the form of *The Waste Land* is doomed because the form is not specific, it is not—to use Blackmur's word—predictive. The poem cries for its form: what it shows forth in itself is not form but the desperate analogy of form, tokens of a virtual form which would be valid if there were such a thing. What holds the several parts of the poem together is the need, which is at once the poet's need and our own, to keep life going, including the life of the poem in the dark spaces between the words. The problem is not that the poem lacks form but that it has a passion for form, largely unfulfilled, and—to make things harder—the memory of lost forms. Those lost forms would not answer the present need, even if they could be recovered: this is what Blackmur meant by saying of Eliot's early poems and *The Waste Land* that 'they measure the present by living standards which most people relegate to the past'.[8] What is present and vivid to us in the poem is the cry for form, the loud lament of that disconsolate chimera, and the cry is so pure that it almost makes up for what is merely lost. If the poem proliferates in little forms, it is because these are variations on an absent theme, a theme of which only the variations are known. The variations are recited from many different sources, and with increasing urgency toward the end of the poem, the sources being older versions of form, present now as broken images. In their bearing upon the reader, these images tell upon his conscience, forcing him to live up to the exactitude of the poem and to reject false consolations. If the poem is to be read as prologomena to

[8] R. P. Blackmur, *Form and Value in Modern Poetry* (New York, 1957), 143.

penance, it is also, in its bearing upon the reader, an incitement to scruple.

So Blackmur on another occasion spoke of Eliot's task as a poet: 'he has in his images to remind reason of its material, to remind order of its disorder, in order to create a sane art almost insane in its predicament.' He has 'to make a confrontation of the rational with the irrational: a deliberate reversal of roles'.[9] But in fact Eliot had to make a double confrontation, the violence going both ways. He had to confront the rational with the irrational, with what is below Nature, and the images used for this violence are mostly those he associated with Conrad's hollow men and *Heart of Darkness*. In the passage which Eliot wanted to use as the epigraph to *The Waste Land* before he came upon Petronius' Sibyl, Conrad's Marlow says of Kurtz:

> Did he live his life again in every detail of desire, temptation, and surrender during that supreme moment of complete knowledge? He cried in a whisper at some image, at some vision,—he cried out twice, a cry that was no more than a breath—'The horror! the horror!'

The confrontation of the rational with the irrational is propelled by the assumption that complete knowledge is possible and its horror inescapable. So I have always believed that the reader of *The Waste Land* ought to take Tiresias seriously as the name of such a possibility, and such a horror. But the other confrontation is equally valid: the irrational is confronted with the rational in all those ways for which, in the poem, the rational imagination is represented by Shakespeare, Spenser, St Augustine, and, in the first version, by a passage from Plato's *Republic* which Pound deleted: 'Not here, O Ademantus, but in another world.'[10] The line comes from a famous passage in Book IX where Glaucon says that the city which has been described is merely verbal, it does not exist anywhere on earth; and Socrates answers,' Well, perhaps there is a pattern of it laid up in heaven for him who wishes to contemplate it and so beholding to constitute himself its citizen.'[11] The contemplation of the City of God is also com-

---

[9] R. P. Blackmur, *Anni Mirabiles 1921–1925* (Washington, Library of Congress, 1956), 31.

[10] *Facsimile*, 31.

[11] *The Republic*, book IX, 592–A–B, quoted from the Loeb edition in *Facsimile*, 128.

plete knowledge, above Nature, its sublimity compelling to the citizen, and its finality is asserted in the repeated Sanscrit word with which the poem ends. A Tiresias would see the City of God as clearly as the Unreal City, its malign counterpart. So the poem moves between *Heart of Darkness* and 'heart of light'. Words stand between reason and madness, touched by both adversaries.

We need an authoritative example; from Section III of *The Waste Land*, 'The Fire Sermon':

> But at my back in a cold blast I hear
> The rattle of the bones, and chuckle spread from ear to ear.
>
> A rat crept softly through the vegetation
> Dragging its slimy belly on the bank
> While I was fishing in the dull canal
> On a winter evening round behind the gashouse
> Musing upon the king my brother's wreck
> And on the king my father's death before him.
> White bodies naked on the low damp ground
> And bones cast in a little low dry garret,
> Rattled by the rat's foot only, year to year.
> But at my back from time to time I hear
> The sound of horns and motors, which shall bring
> Sweeney to Mrs Porter in the spring.
> O the moon shone bright on Mrs Porter
> And on her daughter
> They wash their feet in soda water
> *Et O ces voix d'enfants, chantant dans la coupole!*[12]

It is useless to ask of that passage such questions as the following: who is speaking? what is the point of his narrative? whose white bodies lay naked on the ground? Such questions assume that there is a world-without-words to which Eliot's words pay tribute; as, in common usage, the word 'box' acknowledges the existence of a certain object which does not depend upon a word for its existence. A reader determined to give some kind of answer might say, to the first question: Tiresias; but he somehow includes the Buddha, Ferdinand Prince of Naples, Ovid and Verlaine. And to the second he might say: Well, the narrative is merely ostensible, we are not meant to think of it as a story, the words in that order make a kind of landscape in the reader's mind, Marshall McLuhan calls it psychological landscape, which

[12] *Collected Poems 1909–1962*, 70–71.

is at once subject and object; it has to do with Eliot's theory of the objective correlative or Santayana's theory of the correlative object. And the answerer might say to the third question: The king my brother and the king my father, I suppose, but again the point is verbal and atmospheric rather than denotative. Questions more in accord with the nature of the passage would include the following: what is going on, when 'rat's foot' is preceded by the punning rhyme, 'rattled'? What is going on when the speaker, whoever he is, quotes several fragments from Ovid, Verlaine, the Grail Legend, Australian popular song, Marvell, *The Tempest*, John Day, and Middleton? Why does the passage suddenly change its tone at that first insistent rhyme, 'year' with 'hear'? Why are we given 'wreck' instead of 'wrack' in the quotation from *The Tempest*? These questions are not likely to set anyone's heart astir, but they are more in accord with Eliot's poem because they do not call another world in judgement upon the words. The questions keep strictly to language, and in this respect they follow the rhetoric of the poem. Symbolist poetry yearns for a world governed by the laws of Pure Poetry; internal laws, marking purely internal liaisons between one word and another, without any reference to Nature as a court of appeal. In such a world, time would take the form of prosody. In the passage from 'The Fire Sermon' no effect is allowed to escape from the words, to leave the medium of language. The images and figures do not leave the poem, they refuse to leave a setting which is assertively verbal. It is permissible to say that the speaker here and through-out the poem is Tiresias; but that is like saying that something is the speech of God, it merely replaces one problem by another. The words of the Sermon are not completed by our conceiving for their speaker a personal identity. It is more useful to imagine a possible state of feeling which is secreted in the words. The best way to read the lines is not to ask that each phrase give up its meaning, as if that meaning were then to replace the words; but to ask what quality, in each sequence, the phrases share. That quality may be found to attach itself to a state of feeling which cannot be given in other terms. Not a seamless narrative, but a set of lyric moments, each isolated for consciousness.

It is customary to say that the explanation for this use of language is to be found in the works of F. H. Bradley and in Eliot's thesis, *Knowledge and Experience in the Philosophy of F. H. Bradley*. I quote a few sentences in which Eliot summarizes

Bradley's argument: kinship between Eliot's prose and Bradley's has been noted. 'It is only in immediate experience that knowledge and its object are one.' 'We have no right, except in the most provisional way, to speak of *my* experience, since the I is a construction out of experience, an abstraction from it; and the *thats*, the browns and hards and flats, are equally ideal constructions from experience, as ideal as atoms.' 'The only independent reality is immediate experience or feeling.' ' "My" feeling is certainly in a sense mine. But this is because and in so far as I am the feeling.' 'Experience is non-relational.'[13] These sentences refer to Bradley's general philosophical position but more especially to certain passages in his *Essays on Truth and Reality*, including this one:

> Now consciousness, to my mind, is not original. What comes first in each of us is rather feeling, a state as yet without either an object or subject. . . . Feeling is immediate experience without distinction or relation in itself. It is a unity, complex but without relations. And there is here no difference between the state and its content, since, in a word, the experienced and the experience are one.[14]

In Eliot's version, 'feeling is more than either object or subject, since in a way it includes both'. Furthermore,

> In describing immediate experience we must use terms which offer a surreptitious suggestion of subject or object. If we say presentation, we think of a subject to which the presentation is present as an object. And if we say feeling, we think of it as the feeling of a subject about an object. . . . It may accordingly be said that the real situation is an experience which can never be wholly defined as an object nor wholly enjoyed as a feeling, but in which any of the observed constituents may take on the one or the other aspect.[15]

Perhaps this is enough to suggest what Eliot means when he speaks of 'the continuous transition by which feeling becomes object and object becomes feeling'. The language of 'The Fire Sermon' is surreptitious in the sense that its objectivity is merely ostensible. The rat creeping through the vegetation has only as

---

[13] *Knowledge and Experience in the Philosophy of F. H. Bradley* (London, 1964), 19, 30, 31, 27.

[14] F. H. Bradley, *Essays on Truth and Reality* (Oxford, 1914), 194.

[15] *Knowledge and Experience*, 22, 25.

much to do with animal life as is required to incite a certain feeling in the speaker. The rat has crept into the words and lost itself there; what transpires in the words is a certain feeling, in this case more subject than object. The meaning of a phrase, a line, a word, in 'The Fire Sermon' is every impression that attaches itself to those sounds under the pressure of consciousness; an assertion which reminds us that the famous Chapter XIV of Bradley's *Essays on Truth and Reality* is called 'What is the real Julius Caesar?' The real *Waste Land* is a sequence of those impressions, incited by the sequence of words: the impressions are different for each reader.

There is nothing unorthodox in this, from the standpoint of a philosophical idealist. It would be possible to quote Susanne Langer or Cassirer just as relevantly as Bradley. It is also orthodox Symbolism, of the kind which Valéry treats in 'Analecta, Tel Quel II', where he says that 'the self flees all created things, it withdraws from negation to negation: one might give the name "Universe" to everything in which the self refuses to recognize itself'. The self refuses to recognize itself in any part of the objective world, so called, until the world is transformed into subjective terms, every apprehended object become subject. But the self is always willing to recognize itself in language and symbols. Thinking of Eliot's poem, one might give the name 'language' to that alone in which the self recognizes itself. As for Eliot himself, recognition may be willing or desperate: willing if we emphasize the luxury of the words, the gypsy phrases and cadences, the impression that a man who passes his entire life among such words is the happiest of men; desperate, if we emphasize the allusions, and Eliot's need of them, the accepted weight of responsibility, those fragments shored against his ruin. The allusions are Eliot's insignia, and they have this further point; they give his sensibility other ground than itself, ground in history, literature, religion, revelation, through the words, the ground of our beseeching.

For while the self flees every created thing and refuses to recognize itself anywhere but in words, it needs something besides itself. Perhaps language is enough, but we must leave that question open. In a chapter on solipsism Eliot writes:

The point of view (or finite centre) has for its object one consistent world, and accordingly no finite centre can be self-sufficient, for the life of a soul does not consist in the contemplation of one consistent world but in the painful task of unifying (to a greater or less extent) jarring and incompatible ones, and passing, when possible, from two or more discordant viewpoints to a higher which shall somehow include and transmute them.[16]

In *The Waste Land* Eliot calls this higher perspective Tiresias: 'we are led to the conception of an all-inclusive experience outside of which nothing shall fall', he says in the thesis on Bradley.

A year after the publication of *The Waste Land* Eliot reviewed Joyce's *Ulysses*, and proposed there a distinction which depends upon the idea of greater and lesser perspectives. In this distinction between two methods of fiction, 'narrative method' is based upon the commonly accepted separation of subject and object. The personal equivalent is the notion of a literary character, cut out from his surroundings and endowed with certain qualities. The medium is words, but most of them are common and they are placed in accepted arrangements. Books based upon these arrangements are called novels, so the novel as a form of art came to an end, according to Eliot in 1923, with Flaubert and James. (He later repudiated this obituary, by the way.) The 'mythical method' of fiction, on the other hand, is based upon immediate experience, the primacy of feeling, the idea of subject and object melting into each other beyond positivist redemption, and at last transcended in a quasi-divine perspective, Tiresias in *The Waste Land*, the Homeric archetype in *Ulysses*. But we should not identify Tiresias with the ultimate form of consciousness. It is necessary to think of language (Valéry's 'Saint Langage' in 'La Pythie') as issuing from a perspective grander even than Tiresias', since Tiresias can only see the world as one alienated from it: he does not give or sympathize, he does not participate in the suffering and transformation of 'What the Thunder Said'. It is necessary for the poem, and for poetry, to go beyond the phase of consciousness which Eliot calls Tiresias. The 'going beyond' has no name, it is the action of the poem itself. Instead of common words in common places there is language itself, construed now as a great treasury of images and figures and, increasingly in Eliot, identified with the Word of God. Using language in this way, it seems natural to have Ferdinand Prince of Naples, the Phoenician sailor, the one-eyed seller of currants,

[16] *Ibid.*, 147–8.

and all the women in the world becoming Tiresias. For Eliot, as for Bradley, there is no question of a Wordsworthian liaison between man and Nature. The only part of Bradley's *Appearance and Reality* which Eliot chose to quote in his notes to *The Waste Land* disengages itself from any such hope. In Ch. XXIII Bradley says that 'we behave as if our internal worlds were the same'. But we err:

Our inner worlds, I may be told, are divided from each other, but the outer world of experience is common to all; and it is by standing on this basis that we are able to communicate. Such a statement would be incorrect. My external sensations are no less private to myself than are my thoughts or my feelings. In either case my experience falls within my own circle, a circle closed on the outside; and, with all its elements alike, every sphere is opaque to the others which surround it. . . . In brief, regarded as an existence which appears in a soul, the whole world for each is peculiar and private to that soul.[17]

Perhaps our first impression here is wonder that such a view of the mind's predicament could ever have secreted, in Bradley's pupil, a major poem. But the second impression is better, that for such a poet language is the only possible home: either language or that metalanguage we call silence. But we are in danger of confounding the pupil with his master. Just as Bradley cleared himself of a charge of solipsism by arguing, in *Appearance and Reality*, that 'we can go to foreign selves by a process no worse than the construction which establishes our own self',[18] so Eliot cleared himself of a charge of philosophy by becoming a poet; that is, by attending to all the affiliations of words, including their old hankering after objects. Against the persuasion of his idealism, there are the deep persuasions of Dante, Shakespeare, Virgil; and there is eventually the persuasion of Christian belief in which time is redeemed and the higher dream is made flesh. Perhaps these are the necessary qualifications to make while returning to the poem. Without them, we are in danger of turning the poem into a set of more or less interesting ideas; forgetting that to Eliot, as to Bradley, 'a mere idea is but a ruinous abstraction'; forgetting, too, that it was Eliot who praised Henry James for possessing a mind so fine that no idea could violate it. With

[17] F. H. Bradley, *Appearance and Reality* (London, 1902), 346.
[18] *Ibid.*, 258.

the passage from 'The Fire Sermon' in front of us again, we see that what came first was not an idea but feeling, 'a state as yet without either an object or subject'. The nearest expressive equivalent is rhythm, at this stage not yet resolved in words. In 'The Music of Poetry' Eliot reported that in his own experience 'a poem, or a passage from a poem, may tend to realize itself first as a particular rhythm before it reaches expression in words, and that this rhythm may bring to birth the idea and the image'.[19] An account of our passage would be a blunt affair if it did not point to the changes of rhythm as among the chief moments; where the echo of Marvell's 'To His Coy Mistress' imposes a new and deeper tone upon the verse; and from there until the line from Verlaine the transitions become more abrupt. Eliot remains true to the original feeling by remaining true to its rhythm. The words, when they are found, maintain a double allegiance: they are required to define the rhythm of the first feeling, and they must also allow for the melting of one experience into another.

The first consequence is that, to a reader sceptical of idealist assumptions, many of these lines appear wilfully arch and secretive: they appear to go through the motions of grammar and syntax without committing themselves to these agencies. They are neither one thing nor the other, neither wholly subject nor wholly object: without proposing themselves as paradoxes, they are paradoxical. A further result is that, in verse of this kind, incidents drawn from whatever source cannot have the status which they would have in a novel or in another poem. In the *Metamorphoses* Ovid tells the story of the rape of Philomela by King Tereus of Thrace. Eliot recalls the story in 'A Game of Chess'. Trico's song in Lyly's *Alexander and Campaspe* has the lines:

> Oh, 'tis the ravished nightingale.
> *Jug, jug, jug, jug, tereu*! she cries.

Matthew Arnold's 'Philomela' is one story, John Crowe Ransom's is another, the story is diversely told. How it appears in the mind of God, there is no knowing; what is the real Philomela is a hard question. How it appears in the inordinate mind of Tiresias is given in *The Waste Land*:

---

[19] *On Poetry and Poets*, 38.

> Twit twit twit
> Jug jug jug jug jug jug
> So rudely forc'd.
> Tereu

—being the twit of the swallow, the Elizabethan nightingale-call and, by curious association, the word for 'slut', a fine phrase of justice from Middleton's *A Game at Chess*, and lastly the simple vocative, 'Tereu'. Ovid's story is given, indeed, but only the gist of it, the story insofar as it survives transposition in the inclusive consciousness of Tiresias. In that strange place, one image melts into another; hence Eliot's idiom of melting, transition, becoming, deliquescence, and so forth.

To resume a long story: it is easy to think of Eliot as he thought of Swinburne: 'only a man of genius could dwell so exclusively and consistently among words.' In Swinburne, as in Poe, words alone are certain good. But it is well to qualify that report by adding another, from 'The Music of Poetry', where Eliot speaks of the poet as occupied with 'frontiers of consciousness beyond which words fail, though meanings still exist'. In the plays this exorbitant work is done by miracle, 'the way of illumination'. Tiresias is the Unidentified Guest, until he too is transcended in Celia. The effort of the plays is to allow people to live by a holy language. Language, the ancient place of wisdom, is guaranteed by conscience and consciousness, as in *Four Quartets*. That is why, at last, 'the poetry does not matter'. The procedures of *The Waste Land*, which were sustained by the force of language itself, are transposed into the idiom of characters acting and suffering: transitions and perspectives, verbal in *The Waste Land*, take more specific forms in the later poems and plays, the forms of personal action, chances and choices. The frontier of consciousness is not the place where words fail but where self dies, in the awful surrender of faith. Bradley is not repudiated, but he is forced to accommodate himself to the Shakespeare of *A Winter's Tale* and *The Tempest*: that is one way of putting it.

I have been arguing that it is characteristic of Eliot's language in *The Waste Land* to effect an 'absence in reality', and to move words into the resultant vacuum. At first, the words seem to denote things, *sensibilia* beyond the lexicon, but it soon appears that their allegiance to reality is deceptive, they are traitors in reality. So far as the relation between word and thing is deceptive, so far also is 'objective' reality undermined. The only certainty is that the absence in reality has been effected by the words, and now the same words are enforcing themselves as the only presences. What we respond to is the presence of the words. In this way the words acquire the kind of aura, or the kind of reverberation, which we feel in proverbs; with this difference, that proverbs appeal to our sense of life, an inherited wisdom in our sense of things; Eliot's words appeal to primordial images and rhythms which can be felt, though they cannot well be called in evidence. I cannot explain this use of language except by suggesting that if the common arrangements of words issue from the common sense of time, Eliot's arrangements issue from the quarrel between time and myth: I assume that myth is a way of breaking the chain of time, the chain of one thing after another. Eliot is using words as if their first obligation were neither to things nor to time. Philip Wheelwright has called this kind of imagination 'archetypal', the imagination 'which sees the particular object in the light of a larger conception or of a higher concern'. Nearly everything in Eliot's language can be explained by his feeling that the truth of things resides in an indeterminate area: neither subject nor object, but a state compounded of both; neither time nor eternity, but a state in which the double obligation is registered; neither man nor God, but a being, conceivable in words but not in fact, who is vouched for not in identifiable speech but in language itself, eventually to be invoked as Logos. I am not indeed maintaining that the word 'rat', in 'The Fire Sermon', has ceased to observe all relation to a certain rodent, but rather that the word is a double agent, it accepts the friction between reality and language, but it does not give total allegiance to either party. On one side stands the world of things; on the other, a rival world of dissociated forms, Platonic cities. Between these worlds stands the individual word, maintaining a secret life, double allegiance or double treachery.

It is characteristically American of Eliot to place these inordinate burdens upon language and the poetic imagination. The imagination must do nearly everything because reality cannot be relied on to do much. In the relation between reality and the imagination, he has established conditions extremely favourable to the imagination. This is only another way of saying that language commands the otherwise empty space between consciousness and experience, consciousness and action, consciousness and the earth.

Ideology and Poetry

Kathleen Nott

In what follows I shall try to isolate a structure in Eliot's beliefs and opinions. I shall confine myself mainly to his critical works and lectures. In reading and re-reading his poetry and plays it appears to me that this structure is an organic whole; that is to say that the intellectual integration continues into the poetic; but that is an analysis of greater scope than I am able to undertake at the moment. I shall therefore not attempt to make out a detailed case.

I shall not disguise my antipathy to the general tenor of Eliot's views and beliefs, nor my opinion that the world in which we live has shown that many of them are unworkable. But that opinion is not a claim that they are necessarily and always false or mistaken, nor that the world has always shown that it knows better. That world remains chaotic and lacks a common concept of human existence, and therefore a common aim for human development. But if here we can in part agree with Eliot's diagnosis, that does not entail agreeing with his ideas for remedial treatment nor indeed with his description of the etiology of the disease.

As a particular example of the diagnosis we may take what he says in 'Thoughts After Lambeth' (1931):

> The world is trying the experiment of attempting to form a civilized but non-Christian mentality. The experiment will fail.

To say that the world is trying any kind of experiment appears, if not quite emotive, hardly accurate. More importantly, and perhaps more unfortunately, it removes a possible ground of diagnosis of our present evils which might be common to those who take a theological view of them and to those who do not. The real common ground would be the complaint that the world—whatever that may be, but let us assume it means all of the people including ourselves—is not yet in any condition to experiment with forming any kind of common mentality, if by that is meant making a conscious, agreed and co-ordinated effort to understand, and extend realistically within their natural limits, our powers and aims. The 'world', one may say, is not doing very much about forming even a civilized mentality, let alone something so specialized and apparently indefinable as a Christian one.

To interpret Eliot's statement as something other than the rather fraught and cryptic kind that abounds in his writing, we need to know what he means by a Christian mentality so that we can know what a non-Christian mentality excludes. I believe I have some idea what *I* mean by a Christian mentality (confining that for the moment to the aspects I not only recognize but applaud). That would even so be easier to define by what it is not than by what it is—it is characterized in my mind chiefly by a lack of false beliefs and claims about one's own importance, or perhaps by the continuing and maturing effort to discard those claims as they arise spontaneously. Insofar as we have ever been able to meet it in history, this maturity has not been exclusively Christian. Furthermore, and more significantly, it has never historically characterized a whole society or, as a mentality, even predominated.

Eliot's prophecy seems to be based less on diagnosis than on propaganda. The word 'propaganda' is used here not in the journalistic or popular acceptance of lying or false persuasion. It is *Propaganda Fide*—propaganda of the Faith. Eliot was a genuinely committed man, intellectually committed moreover. He believed that his theological and religious beliefs were true, and that would imply that like any other committed person he had not only the right but the duty to present them as powerfully and convincingly as possible. The claim to truth (if not verifiability) is frequent. For instance, in a reference to his conversion— perhaps we should say his registration of conversion, for it appears that he never deliberately left the Christian fold—he says, with more than an echo of Newman:

> The Christian thinker [this is in an essay on Pascal of 1931] proceeds by rejection and elimination. He finds the world to be so and so; he finds its character inexplicable by any non-religious theory; among religions he finds Christianity, and Catholic Christianity, to account most satisfactorily for the

world, and especially for the moral world within: and thus, by what Newman calls 'powerful and concurrent' reasons, he finds himself inexorably committed to the dogma of the Incarnation. To the unbeliever this method seems disingenuous and perverse: for the unbeliever is, as a rule, not so greatly troubled to explain the world to himself, nor so greatly distressed by its disorder: nor is he generally concerned (in modern terms) to 'preserve values'.

And again (from *The Idea of a Christian Society*, 1939):

To justify Christianity because it provides a foundation of morality instead of showing the necessity of Christian morality from the truth of Christianity, is a very dangerous inversion. . . . It is not enthusiasm but dogma that differentiates a Christian from a pagan society.

Elsewhere Eliot refers with approval to T. E. Hulme's *Speculations*, a book which strongly affected a number of writers as well as Eliot, after the end of World War I, and helped at least to confirm them in their belief in a theological Absolute, in the dogma of Original Sin, and in the radical imperfectibility of mankind—all of which amounted to a deliberate and professed anti-humanism. According to Hulme, it was 'the duty of every honest man to cleanse the world of these sloppy dregs of the Renaissance', meaning to cleanse it of all humanist and liberal philosophies, which all of necessity strive to be rational, reaching their conclusions and attempting to demonstrate the probability or the truth of these by reasonable and evidential argument. Approving Hulme ('Second Thoughts on Humanism', *Selected Essays*, 1932), Eliot quotes him in repudiation of any emotional foundation to Christian belief:

Most people [says Eliot] suppose that some people, because they enjoy the luxury of Christian sentiments . . . swallow or pretend to swallow incredible dogma. For some the process is exactly opposite.

And here comes the quotation from Hulme:

It is not then that I put up with the dogma for the sake of the sentiment but that I may possibly swallow the sentiment for the sake of the dogma.

It is worth noting that in the quotations just given, Eliot makes a kind of verbal opposition—between his own views and assumptions, on the one hand, and those he attributes to other or 'most' people—which we are justified in calling pre-selected or even projected. The assumption is that there is only one intellectual approach—that of Eliot and his fellow-believers and all the rest are emotional; the dogma, on the one hand, a hard intellectual statement free of any dregs of sloppiness and, on the other, attitudes variously named 'enthusiasm', 'sentiment' or some other term denoting subjective emotion. That is combined with a general attribution of social and moral deficiency to the host of unspecified non-believers—that they are in general 'not so greatly troubled to explain the world, nor so greatly distressed by its disorder'.

One need not dwell here on what, nevertheless, seems to be the self-righteous superciliousness of this proposition, because it also appears to be visibly false: with very little trouble we can all point to innumerable examples of unbelievers, both in the present and in history, who have been almost too greatly distressed by the state of the world and have almost fallen over themselves to try to do something about it. Jeremiads about Original Sin and radical imperfectibility more often indicate a thunderous disapproval than a humble distress.

But what is at present more important in these quotations is the method they illustrate. In an earlier study of Eliot, I said of his theological and anti-heretical commitments:

> Mr Eliot reminds me of a dignified landlady who without a word retrieves the tribal ornaments from the cupboard where the guest has hidden them, and puts them back upon the mantelpiece. (*The Emperor's Clothes,* London, 1953)

That is a flippant but still, to my mind, a fair description both of a singular mutation and its likely general effect. It was a reference to the lectures published as *After Strange Gods* where Eliot introduces us to his notions of orthodoxy and heresy. That book certainly could not but disquiet, and even shock, those of us who still obstinately believed that the liberal humanist tradition of free inquiry was not dead, but might even still be fruitful whether or not it was generally felt to constitute a moral demand. But the manner of the book appears to be a method too, and to embody a kind of teleology or even a tendentious orientation. The attitude is not merely passive—it is not a way of saying that the Defence (or the Prosecution) rests, and is waiting for the opposing case to be stated. It is on the contrary a pole-mical method of argument by not arguing or by refusing to argue. And one can trace its development throughout the rest of Eliot's critical and theoretical work. Here and elsewhere Eliot intimates that his differences with his contemporaries are so profound that controversy is useless—meaning that logical conversion of either side by the other is inconceivable. It is sufficient, he concludes, to state a point of view and 'leave it at that'.

This method develops into something we might almost call a 'negative way'. Again and again in these essays we meet an almost pedantically precise enumeration of all the topics he does *not* propose to take up, and of all the themes and ramifications he will not pursue. Over the years of work the cumulative effect of this process of elimination is almost comic. Nevertheless, it can also suggest evasiveness. For to many people the topics and arguments which are rejected, postponed or skirted appear pressingly relevant to the state of the world in which we live (a state which, as we saw, is a matter of distress to Eliot and to his fellow-believers) and to the topics which Eliot himself has chosen for discussion.

The method then is not only a way of stating a case; it is tele-ological, directed towards organizing a goal. I do not say that it is wrong of Eliot to state a point of view and 'leave it at that'. But we should be aware that the stated point of view is deeply and widely ramified and that it also has a direction and a goal—which he both defines and approaches by this method of exclusion.

It may well be argued that Eliot has been entirely open. He has taken a firmly committed stand on Christian theological dogma, which represents to him the touchstone of truth. One might say that he has stated his axioms and that within them his argument is coherent and demonstrative. But in that case there is not much room for anything but exegesis of what the Christian Fathers and other accredited theologians have said—a great deal admittedly—on esthetics and on morals, private and social. One must step down into the arena of ordinary logical dialogue or keep out of it.

If Eliot had chosen the first, or exegetical method, and stuck to it, we should all of us have arrived at a much clearer notion of what he means by orthodoxy and heresy, and also of the distinc-tion as it applies to literature—the main theme of *After Strange*

Gods where he advances the claim that Christian readers ought
to scrutinize all their reading by precise theological standards.

In 'Religion and Literature' (1934) Eliot writes:

> The 'greatness' of literature cannot be determined solely by
> literary standards; though we must remember that whether
> it is literature or not can be determined only by literary standards.

Admittedly Eliot does not deduce that writers too should be
subject to limitations of such fine precision, nor that orthodoxy
will help anyone to write better or even well, nor does he deny
that some heretics have performed very creditably; while in
Notes towards a Definition of Culture, a book primarily devoted to
establishing the unity or necessary association of religion and
culture, he even acknowledges

> that many of the most remarkable achievements of culture have
> been made since the sixteenth century in conditions of disunity;
> and that some . . . appear after the religious foundation for
> culture seems to have crumbled away. We cannot affirm that
> if the religious unity of Europe had continued, these or equally
> brilliant achievements would have been realized. Either
> religious unity or religious division may coincide with cultural
> efflorescence or cultural decay.

Nevertheless, categories of orthodoxy and heresy in literature
have been framed and must be filled. But to do this requires a
certain sleight of definition—orthodoxy becomes not merely or
even necessarily orthodoxy of religious belief, but an orthodox
Christian *sensibility*.

I have already questioned the assumption about a Christian
mentality, and the same doubts apply here. That James Joyce is
given as the only example of either this mentality or this sensibility may seem an odd or obscure choice on all counts. And we
might assume that Eliot is adopting the term 'sensibility' because
orthodoxy of theological belief is so clearly ruled out in Joyce's
case. But that in turn obscures the distinction Eliot himself has
made between the hard necessary intellectual structure, the
dogma, and the emotional and moral uses and advantages of
Christianity. Here we have one of Eliot's categories which for the
exposition of his beliefs should be essential, and he avoids or
finds difficulty in defining it. About 'heresy' on the other hand he
comes to a definition elsewhere—in *The Idea of a Christian Society*:

Heresy is often defined as an insistence upon one half of the truth; it can also be an attempt to simplify the truth by reducing it to the limits of our ordinary understanding, instead of enlarging our reason to the apprehension of truth.

That is not the ordinary definition or anything like it. The common definition of heresy is something like denying or countering established opinion, particularly religious or orthodox opinion. That boils down to being the opposite of orthodox or, in other words, resisting or trying to inquire into dogmatic belief. On its own ground and in disguise, Eliot's definition of heresy amounts to the same thing. It only has to be seen in the context of his assumptions about orthodoxy. Orthodoxy has pre-empted the entire truth. Obviously then we have to 'enlarge our reason'— Eliot's expression—which has been defined as capable only of dealing with half the truth, whichever that may be, until it is capable of moving into the other half—whatever *that* may be. In fact, if our reason—which is after all the only instrument we possess for inquiring into all the categories and concepts of the understanding—behaved in this odd and submissive fashion, it would lead us not into some kind of higher truth, but into some accepted convention of a body of believers, or into the opinion of some majority.

How precise, for orthodoxy, does a theological standard have to be? We may even ask: Who are the elect who determine it? (And how are they elected?) The preciseness, it could be thought, might be narrowly sectarian. Remember, for illustration, the 'Anglo-Catholic' of the famous manifesto of 1928. Older, maturer, more mellow perhaps, whether from conviction or from worldly success, the later Eliot somewhat widened the category of acceptable belief which, as it stood at the time of *For Lancelot Andrewes* (1928), may well have confused a wide and earnest audience of Christian readers.

It is not only our reading that requires to be scrutinized by theological standards. For elsewhere (in the Chicago lectures on education of 1950) where he sees, rightly I should say, that a true education must be an honest attempt to make a relevant response to a question that underlies all human being—'What is Man?'— Eliot assumes that this question is essentially a theological one.

That again seems to be primarily an example of the assumptive method which precludes discussion. I believe that even Eliot would hardly have denied that the question 'What is Man?'

invites and requires a great variety of answers, being a natural and spontaneous as well as a deliberate and formal response to our continued existence on this planet. It may come in some more or less recognizable shape from private and unprofessional persons and then, whatever verbal formulation it finds, it is often a cry of distress or bewilderment at an inevitably lonely confrontation with an inevitable human predicament. Or the question 'What is Man?' may be implied, often more complacently, in the intellectual pattern of inquiry of those who have chosen to look at the world in the frame of some particular discipline—philosophy, sociology, anthropology, psychology, biology. Each of these departmental studies, I believe, is likely to come up with a partial answer which, implicitly rather than overtly, but with some favouritism, it puts forward as if sufficient, exclusive and final. That does not mean that Plato or Bradley or Rousseau, or Marx or Keynes, Comte or Durkheim, Lévi-Strauss, or someone like Margaret Mead, Huxley or Waddington would, if challenged, deny that they had not reached and could not reach, an exhaustive definition—agreeing that Man had other essential characteristics which their definition could not cover. Nevertheless, they have to proceed by ignoring the majority of these characteristics, leaving them, hopefully perhaps, to one of the other studies or sciences—because they can achieve their own generalizations only by a process of abstraction from the whole welter of human existence and material.

It would however be a very fond hope that all the sciences of man could ever be totted up together so that we, their subject-matter, could ever receive a synoptic view, or even a glimpse, of our own nature, in its whole and real being and its phenomenal enactments. And we must remember that the sciences of man are seldom for long, if ever, in a happy state of internal agreement. Thus it seems that we need a supra- or inter-study, or philosophy, of man which is also a living and moving picture of men and women, and a mirror too to each one of us, of his individual self in its individual and common aspects.

I have little doubt that Eliot and those who are similarly persuaded would say that that is precisely the human function of theology—to show us ourselves in our essential nature; and also—because, as they believe, that nature has fallen away from the Divine which provides its only standard and hope of perfection—to account for the unsatisfactoriness and disillusion that wait on all secular projects for human understanding and improvement, including those of the human sciences.

But is it not the case that such a proposition is only acceptable if you already more or less accept it? For theology is just as or rather more abstract than any science and thus no richer in human content.

If we want a binding and intuitional scheme of human existence, we are more likely to find it in poetry, but also of course in religion before it can be imprisoned in institutions and theologies. I suggest that the content to which a theology refers, if we find it humanly persuasive, is always a purely naturalistic psychology which we can test in our daily practice of living. And for theology here understand all the other constructs I have mentioned where they go beyond hypothesis into speculation.

Eliot praised an idea of T. E. Hulme that there is an absolute discontinuity between two orders—each of which is knowledge or truth in its own sphere—the religious or theological on the one hand, the knowledge of physical nature on the other; a supernatural order opposed to a natural one. The knowledge of the truth of the supernatural order is revealed in theological dogma—that no doubt accounts for Eliot's unwillingness to enter into controversy. Over against this lies the zone of scientific and natural knowledge which is true as far as it goes but whose field is limited to the measurable or quantifiable. Hulme allowed for what he called a 'muddy mixed zone' in between, where what we should now call the 'sciences of life' are located. Supported by the fact that Hulme failed to notice that all his arguments were metaphoric, we might allow ourselves to call the middle zone a no-man's-land between the supernatural and the natural, except that a 'man's-land' would be more appropriate, because Hulme seems to see the zone of the vital as trampled over by hordes of humanists with their muddy boots as well as their muddy theories, their -ologies and their -isms, thus beating the bounds of human nature and mind which has already been pre-empted by theology. Hulme worked out a theory of time and mind based on Bergson which need not be discussed here. It was simply designed to rescue the human intellect and understanding from their dependence on experience and logic, which fortunately or unfortunately are still our best guarantee of arriving at realistic and testable results.

It must be noted that Hulme had great difficulty with the middle

zone of knowledge, relating to human mind when we consider
it in both its intellectual and moral aspects. His difficulty was no
less than that of Descartes, to which it was analogous. Having
split mind from body, Descartes had to resort to the oddest
expedients to account for the way the one operated through the
other, as it appeared to do. Similarly Hulme, having established
to his own satisfaction an absolute discontinuity between the
Divine and the human, each as defining realms of truth or knowledge, hardly succeeded in showing how the supernatural did or
could operate on our human nature or on man in the ordinary
naturalistic sense of the word.

Eliot, I think, took over the idea of discontinuity with all its
difficulties not only unresolved but unexamined, if not unnoticed
—although the last is difficult to swallow.

To put this another way, he wants to show that any natural
order which we think we can discover or make depends on a
supernatural order, if it is to have any meaning or value, if it is
indeed to be recognized as an order. Unfortunately he does not
know how the connection operates and, unlike Hulme, he does
not try to force, or even to find, an explanation. In his own terms
he may be allowed to regard this as a legitimate mystery, like
the Incarnation. But the idea of a supernatural order or a supernatural point of reference is implicit in his whole body of work,
both theoretical and poetic—not least in the plays. And here
there seems to be some deception, self-deception anyway, which
is not so legitimate. In all these works Eliot has really nothing
which intimates a distinct or personal intuition of the Divine
that one could respect or even accept on its own terms as one
accepts the religious vision of a Vaughan or a Herbert (though
not necessarily with any intellectual identification).

In the theoretical work he has nothing of theological content
to reveal, therefore he can convey no personal conviction nor
any argument that might convince *us* how institutional orthodoxy
can have any immediate bearing on our social or moral problems.
His own analysis of those problems, particularly the cultural and
educational, is often both acute and sound—but that is when his
psychological observation, of himself and others, is also acute and
sound. In other words, what we admire in him, when we do, is
naturalistic observation and awareness of some kinds of natural
order—a capacity in short which, in combination with other
qualities, makes him a good poet. But Eliot was much concerned

with order in itself; and here I think the concept of a supernatural order, or even an ideal order, which he always kept in mind if not in direct view, was misleading to himself and to us, and for himself in some degree stultifying. If you believe in an ideal order you can easily fail to discern that human and social impulse to the ordering of living which really exists, even if only tentatively, and here and there, or from time to time: and you may see total disorder where there is instead a necessary change to a new order. Moreover you may easily fail to see that there are new and formative concepts, even in the sciences, which if all men and women of good intellect and realistic moral sense would come to their aid, to their understanding and dissemination, might not miss their incarnation in human action, and might even socialize and civilize the human psyche.

Eliot's construction of order was both artificial and nostalgic. True, we can only distinguish the growth of new order, if at all, by looking at the past—that is when we have already grown beyond it. Nevertheless, that is no excuse for idealizing the past, for making custom-built specifications of order to fit our own necessarily restricted view, still less for pretending that they are organic or that they all command the same degree of common and verifiable agreement.

Let us look at the idea of order as it emerges first in the essay 'Tradition and the Individual Talent', which was a kind of early manifesto:

> We dwell with satisfaction upon the poet's difference from his predecessors . . . whereas if we approach him without this prejudice we shall often find that not only the best, but the most individual parts of his work may be those in which the dead poets, his ancestors, assert their immortality most vigorously.

Two others define or delimit the concept of tradition: 'Someone said,' writes Eliot, ' "The dead writers are remote from us because we *know* so much more than they did." Precisely, and they are that which we know,' he comments. The remaining quotation gives the essential structure of the idea:

> . . . what happens when a new work of art is created is something that happens simultaneously to all the works of art which preceded it. The existing monuments form an ideal order

among themselves, which is modified by the introduction of the new (the really new) work of art among them. The existing order is complete before the new work arrives; for order to persist after the supervention of novelty, the *whole* existing order must be, if ever so slightly, altered; and so the relations, proportions, values of each work of art toward the whole are readjusted; and this is conformity between the old and the new. Whoever has approved this idea of order, of the form of European, of English literature, will not find it preposterous that the past should be altered by the present as much as the present directed by the past.

I admit that I for one do find this preposterous, I suppose among other reasons because I find it difficult to admit or even to understand Eliot's idea of an ideal European order. It strikes me as a very mystical body. Or does Eliot mean that the new major and of course very learned poet provides us with a new way of looking at all poetry which at the same time reveals to us that his dead ancestors were doing something significantly different from what any of us thought before his time? I can see how it is possible for a tradition to expand thus critically or evolve in a forward direction while still retaining perhaps a preponderance of traditional elements, but I do not see how the novel stage can be retrospective any more than I can see how, by thinking about a chimpanzee or even training it, we can make it reveal human potentialities it did not already possess. Of course language, in the usage of poets, contains unexplored possibilities—otherwise the art of poetry would die. But as far as the poets, our dead ancestors, are concerned, we shall be more illuminated and illuminating if we study them in their own terms and times, and try to discover what they themselves thought they were doing, to communicate what they saw, felt, heard, smelt, in the language at their disposal. Otherwise we arrive at a curious Messianic attitude implying that they were somehow waiting for us to arrive in order to fulfil themselves: that would suggest that the moderns have some progressive advantage, a notion which Eliot would have been the first to reject. Has he not stated that 'Art does not progress'?

As a corpus of nourishment for the individual poet, Eliot's ideal order of tradition may appear highly artificial, or even arbitrarily selected. And it leaves him with some awkward cases to explain, not least important that of Shakespeare.

Some can absorb knowledge; the more tardy have to sweat for it. Shakespeare acquired more essential history from Plutarch than most men could from the whole British Museum.

But we must not confine our idea of knowledge to knowledge of the past, as in the context Eliot seems to do. Shakespeare had a great gift for absorbing all kinds of knowledge: look at the legal vocabulary which has, among other things, misled some Baconians. No doubt he had developed to an unusual degree what Robert Graves calls the poet's 'proleptic' or anticipatory instinct, the squirrel-like foreknowledge of what he will need to know and what is likely to come in handy. This often reveals a genuine spirit of prophecy: the poet, in need of some fact or information to lend verisimilitude to his composition, will often invent it, and then go and look it up in the encyclopedia where, as like as not, he will find that he had guessed right. I believed that this is not much exaggerated and that you can say the poet's mind continually and unreflectingly selects and cherishes forms and patterns, multi-dimensional words, metaphors which reveal the homologies of nature, concepts which suggest some hidden but inherent dialogue—all kinds of structures, especially if they have some dramatic value.

The essential faculty does not depend on commitment to any external authority or alien order of belief or concept. Most poets have done with the directly formative influence of their dead ancestors in youth. That may be a passionately exciting love-affair, and therefore somewhat haphazard. At the end of the affair, the poet has absorbed what he must, and also most of his other direct influences. He then goes on to write as well as he can and most probably to live in the world, whose influences will be much more powerful and immediate than any reading. He will also spend a lot of the leisure that remains from the BBC or the bank, in pubs and in the society of other poetic aspirants. That will produce for him a lot of new structures or ideologies which are not necessarily organic or even sensible, and which are certainly not rooted in any ideal order. It is arguable that they might be better if they were, better even for the poet. It is equally arguable that the poet might be better if he kept himself more to himself, neglecting movements, groups and influences, and continuing to hammer out his own vision.

I do not doubt that Eliot was following his own formula. We

might even say that his critical prescriptions express a workshop criticism, describing his own practice. Certainly in *The Waste Land*, and also in many of his later poems, his dead ancestors are notably present. We might almost dare to say that they constitute a Great Majority. *The Waste Land*, as we all know, is full of quotations in a way that was never implied of *Hamlet*. I admit that I do not know if quotations actually preponderate over original lines. But certainly re-reading the poem over the years I am always spotting a new one.

I enjoy *The Waste Land* very much indeed and I think that it is a brilliant poem. I prefer it to any whole poem or play that Eliot wrote. But I enjoy it, apart from its musical and rhythmic skill, which is considerable, rather as a poetic montage that is eclectic and arbitrary—like Eliot's tradition of ideal order. *The Waste Land* makes me wonder how much of a poetic ancestor Eliot himself will prove to be. For the selection of dead ancestors strikes me at least as inorganic and not likely to provide the kind of compost in which other poetic organisms can be nourished.

Insofar as it bears on the body of writing which, with all its variations, we recognize as 'poetry' or having a common poetic factor, Eliot's notion of a traditional ideal order shows at best that there are two kinds of poet, rather sharply distinct—those who learn their art chiefly from reading, and so from dead ancestors, and those who start from scratch and develop a native vision which may, and probably will, be modified by available literature (though not by literature as any 'body' or 'entity'). Some people might describe this opposition as that between the Classical and the Romantic. But that is too wide and too vague and it takes no account of the overlapping of the two kinds of poet, here of course classified into extreme cases.

We are talking about two kinds of poetic *mind*. The difference stands among other things for two kinds of tradition within English poetry, as Eliot was himself aware. He was also aware, regretfully, that one of these traditions had been lost or at least for long years mislaid.

Of this important matter he gives us I believe an insufficient explanation, even a misinterpretation. In 'Tradition and the Individual Talent', Eliot in effect describes the poet's mind as a kind of compression-instrument which fuses the most heterogeneous material into a new poetic unity; that associates, as he puts it elsewhere, 'Spinoza with the smell of the cooking'. I am not denying that this is a faculty which the poet may have developed in a very high degree, but it is not poetically definitive. It is universally characteristic of human mind, especially of the way we remember; we all know how a particular sensuous impression, most markedly a smell or a sound, will bring back a recollection of past experience, remote maybe, though often in sharp visual and auditory detail. Someone who develops as a poet has a heightened capacity for sensibility and hence a highly developed and accurate memory for his emotional and perceptual experiences, often reaching back into early childhood. But that is universal mind-stuff (though I should guess that the poet's mind has much more of it much more readily available), and to make use of it as a poet needs a special faculty. I do not take the view that poets are born, not made, though it might be true that a special intensity of this universal faculty is something one is born with or not; it is much more likely, I should say, that in someone who becomes a poet it persists relatively uncorrupted and unthwarted.

In one sense, nevertheless, a poet *is* made—as well—by his determined persistence in subjecting this basic or common material to the forms of perception and sensibility which his developing identity and mind oblige him to extract from his experience of living, and which becomes a personal vision, a whole individual way of seeing, This we can learn to recognize as authentic and peculiar.

I mean that the poetic capacity is a formal or structural one. It is the poet's special form of perception, not the material of sensibility, that counts; not merely the vividness of associational memory, as Eliot's illustration of Spinoza and the cooking implies. That there is no special poetical stuff in experience, and that the poem is a new unity, is admitted by Eliot but he does not tell us satisfactorily how this new unity comes about, what *is* the poet's instrument of compression. He simply says that up to the seventeenth century and the Metaphysical poets, feeling or emotion, and thought, were one; to the poet a thought was immediately a feeling, so that he could digest any kind of experience into poetry. All that is no doubt acceptable. But I think there is a point of greater significance which Eliot neglects. The poet's method is structural and therefore logical; it does not only work on arbitrary and private association. It is not that he can associate thought with feeling or sensation, or thought with emotion, in a peculiar union, that is most characteristic of a poet, but how he does it. What chiefly characterizes a poet's mind is that, maturing in complexity, it senses more quickly and subtly the analogies and homologies, and the rhythms and patterns which can be extracted from the living world around him and the personal life within him.

It is the poet's metaphoric capacity, then, that provides the instrument for compressing his mind-stuff, his heterogeneous associations, and which also provides the unity of the poem and the unity of the poet's lasting personal vision. The metaphors do not have to be startling or obtrusive; probably, as the poet matures, his metaphoric apperception, his awareness of the analogies (or likenesses of function) and of the homologies (the likenesses of structure and of concepts) in the phenomenal world around him, will move easily beneath the surface of a personal style and we may hardly be aware of them. (Under metaphor I include awareness of all contrasts and similarities of a structural kind, that may be expressed in contrasts of diction—for example, between intense simplicity and great complexity, or in balancing rhythms and kinds of musicality.)

I think that this is not irrelevant either to Eliot's own poetry or to his criticism. He wanted to fit the Metaphysical poets into the mainstream of English tradition. About this he was—respectfully of course—prepared to disagree even with Dr Johnson who admittedly thought they were an odd strain in English poetry but who did at least see that poetic wit was their characteristic method.

Eliot, I think, underestimated the importance of this witty faculty—which I have been identifying with the natural and fundamental poetic mode of metaphorical apperception. The poet uses it to find his own poetic logic, his own structure of knowledge which is both available and useful to him as a poet. That makes him the arbiter of his own peculiar vision, spontaneously selecting at the same time his own intellectual tradition.

That individualism is something Eliot cannot afford to allow. In the same essay on the Metaphysical poets he refers again to the poet's need for erudition, and even for some philosophical learning. But we must note that he never recommends the poet to be critical of ideas. Here, as on one or two other occasions, he asserts that poetically it does not matter if the poet believes or disbelieves the beliefs he has adopted, as long as they can be digested into the poetry—that will be truth enough; which amounts almost to saying that 'Beauty is truth, truth beauty'— something that Eliot would hardly have meant.

For although (in discussing philosophical poetry, as he does in his essays on Dante, on Shakespeare and Seneca, and on Blake)— he implies that it does not matter if either the poet or the reader believes or disbelieves the philosophy or the intellectual framework the poet uses in his poetry, I think it is improbable that Eliot took a purely esthetic view of truth or belief. And I would add that we should not fail to note that what in this respect was possible for Dante or Shakespeare, or what was possible for a contemporary reader, just is not possible nowadays. I would say that both Shakespeare and Dante believed their beliefs because, in their times, there was no very cogent reason for disbelieving them.

Behind Eliot's discussion of Dante's beliefs we can see looming once again the ideal order of tradition. It is interesting that he does not find it necessary or perhaps possible to tell us clearly *why* this essential poetic power of intellectual and emotional fusion was overlaid as it were, why it deserted, even for a time, the English tradition, though it is obvious throughout the rest of his work that he was trying to save a kind of Christian unity of knowledge, and that he had no quarrel with those later writers who have suggested that the failure of poetic nerve, if there was one, was caused by the tremendous impact of scientific thought and language on the seventeenth century, so that poets, like other people, became troubled about truth and the objective validity of their beliefs.

I think this may have happened, and might happen again. Nevertheless, poets very readily recover their natural and spontaneous unity of apperception and their confidence in its power of revealing a natural structuring in the observable world which convinces us as a way of seeing, and introduces us to a new reality of vision. Poets, whatever else they are doing *ex officio*, are trying in their very language, natural and developing, to treat the many forms of schizophrenia from which we suffer in the human world, not least today. Not of course deliberately or even consciously, or with any therapeutic or moral intention. It is something more complex, but it is really no stranger or more arguable than our ordinary acts of physical vision which we accept as giving us a common world. Unlike both scientific and theological cosmologies, that common vision is not subject to proof or to falsification, but works by a kind of revelation—we reveal by our tacit behaviour and by our involuntary acts that we accept it as common.

All that amounts to saying that it is the poetry, indeed the poet, that forms the tradition, and not the other way about.

But that poetry, however the habit is acquired or learnt, is the holistic activity of a peculiar kind of mind or person is something that people find very hard to admit. People, especially those who seldom or never read the actual stuff, are always trying to fit the poet into their preferred ideologies and dogmas. From Plato to Hobbes, philosophers of various abstract persuasions have been trying thus to incorporate him, or to admonish or reject him, on the ground that what they believe to be fact is somehow morally superior to what they call his fictions.

However high we may rank him as a practitioner, Eliot's main structure of ideas—the theory of a traditional and objective ideal order—can be seen as similarly Procrustean towards poets. Not the least important reason is that the 'ideal order', as Eliot's later work substantiates, must be seen as in continuity with a supernatural and theological order.

Theoretically at least, Eliot recognized that this continuity has to be made by the poem—it can't be done by any artificial join with whatever may be the intellectual scheme of reference. We can say that Dante's *Paradiso* in large part made his theological and supernatural framework poetically real—the fusion had taken place. But that is a supreme and therefore unlikely achievement. And to confound two orders, the supernatural or the theological with the natural, or to obtrude the supernatural, with its implied priority, upon the poetic, hardly seems legitimate art, nor is it likely to be successful in manifesting that unity of sensibility by which Eliot sets so much store; while the attempt may discriminate against natural and human sympathies in a way that may be dangerous for a poet.

Eliot in One Poet's Life

Donald Davie

What I have to say may sound egotistical and self-regarding. And so I owe it to myself to say at the start that these were the terms of the assignment I was given—I was to be personal, almost confessional. And it's no good pretending that I find this unpleasant. On the contrary, I feel a happy gratitude to the University of York for inviting me to come here unequivocally as a man who has written poems, very much on holiday from my avocations as critic and journalist and teacher.

One reason for having such avocations, or at least for pursuing them as strenuously as I do, is to keep a man so busy that he needn't at all often pause to make sense of himself and of his life so far as he has lived it. For that sort of taking stock is inevitably, in the very nature of the case, depressing or deflating. Thinking about what I was to say today has compelled me to this sort of salutary exercise, and if it has been a little lowering to the spirits, it could have been much worse. In fact I found it much less depressing than surprising: once I bent my mind to the question of T. S. Eliot in my life, I was very surprised.

The surprise was that I discovered, as soon as I thought about it, that the late Mr Eliot has been a presence in my life more insistently influential than any other writer whatever. There is no doubt of this; and yet I recognized it with astonishment. Without being conscious of doing so, I had got into the habit of regarding him as just one of the larger-than-life effigies which are disposed, as inspiring or minatory presences, in the vaguely apprehended landscape of my imaginative world. But it isn't so, I realize; more than Shakespeare or Samuel Johnson, more than Pasternak or Wordsworth or whoever else, it is Eliot who presides densely over my sense of myself, and not just my sense of myself as writer.

To begin with, his effigy has stood there longer than any other.

It has been there ever since I was a schoolboy. This does not mean, alas, that as a pupil of Barnsley Grammar School I discovered Eliot's poetry for myself, still less (what would be more extraordinary and interesting) that I discovered the whole of English poetry through first responding to Eliot's. No, I discovered English poetry through Walter de la Mare—a far more likely way of discovering it, and not a bad way either. And if *The Waste Land* and *Prufrock* were already known to me by 1938, when I was sixteen, it was because alert and ambitious schoolmasters had pressed them upon me. And I was a very ambitious schoolboy, in those days when British education was more élitist and competitive than it is today. So I responded very readily to Eliot's early poems, in the terms in which my schoolmasters presented them to me—that is to say, as commando obstacle-courses which one was not expected to complete, only to fail at more or less creditably. And I have to confess that even today *The Waste Land* as a whole lives in my mind in rather this way—as a famous challenge and ordeal, a sphinx's riddle; which is to say, not (strictly speaking) as a poem at all. Now that the publication of the famous drafts of this poem has made it a focus of argument once again, I see others confessing in print that it is a sphinx's riddle to them too, and often enough they complain of Eliot, or of Eliot and Pound together, for having made a frustrating tease out of what should have been complete and satisfying. This may well be right. On the other hand it may be that what seems unsatisfying about *The Waste Land* is nothing intrinsic to the poem, but has to do with the poem's reputation, with how that reputation was first made and has been sustained ever since, in large part as an excitingly advanced exercise for the Modern Sixth. (I do not need to spell out the implications of this for teachers of literature, for their pupils, and for those who construct the syllabus for an examination or the curriculum of a course—to put modern or near-contemporary books on the syllabus is not always proof of enlightenment, and it may harm the authors that it means to help.)

Thus the Eliot who stood in effigy in the landscape of my young mind was not the author of *The Waste Land*, of 'Gerontion', of *Ash-Wednesday*. At some point (I think after I left Barnsley for Cambridge) the look in the eyes of the statue changed a little, and he became the author of 'Marina'. For that is the first poem of Eliot's that I discovered as it were for myself, and so I cherished it, as I cherish it still. But originally the effigy was not of Eliot the poet, but of Eliot the author of those influential essays, 'The Metaphysical Poets', 'Andrew Marvell', and 'Homage to John Dryden'. I don't like to confess this, but I fear there is no doubt of it. The proof is in the poems of mine, all long ago destroyed, which I was writing in the 1940s, when I had joined the Royal Navy after a year at Cambridge. For those poems, as I distastefully recall them, had nothing to do with Eliot's practice as a poet, but had everything to do with what he was taken to have recommended in theory. Had he not re-established connections for us with the seventeenth-century poets of strenuous wit—with Donne and Herbert and Marvell? And so the poems that I wrote at that time were painstakingly structured on the extended comparisons and the farfetched hyperbolical conceits of John Donne's 'The Good-morrow' or Marvell's 'To his Coy Mistress'. Nor was I alone, I think—as late as 1954, when Thom Gunn published his first collection, *Fighting Terms*, we could see a serious and ambitious poet still strenuously acting the part (brought up to date of course) of mad Jack Donne, the libertine of the Elizabethan stews and lawcourts.

I want to dwell on this, even though it takes us further still from what Eliot wrote as a poet, to what he wrote (or was thought to have written) as a critic. I should like to be helpful if I can, and it may be there are still young writers who can be sidetracked for years, as I was, into thinking that the seventeenth century (or the eighteenth, the sixteenth, the fourteenth) is immediately accessible to us if only we will exert ourselves. Accessible, I mean, *creatively*. For that delusion was what had me balked and at a standstill, in my own writing, through most of the 1940s. I thought that since John Donne had a valuably unified sensibility (to use the jargonish phrase that Eliot was embarrassed by later on)—since I was told that, and I was persuaded, and could see it for myself—a sort of duty was laid upon me to regain it in my poems, and help others to regain it. If any one had murmured that a lot of water had flowed under the bridge since the deaths of John Donne and George Herbert, I should have known how to reply. For that turbid water which had flowed by was 'Romanticism', and I knew that duty required me to have no truck with *that*! 'Romantic' was for me and my friends the ugliest imputation that could be thrown at any one or anything, a sentence of death from which there was no appeal. There is a well-written early poem by Kingsley Amis, called 'Against Romanticism', which catches the note very accurately. And yet why should I treat such nonsense as a thing of the past? For I notice that in the mouths of my students today 'Romantic' seems to mean just what it meant in our mouths thirty years ago. And if this is so, there is the more reason for me to say this: that what liberated me into writing to some purpose was the sudden realization that what we call 'the Romantic movement' was not a fad or a fashion or an aberration, but something which happened to the mind of Europe and the Americas about the end of the last century, and that what happened was—like it or lump it— irreversible. We are not called upon to approve or disapprove; one does not approve or disapprove of a landslide, one notes that it has happened and begins to try putting life together in the new landscape which it has created. Just thus, as a drastic breach or geological fault, does Romanticism exist in the cultural past of each one of us. We are all post-Romantic people; there are no exceptions or exemptions. And in particular no one can climb back into some lost garden of the seventeenth or eighteenth centuries except by crossing that fault-line, and arriving permanently travel-stained from the long trek. Which means, I take it, that no twentieth-century poem that is worth anything will be structured like a poem of John Donne's.

And no poem by T. S. Eliot is thus structured. But as I've explained, my friends and I in the 1940s weren't looking at the poems but at the criticism. And Eliot the critic had declared himself 'a Classicist'. Not altogether foolishly, we took that to mean that we not only could but *should* pretend that the nineteenth century had never happened; that it could be erased from the historical record by a sheer act of will; and that it could somehow be by-passed as we threaded our way back to Boileau or Pope, to Shakespeare or Donne, ultimately to Dante. This was a damaging delusion that we laboured under, and I owe Eliot a grudge for having, more than any one else, foisted it upon us.

You may recall that at the same time as he declared himself a Classicist (he wasn't of course—it was just a coat-trailing manoeuvre), Eliot announced that he was Royalist in politics and Anglo-Catholic in religion. And you may wonder that we were not offended and alienated by this provocative espousal of positions that were unblushingly conservative, if not indeed reactionary. But I would ask you to remember rather precisely the generation that I belong to. I was seventeen in the year of the Molotov–Ribbentrop pact, when Hitler's Germany and Stalin's Russia agreed to carve up Poland between them. A year later, when I went to Cambridge, there was still in Rose Crescent the Left Bookshop to remind me that this was the university from which John Cornford and Julian Bell had gone to die in Spain. But that bookshop did not survive for long; current affairs, and the news of the war, as we heard them over the radio, belied all too evidently the utopianism of the Left. And this was the time too when Orwell and Koestler and others began to reveal the duplicity of Russian policies and promises in Spain and elsewhere. The break between the generations was very sharp; for men and women who had gone up to university only eighteen months before me had had that much time to invest something in the ideology of the Popular Front, and to this day that investment (as I know, for I am speaking of my closest friends) makes them wryly suspicious and resentful of Eliot as a thinker about society and as a force in politics. I had no such difficulties; for me, growing up when I did, Eliot's pessimistic conservatism seemed tough-minded and straight-talking, a bleak but welcome wind to sweep away the tergiversations, the sentimental contradictions and self-deceptions of what Auden called 'a low dishonest decade'. And just as for my Leftist friends a couple of years older than me, so I must suppose that for me too this experience was definitive; and sure enough, even today I am more readily exasperated by the sentimentalities of the Left than of the Right. No doubt my growing up as a petty bourgeois in the overwhelmingly proletarian society of Barnsley had already inoculated me against the rhetoric of the Left. (Had I not myself collected signatures for the Peace Pledge Union? Yes, I had.) Still, I was glad to be emboldened by having a figure like Eliot, widely revered on other counts, asserting in British politics what looked like a plausible alternative.

(I make no excuse for touching on politics thus explicitly: so far as I can see, every estimate of Eliot that is offered today in Britain is politically tendentious, consciously or not; and I do not except my own estimate. I shall suggest later on how Eliot's stock began to fall when the climate of opinion changed once again. Eliot would not have expected anything else; one of the strengths of his tough-minded criticism is that he never supposes æsthetic judgements are passed in a political or religious vacuum.)

And now I have reached at last the poet, rather than the brilliantly evasive critic or the opinion-maker and trend-setter. I have reached the *Four Quartets*, poems of a nation at war; and poems which I, myself at war (I remember reading them in Arctic Russia), discovered for myself and savoured for myself, without the dubious mediation of commentators, pedagogues, exegetes. I leave aside 'Burnt Norton', the first of the Quartets, because it was written and published before the war began. For that matter I find I don't know just when 'East Coker' and the others were composed, if indeed that information is available. Never mind: the poems appeared in the years of the war and were surely read by others as well as me, as war poems. I suppose it would still be a bold anthologist who would represent Eliot as a poet of the Second World War, along with Drummond Allison and John Pudney and Alun Lewis; and if Eliot were to be represented in such an anthology, it would have to be by 'Little Gidding', the last and without doubt the most consistently splendid of the Quartets, which includes not only the famous Dantesque imitation set in London at dawn after a bombing-raid, but also—

> There are other places
> Which also are the world's end, some at the sea jaws,
> Or over a dark lake, in a desert or a city—
> But this is the nearest, in place and time,
> Now and in England.

Equally, however, when I read in 'East Coker',

> And so each venture
> Is a new beginning, a raid on the inarticulate
> With shabby equipment always deteriorating
> In the general mess of imprecision of feeling,
> Undisciplined squads of emotion. . . .

I reflect that 'raid' and 'equipment' and 'squads' are words of wartime, perhaps of that particular wartime, 1939–45. And even in 'The Dry Salvages', the least satisfactory of the Quartets and the most American, there is the crackling vividness of the concluding section:

> To communicate with Mars, converse with spirits,
> To report the behaviour of the sea monster,
> Describe the horoscope, haruspicate or scry,
> Observe disease in signatures, evoke
> Biography from the wrinkles of the palm

And tragedy from fingers; release omens
By sortilege, or tea leaves, riddle the inevitable
With playing cards, fiddle with pentagrams
Or barbituric acids, or dissect
The recurrent image into pre-conscious terrors—
To explore the womb, or tomb, or dreams; all these are usual
Pastimes and drugs, and features of the press:
And always will be, some of them especially
When there is distress of nations and perplexity
Whether on the shores of Asia, or in the Edgware Road. . . .

where that juxtaposition of Asia with the Edgware Road, so
oddly but effectively formal in its phrasing, I identify as once
again a sentiment of wartime.

This passage begins with a dozen lines of rapid and yet languid
catalogue, such as may remind us of Auden at his best—consider
the inventiveness, at once lexical and phonetic, of the sequence
'horoscope, haruspicate or scry'. But it modulates from this
into something very different, a style of flat asseveration which
confidently takes the risk of being flat in a different, more damaging sense:

> all these are usual
> Pastimes and drugs, and features of the press:
> And always will be. . . .

This bleakness and explicitness, this daring to seem pedestrian,
is a note which Auden at that time had always fought shy of.
And I do not mean to inflame an old resentment when I suggest
that Auden, if he ever wanted to strike this note, forfeited the
chance of doing so when he left England in the year the war
started. However that may be, in the *Four Quartets* it is everywhere, this passionate explicitness:

> We are only undeceived
> Of that which, deceiving, could no longer harm.
> In the middle, not only in the middle of the way
> But all the way, in a dark wood, in a bramble,
> On the edge of a grimpen, where is no secure foothold,
> And menaced by monsters, fancy lights,
> Risking enchantment. Do not let me hear
> Of the wisdom of old men, but rather of their folly,
> Their fear of fear and frenzy, their fear of possession,
> Of belonging to another, or to others, or to God.

Here the blankly rhetorical explicitness of 'Do not let me hear' is worked up to through lines in which the language is more exuberant, for instance in the daring juxtaposition of the nonce-word, 'a grimpen', with the impatiently thrown away 'fancy lights'. And this is just the same progress as when 'all these are usual' was worked up to through 'haruspicate or scry' and similar inventions. It is my firm impression, which there is however no way of proving, that this explicitness was possible only for a poet who conceived himself to be speaking for his adopted nation when that nation was united in desperation and resolve.

I am aware that it is precisely this tone which some readers of *Four Quartets* find insupportable. They call it 'pontificating', and so it is; I can only record that when the poems first came out I was ready to accept Eliot as my *pontifex*, and thought that he had earned the right to that office. I think the same now.

It is in any case astonishing that the poet of *The Waste Land* or of *Coriolan*, a poet so enamoured of baffling obliquities and discontinuities, should have developed to a point where some readers can complain that he isn't oblique *enough*. In this respect the contrast between early and late Eliot is so startling that critics, myself among them, have been at pains to show that the Quartets do not represent a radically new departure for the poet. On the contrary the poems advertise by their very title, as well as by repeated excursions to Mallarmé, that they belong to the same endeavour as had engaged Eliot from the first, the endeavour to find, or make, analogues in English for the achievements and procedures of the French symbolist poets, vowed to making poetry approach the condition of music. This is certainly true; and the delay in recognizing Eliot's French affinities is woeful evidence of the Englishman's stubborn and self-congratulating insularity. All the same, although the structure of *Four Quartets* both severally and as a whole is in this way musical, non-discursive (so that they are not for instance treatises of Christian apologetics or mystical theology), what must strike us is that over long stretches—sometimes throughout one entire 'movement' of a Quartet—the writing *is* very markedly explicit and discursive. If it were not so, we should not hear the poems objected to as 'didactic' or 'pontificating'. And when I began to think of my own writing in relation to the Quartets, it was this aspect of their style which I found most arresting and most profitable. They seemed to show that poetry could be explicit, that it could work by statement and bare asseveration as well as through implications and overtones. It could do so if the writer was alert to the metaphors buried in the etymology of abstract words, and to the articulate beauty of sustained and elaborately correct syntax. Not before time, this liberated me very fruitfully from a bundle of notions I had picked up somewhere to the effect that poetry could and should convey meaning only through overt metaphor and what in those days we called 'image-clusters'.

But it was still impossible for me to draw directly on Eliot as a model. At the end of the 1940s I was still a ventriloquist's doll, squeaking out poems which Eliot of the Quartets had put in my mouth just as some years before others had been put there by the ghost of Donne. And I don't believe this was inevitable, or due simply to my obtuseness; what prevents the Quartets from being a *directly* fruitful influence on me or any poet is the laxity of their rhythms, at best no more than adequate. It still seems to me that their prosody is profoundly uninteresting—the accentual line that Eliot mostly uses is too capacious to create cadences that are sharp and distinct. And so, before I could profit from what the Quartets had to teach me about diction, I had to go to other masters to learn about versification.

However, rather than pursue these technicalities, we ought to dwell on how astonishing it was for Eliot to have achieved in England the unquestioned pre-eminence that he had for all of us in the 1940s. How did it come about that a reticent and elegantly evasive, over-educated American came to occupy this position, and to go on to an Order of Merit and a tomb in Westminster Abbey? Hugh Kenner has ventured an answer to this by pressing hard on Pound's nickname for Eliot, 'the possum'. Eliot got where he did, so Kenner suggests, by 'playing possum', by lying low and shamming dead. As a foreigner moving in English life, Eliot's great talent was for protective colouration; and Kenner, both entertainingly and justly, shows for instance how Eliot evolved for his criticism a prose style of just the decorous anonymity proper to *The Athenæum* and *The Times Literary Supplement* in the 1920s. A similar talent for the inconspicuously acceptable tone may have been what recommended him in the circles of 'Bloomsbury'. And so it may be thought that when he joined the Church of England (in a discreetly well-publicized conversion), this patiently adroit interloper from St Louis,

Missouri, had penetrated by these methods to the very arcanum of the English Establishment. But of course this is to misunderstand the status of the Established Church in England. If we can speak of a literary and intellectual 'Establishment' in this country, the Church of England is not the ark of its covenant—quite the contrary; to the Bloomsbury of the 1920s, as to the opinion-makers of every decade since, a profession of Christianity was very un-smart indeed. And if one has to become Christian, let it be theatrically Papist or eccentrically Calvinist Christianity, not at all events in that Church which has been called 'the Tory party at prayer'. From the standpoint of the literary intelligentsia, Eliot's churchmanship was not a penetration into the holy of holies but on the contrary a voluntary departure into the wilderness—as Eliot himself recognized, in one of the most vivacious of his prose polemics, 'Thoughts after Lambeth'.

Thus it will not do to envisage a wily American serpent worming his way into our trusting or mistrustful bosoms. The facts won't fit this fable. But it won't do in any case. For it rests upon the complacent assumption that London must be the metropolis towards which any ambitious American artist will naturally gravitate. Why should Eliot, however serpentine, have sought an English bosom in any case? I began to ask myself this question when, in the 1950s, my conscious concerns turned to Ezra Pound. For Pound, about 1920 when his association with Eliot was at its closest, quite consciously repudiated England as a milieu in which concertedly creative practice of the arts could be carried on. He went to Paris, and then to Italy; and of course in the 1920s it was pre-eminently Paris, not London, where the American expatriates foregathered, to be joined there by English expatriates like Ford Madox Ford. It has been plausibly argued that American poetry, perhaps American literature in general, came brilliantly to maturity in this century only when American writers broke the ties of ex-colonial dependence which had bound them to London, and betook themselves instead to Paris or Vienna or Rapallo. From this point of view Eliot's determination through the 1920s and 1930s to bed himself ever more deeply in English life is anomalous, and was seen to be so by Pound. And when we consider the English-born poets who in the same decades were finding England sterile and sterilizing—one thinks of D. H. Lawrence, of Robert Graves, ultimately of Auden—we might from time to time feel a sort of sneaking gratitude to Eliot for sticking with us, as it were. Instead, I'm afraid we put the meanest possible construction on his fidelity, and we call him an Anglophile snob.

Early in the 1950s I imposed a self-denying ordinace on myself, and quite deliberately read no verse by Eliot at all over a period of several years—all in a drastic attempt to root out of my own style the Eliotic cadences which were making it not mine at all. In any case by this time I was in Dublin, where the master-ventriloquist was, as you might expect, not Eliot but Yeats; where Tom Kinsella for instance, that gifted and admirably serious poet, was trying to get out of range of that organ-voice as I was fighting free of Eliot's.

When I returned to England in 1958, I found a changed climate of opinion and feeling. The younger intellectuals were turning Left once more, taking up the vaguely populist attitudes which I had been glad to see discredited at the end of the 1930s. And so the tide of sentiment had turned against Eliot once more. There was a difference however. Leftist sentiment of the 1930s, as one may see it in the Auden of those years or as surviving to the present day in Geoffrey Grigson, voiced its distrust of Eliot in overtly political terms, thinking of him for instance as the English Paul Claudel. In the 1950s and 1960s, however, this political animus against him was very often disguised behind what seemed to be a more general indictment, levelled on behalf of a guileless preference for generosity of temperament, magnanimity, for being 'on the side of life'. Eliot's attitudes, it was said, were constricted, mean-spirited; he seemed not to like people very much, in particular he showed no disposition to celebrate a joyous sexuality.

I could, as I still can, see what people meant when they said this kind of thing—though it so happened that the generously impulsive and foolhardy poet whom I would set up against Eliot was Ezra Pound, rather than D. H. Lawrence. It was, and is, a real dilemma. One would like to love where one is compelled to praise; and Eliot is the least lovable of poets. What makes the nerves tingle and the mind assent, should warm the heart; and in Eliot's case it doesn't. We respect, we admire, we do not love. A pity. And yet there is no rule which says that a great poet has to be likeable. Wordsworth strikes most of us as an unlikeable man, yet a very great poet indeed. What's more, the one may be the condition of the other; without the stiff-necked self-compla-cency that repels us in Wordsworth, he could never have persisted

in the face of the obloquy and ridicule which he ran into initially.
And in the same way the self-possession and bleak self-control
which exhale a chill from Eliot's pages are the condition of his
rare and fastidious accomplishment.

Moreover, when we reproach Eliot or Eliot's shade with
being too guarded towards experience, not generous enough,
he has anticipated us—in lines I have quoted already:

> Do not let me hear
> Of the wisdom of old men, but rather of their folly,
> Their fear of fear and frenzy, their fear of possession,
> Of belonging to another, or to others, or to God.

If one of the old men that Eliot here castigates is the old man
that he saw himself becoming, that surely makes the lines all
the more poignant and admirable and compelling. For fear of
being possessed, fear of belonging to another, is just what we
accuse Eliot of, when we compare him to his disparagement with
incautious writers like Lawrence or Pound. And so this passage
may well be self-accusing. But if it is, people will still resist
giving him credit for it, because of the sorts of 'belonging' that
he specifies:

> Of belonging to another, or to others, or to God.

That 'or to God' outrages our militantly secular culture, as of
course Eliot intended that it should. We want to believe, it seems
we obscurely *need* to believe, that belonging to God precludes
belonging to another or to others. And Eliot won't have that,
any more than the Scriptures will.

I have got to a point where I am speaking no longer of Eliot's
churchmanship, but of his faith, his Christian beliefs. And
although it is high time I got back on the wavelength of personal
testimony, this is the most awkward point at which to do so.
And in fact I must duck the challenge; for bearing witness to
one's religious experience and apprehensions is an exercise in
rhetorical candour which calls for skills I don't have. I will say
only this: that whereas through most of the years when I have
been reading Eliot I would not have professed myself a practising
and believing Christian, yet on the other hand I have never
shared nor understood the animus against Christianity as a
hypocritical cheat, which I find so common, so all but universal,
among my friends and contemporaries. As I try to understand

this, I think again of that one poem of early or middle Eliot which
I have said that I came across and responded to as a very young
man. This is the 'Ariel' poem, 'Marina'. And someone—I think
it may have been the late lamented friend of my youth, Douglas
Brown—provided me with the minimal orientation that I needed,
by saying that this poem presents allegorically or in symbol the
movement towards conversion of a man not yet converted, who
does not know what conversion will mean, who yet knows that
he is being impelled towards it:

>   What seas what shores what grey rocks and what islands
> What water lapping the bow
> And scent of pine and the woodthrush singing through the fog
> What images return
> O my daughter.
>
>   Those who sharpen the tooth of the dog, meaning
> Death
> Those who glitter with the glory of the hummingbird, meaning
> Death
> Those who sit in the sty of contentment, meaning
> Death
> Those who suffer the ecstasy of the animals, meaning
> Death
>
>   Are become unsubstantial, reduced by a wind,
> A breath of pine, and the woodsong fog
> By this grace dissolved in place
>
>   What is this face, less clear and clearer
> The pulse in the arm, less strong and stronger—
> Given or lent? more distant than stars and nearer than the eye
>
>   Whispers and small laughter between leaves and
>   hurrying feet
> Under sleep, where all the waters meet.
>
>   Bowsprit cracked with ice and paint cracked with heat.
> I made this, I have forgotten
> And remember.
> The rigging weak and the canvas rotten
> Between one June and another September.
> Made this unknowing, half conscious, unknown, my own.
> The garboard strake leaks, the seams need caulking.
> This form, this face, this life
> Living to live in a world of time beyond me; let me

Resign my life for this life, my speech for that unspoken,
The awakened, lips parted, the hope, the new ships.

What seas what shores what granite islands towards
    my timbers
And woodthrush calling through the fog
My daughter.

I shall never write like this. I don't mean I shall never write as
well as this, but I shall never write *like* this, in this symbolist
manner. (I know, for I have tried and disliked the outcome.)
What does seem quite clear, however, is that this way of writing—
in the Quartets as in 'Marina'—enables the poet's sensibility to
meet with his reader's at a level far below whatever dogmas may
be consciously espoused by either one of them. Why, the conversion spoken of here isn't even a specifically *Christian* conversion!
And so I can say, out of my own experience, that Eliot's piety
is not just no more of a stumbling-block than is George Herbert's,
it is infinitely *less* of a stumbling-block. And yet, for as long as
I can remember, agnostic readers have been explaining how they
can enjoy and participate in the devout poetry of George Herbert
while still rejecting all the objects of Herbert's devotions. The
latest I have come across is Geoffrey Grigson, in a book published
four years ago:[1]

> Why can I accept the Christianity of George Herbert—though
> 'accept' may beg the question—and not the Christianity of
> Eliot or Auden, or Claudel, or any television apologist?
>   Because Herbert had no option. He had no possible, no
> sensible alternative. It was his inevitable mode of evaluation.

Grigson's honesty is something to be grateful for. He says quite
plainly that what affronts him in Eliot and Auden is not what
they choose to believe, but what they choose to disbelieve—the
sectarian alternatives to Christianity such as are in our enlightened
age so abundantly on offer. What he cannot stomach is the poets'
refusal to buy any of these goods. What outrages him is not their
credulity but their scepticism. And on the other side of the
Atlantic Helen Vendler concurs,[2] speaking of 'the religiosity
of the *Four Quartets*', and asking rhetorically, 'Is nervousness
cured by ethics? Can "the heap of broken images" be put together

---

[1] Geoffrey Grigson, *Notes from an Odd Country* (London, 1970). 192.
[2] *The New York Times Book Review* (7 November 1971).

again, like Humpty-Dumpty, by a heap of moral injunctions?'
Well, we may reply, Dr Johnson thought so. And what is Mrs
Vendler's alternative? Psychotherapy? As for me I will plead
guilty to being too ready to believe in the bankruptcy of the
secular alternatives. I want to believe, and have always wanted to
believe, that psychotherapy mostly wouldn't work. And so I have
always been ready, doubtless *too* ready, to be persuaded by Eliot
that psychologists and other social engineers are 'Those who
sharpen the tooth of the dog'.

So far as I can understand my motives they have to do with
believing in the right to personal privacy, and the respectability
of reticence. When I was still a boy I remember I read with a
spasm of delighted assent an angry letter from Joseph Conrad in
which he repudiated an invitation to let his hair down in public,
saying proudly that if he could help it no one should see 'Conrad
en pantoufles', Conrad in carpet-slippers. And this was quite
plainly Eliot's attitude also; some of the chill that rises from his
pages is the proper and bracing chill of a man who says, 'Keep
your distance. I have a right to a private life, even if I *am* a
writer.' The doctrine of impersonality in art which Eliot promul-
gated in a famous and influential and sadly muddled essay (he
seems to have meant to say not that art is impersonal but that it
de-personalizes), is plainly a product of the same justified *hauteur*
as Conrad's angry letter. And consider the success with which
Eliot maintained an ironclad reticence about the first Mrs Eliot.
Eliot's tone is never intimate; he invites no intimacies and allows
of none, and this is where he and Lawrence are poles apart. In a
time like ours when 'personalities' are fabricated and peddled
daily, when in many quarters poetry is thought to be undressing
in public, when as we probe for sincerity in our artists we demand
the right to follow them into their bedrooms and bathrooms
and onto the analyst's couch, it is no wonder if Eliot affronts us.

And yet democracy, as it used to be understood in this country
perhaps more than in any other, consisted precisely in the right
of the householder to slam his door in the face of the Nosey
Parker, to tear up the questionnaire and put it in the wastepaper
basket, the right *not* to join the Union or the Club if he didn't
want to, and the right *not* to send his child to the school that a
bureaucrat had decided for him. In that perhaps obsolete sense of
democracy Eliot was a democrat. And I am prepared to wonder
whether it wasn't this quality in English life which made this

American prefer it to America. These are homespun speculations; but they seem to be called for, now that on all sides heads are angrily or regretfully shaken over his allegedly reactionary politics—which were, incidentally, by any objective measure, much less reactionary than Yeats's, though Yeats's are excused where Eliot's are not.

Let me try once more, for my own satisfaction, to justify my sense that Eliot has meant more to me than any other writer. It has everything to do with when I grew up. If I had been eighteen in 1920, with my heart set on some day writing memorable poems, my master would have been—would have had to be—Thomas Hardy. If I could have overcome my diffidence I would have made the pilgrimage to Max Gate, as Robert Graves did and Siegfried Sassoon and Edmund Blunden. In 1940 on the other hand, or in 1945, I would not have dreamed of penetrating to see Mr Eliot in Russell Square, and would doubtless have got a frosty or at least constrained reception, if I had. *There* is the difference. For Hardy I feel much more affection than for Eliot, but infinitely less professional respect. And the proof of the pudding is in the eating; of the poets who took Hardy for their model, as the accredited master-poet when they grew up, the ones who achieved most were those, like Lawrence and Graves, who departed furthest from Hardy's procedures and precedents. Eliot in the 1940s, precisely because the only possible relationship one could have with him was austerely professional, could be a master in the strict sense, as twenty years before Hardy could not be. If in the end I had to go elsewhere to learn versification and lyric structure (I went first to Robert Graves, and I am glad of the chance to acknowledge it), diction was what l learned from the Eliot of the Quartets. They were my model then; they are my model now. And diction is not just one aspect of poetry among others; it is the very stuff that one works with, the medium itself, language under poetic conditions. Eliot's professionalism—in the end that is what I am most grateful for; though the possum shammed dead, and perfected his English camouflage, he stopped short of adopting that disastrous English habit, indulgence towards the amateur and the amateurish. Between master and apprentice, between the poet of one generation and the poet of the next or the next-but-one, the only proper relationship is cool and distant, professional. For both are servants of another master yet—what Eliot called 'the tradition'. He made that word do many, perhaps too many, tasks. I have in mind one of the meanings he gave to it, when he took it to mean the entire English language as we inherit it, with all the quirks and accretions, the graces and malformations which have accrued to it through the centuries, not least at the hands of the poets of those centuries. That is the master whom both master and raw apprentice are called upon to serve. Eliot was never so American, so properly professional, as when he harped on 'the tradition' in this sense. I am grateful to him, and I count myself lucky that I started my writing career, or rather I groped my way towards it, at a time when he was pre-eminently, in fact unavoidably, the seamark that one had to sail by.